In Search of the Lost World
The Modernist Quest for the Thing, Matter, and Body

Tsaiyi Wu
The Research Center for Comparative Literature and World Literature
Shanghai Normal University

Series in Literary Studies

Vernon Press 2023. This book is licensed under a Creative Commons Attribution 4.0 International license (CC BY 4.0) which is the most open license available and considered the industry 'gold standard' for open access. This license allows you to share, copy, distribute and transmit the text; to adapt the text and to make commercial use of the text provided attribution is made to the authors and a full reference to book as follows:

Tsaiyi Wu, *In Search of the Lost World: The Modernist Quest for the Thing, Matter, and Body*, Vernon Press, 2023. https://vernonpress.com/book/1675

More information about the CC BY license is available at
https://creativecommons.org/licenses/by/4.0/

Copyright, attributions and/or permissions for third party material included in this book may differ, and are noted, as appropriate.

www.vernonpress.com

In the Americas:
Vernon Press
1000 N West Street, Suite 1200
Wilmington, Delaware, 19801
United States

In the rest of the world:
Vernon Press
C/Sancti Espiritu 17,
Malaga, 29006
Spain

Series in Literary Studies

Library of Congress Control Number: 2022950702

ISBN: 978-1-64889-630-9

Also available:
978-1-64889-597-5 [Hardback]
978-1-64889-629-3 [Open Access, PDF, E-Book]. Available for free download:
https://vernonpress.com/book/1708

Cover design by Bill Graham.

Every effort has been made to trace all copyright holders, but if any have been inadvertently overlooked the publisher will be pleased to include any necessary credits in any subsequent reprint or edition.

This publication has been made possible following the award of a research grant from Shanghai City Philosophy and Social Science Research Project (grant number: 2021EWY007), the research awards from the School of Humanities as well as the Innovative Team of International Comparative Literature, Shanghai Normal University.

For whom have truly and bravely, loved

Table of Contents

	Abstract	*vii*
	Acknowledgment	*ix*
	Introduction	*xi*
	I. The Moderns at the Crossways	
	II. The Fields of Conversation, and My Approach to De-anthropocentricism	
	III. The Ethical Significance of Subjective Transformation	
ONE	**Artificiality**	1
	I. Pygmalion's Statue	
	II. A Dream of Stone	
	III. Spirituality of Dandyism, and of Cosmetics	
	IV. The Style of Inorganic Things	
	V. Huysmans's Artificial Paradise	
	VI. Summary of Part One	
TWO	**Auto-Philosophical Fiction**	61
	I. Empiricist Psychology	
	II. Receptivity and Memory	
	III. Pater's Imaginary Portrait	
	IV. Proust's Irony	
	V. Woolf's Universal Sensation, and Her Problems with Writing	
	VI. Remembrance of the House	
	VII. Summary of Part Two	
	Conclusion: Three Requisites to De-anthropocentrism	*129*
	Bibliography	*133*
	Index	*139*

Abstract

Historically, the book studies how modernist artists, as the first generation who began to rethink the legacy of solipsist idealism, sought to check their anthropomorphic impulse and to recognize the alterity of the thing. With intense passion, the moderns recreate the self so as to recreate their relationships with the material world: by loving a marble statue, capturing fleeting impressions, or retrieving sensuous memory. Theoretically, the book converses with the topical de-anthropocentric and materialist interests in the twenty-first century, and proposes that the artist may escape human centeredness through transformation of the self, in one's yearning toward the material world.

De-anthropocentrism, or the attempt to approach the material world in a way that is not already centered upon human perception, is one of the most prominent motifs in the humanities of the twenty-first century. The book engages with contemporary scholarships, including Object-Oriented Ontology, Thing Theory, New Materialism, and Posthumanism, but I focus on yet another dimension that is often overlooked: *the efforts to be made to achieve de-anthropocentrism, as well as the effects of embracing it.* Kantian metaphysics is anthropocentric because he elevates human reason as the measure of knowledge—and to escape anthropocentrism, we must ask, first and foremost, *how we might escape Kantian universal reason. That is, de-anthropocentrism would necessarily involve subjective transformation.* Whereas Bill Brown and Graham Harman argue that art functions to reframe the thing so that we may see other facets of it, my book argues that the other half of the project is to recreate the self so that we see the thing in a new light.

Part One, "Artificiality," begins the discussion with Baudelaire's poem "La Beauté" in which the poet disavows his anthropomorphic impulses by dedicating himself to love the inaccessible stone, and defines this relationship of the unrequited love and perpetual quest as the beautiful. This discussion of the poem is contextualized in the fin-de-siècle cult of artificiality, where artists such as Theophile Gautier, J.K. Huysmans, and Gustave Moreau are fascinated with insensible marble statues and jeweled surfaces. The cult of artificiality is a mischievous subversion to Hegel's maxim that inwardness is superior to matter. In the cult of artificiality, art is superior to nature, but art is now reconfigured as an inorganic, sensuous surface that defies signification and subjugates the feeling heart. Artificiality then is the fin-de-siècle allegory of how imagination might not be defined as transcendental interiority, but rather relate in ingenious ways with materiality.

Part Two, "Auto-philosophical Fiction," explicates how aesthetic cultivation is a major theme for Pater, Proust, and Woolf, for they are all interested in the latest findings of empiricist psychology, which allows the possibility to escape Kantian transcendental reason (at the time already conceived as a barrier against the plenitude of the sensuous world), if one is committed to cultivating her powers of reception in order to register passing thoughts and sensations. Auto-philosophical fiction is a genre where the artists set philosophical ideas in the laboratory of their lives, and therefore translate the aesthetic ideal—the way they wish to relate to the world—into a journey of self-examination and self-cultivation. Auto-philosophical fiction is a unique approach to truth as it renders theory into transformative sentiments, experiences, and practices, while my book argues that de-anthropocentrism cannot be realized without such inquires as to how the theory may mode and fashion the self.

Together, my book argues that de-anthropocentrism, which must involve a transformation of the self so as to escape the human-centered perception, cannot be predicated upon a metaphysics that presumes the conditions of a universal subjectivity, but must be a form of aesthetic inquiry that recreates the self—its desires and perceptions—in order to recreate new relationships with the world.

Keywords: French and British modernism, de-anthropocentrism, aesthetics of the self.

Acknowledgment

I have spent seven years writing this book—four years during my doctoral education at Indiana University Bloomington, U.S.A., and another three years to revise my dissertation into the present form at Shanghai Normal University, China, where I currently serve as a lecturer. These are two beautiful universities that have granted me space, time, and financial security to build this project—to them I am forever grateful. I would like to thank Argiris Legatos, the recruiting editor at Vernon Press, whose patient and adamant support makes the production of the book such a proud and pleasant process; Professor Maurizia Boscagli and Professor Gayle Rogers, the reviewers of the book, whose insightful comments have helped sharpen my language and widened my vision. I appreciate the support of my dear friends, Micah Tewers, whose passion for philosophy has inspired me along the way, and Bill Graham, who designs the cover image for this book.

I am still indebted to my doctoral advisor, Professor Jacob Emery, whose confidence in me in my formative years allowed me to launch this adventurous project, and Professor Scot Barnett, who introduced me to contemporary thoughts, including Object-Oriented Ontology that became the most prominent influence of my study. I would like to thank Professor Graham Harman, who offered to read my work and has written me letters of recommendation. His cordial championship of young scholars truly embodies his metaphysical vision of democracy, and has helped shape academia into a more open and conversational space.

In Joseph Campbell's timeless classic, *The Hero with a Thousand Faces*, he proposes that there is one single universal structure to be found in all myths, fairy tales, and fantasies of all time and cultures. This monomythical structure is one of quest and transformation, where the hero or heroine must willingly crawl into what Campbell calls "the belly of the whale," to grope one's way through an uncharted terrain and to undergo a series of trials so as to eventually achieve a symbolic award—while the purpose of the rite of passage is to develop the young adult into whom she is meant to be. Writing this book is such a rite of passage, and it would not be an exaggeration to say that my advisor and the mentors named above have played active roles in shaping my relationship with academia during my formative years. They have inspired me to finish this ambitious project, cultivated in me a true confidence to overcome obstacles, and instilled in me an abiding sense of gratitude toward the world at large. By what they have given me, I am compelled to return the best I have to my fellow scholars and future students for all my years in academia.

I am also grateful for receiving the funds from Shanghai City Philosophy and Social Science Research Project (grant number: 2021EWY007), the research awards from the School of Humanities as well as the Innovative Team of International Comparative Literature, Shanghai Normal University, which together allow the book to be published in open access format and be translated into Spanish.

Tsaiyi Wu

The Innovative Team of International Comparative Literature

Shanghai Normal University

Fall 2022

Introduction

I. The Moderns at the Crossways

In the poem "L'Homme et la mer,"[1] Baudelaire lays out a very intricate relationship between human and Nature, where, on the one hand, his affirmative tone registers an idealist ideology with which the man considers the sea to be the mirror of his own psyche, and, on the level of the content, a lucid exposition that the sea itself has a depth that we humans cannot touch.

> Homme libre, toujours tu chériras la mer !
> La mer est ton miroir ; tu contemples ton âme
> Dans le déroulement infini de sa lame,
> Et ton esprit n'est pas un gouffre moins amer.

Human and Nature both have their unfathomable inward depth, while the false correspondence happens only on the surface, since the human, much troubled by his tumultuous psyche, takes the sea only as a mirror to contemplate upon his own visage. An alleged correspondence between the man and the sea is suggested by a symmetrical structure as the man's soul ("ton âme") rhymes carefully with the blade of the sea's waves ("sa lame"), and the stanza ends with "amer" that rhymes with "la mer," referring metaphorically both to the man's psychical resentment and the sea's bitter salty water. But then, even as both the man and the sea have a bitter inwardness, their metaphorical resemblance does not foster an empathetic bond. Instead, both are absorbed in their own "gouffre," while the repetitive throaty "r" sounds suggest this self-referentiality: the man broods over his own troubling thoughts, while the sea rejoices in its infinite rolling waves amongst littoral caves.

The man does not embrace or listen to the sea. Rather, if he jumps into the sea, it is to plunge into his own image as reflected by the sea, and to interpret the commotion of the sea as if it were outcries of his own passion.

> Tu te plais à plonger au sein de ton image ;
> Tu l'embrasses des yeux et des bras, et ton cœur

---

[1] Charles Baudelaire, *Les Fleurs Du Mal*, 2nd ed. (Paris: Poulet-Malassis et de Broise, 1861), 36–37.

> Se distrait quelquefois de sa propre rumeur
> Au bruit de cette plainte indomptable et sauvage.

Narcissistic as he is, the man has an aesthetic similar to what Hegel calls Romantic art. For Hegel, the man achieves spiritual victory over nature when he ceases to consider nature as an existence of its own right, but rather appropriates it as an expression of his inwardness. As Hegel remarks in his *Aesthetics*:

> This *inner* world constitutes the content of romantic sphere and must therefore be represented as this inwardness and in the pure appearance of this depth of feeling. Inwardness celebrates its triumph over the external and manifests its victory in and on the external itself.[2]

In Hegel's dialectical scheme, human evolution is marked by the degree of which we are conscious of our Idea, and the three stages of art—symbolic, classical, Romantic—embody the three relationships between spirit and matter in the process of evolution. The Romantic stage is the apex of human evolution, where humans become entirely conscious of their own thoughts, their thinking free from and independent of the sensuous powers of matter, and thus claims victory over matter by reducing its existence into an image of thoughts. Notably, by claiming that the sea is a reflection of his own image, the man seeks not to friendly correspond with the sea, but rather to conquer it. While a genuine correspondence presumes the self to listen to an Other and to understand it in depth and with sympathy, here the man wants to reduce the sea to an appearance that seemingly reflects only his own visage.

The man here is a typical Hegelian poet, but Baudelaire does not uncritically inherit Hegelian idealism. Whereas the man seeks to reduce the sea to an expression of his inwardness, Baudelaire reveals that the sea has its irreducible depth and its own wealth unknown to the man. At one stroke, Baudelaire reveals that such idealist pride is pathetically ignorant.

> Vous êtes tous les deux ténébreux et discrets :
> Homme, nul n'a sondé le fond de tes abîmes ;
> Ô mer, nul ne connaît tes richesses intimes,
> Tant vous êtes jaloux de garder vos secrets !

---

[2] G. W. F. Hegel, *Hegel's Aesthetics: Lectures on Fine Art*, trans. T. M. Knox, vol. I (Oxford: Oxford University Press, 1975), 81. Emphasis original.

The two symmetrical sentences that refer respectively to the man and the sea again rhyme perfectly, but this musical harmony contradicts the syntactical sense. "Intimes," which rhymes but contrasts with "abîmes," here does not mean "intimate" but "private," referring to that the sea hoards in it its precious material wealth, while the man has a psyche that is a bottomless void. The man is preoccupied with his own dark psyche that he would have no extra energy left to explore the sea, let alone to establish an intimate friendship with it. While the Romantics would want to reduce the sea to its surface reflection of the man, the moderns, this book argues, began to realize such an aesthetics is only an anthropocentric hubris, neglecting what is beyond the human kens. Seventy years later, Virginia Woolf, in her novel *To the Lighthouse*, makes a similar comment that the human wish of "making the world reflect the compass of the soul" is only an illusory anthropocentric dream, because the sea is an independent Other that cannot be reduced to a mirror of our psyche:

> That dream, then, of sharing, completing, finding in solitude on the beach an answer, was but a reflection in a mirror, and the mirror itself was but the surface glassiness which forms in quiescence when the nobler powers sleep beneath?[3]

As this book will further explicate, an important aspect of modernism is that artists began to be painfully aware of the fact that much of the idealist legacy is illusory, that what Hegel calls transcendental victory can be achieved only as humans ignore the powers sleeping underneath the sea, surely nobler than our kind as we have proven to be so narrow-minded.

In the final stanza, Baudelaire addresses in apostrophe the man and the sea—"vous vous combattez sans pitié ni remord"—and pronounces in a mythical tone that the relationship between the man and the sea as "frères implacables." The man and the sea are brothers because the man seeks to find similitude in the sea—but they will not stop fighting because this similitude is won by ruthless reduction of the Other as if it were only an image of the self. The poem is a concise philosophical treatise on idealist aesthetics, where the man's wish to transfigure the sea into an expression of his thoughts is revealed as narcissist and naïve, for the man is completely ignorant of the fact that the sea, far from being a passive mirror, has a deep and rich inwardness like that of his own.

---

[3] Virginia Woolf, *To the Lighthouse* (Harcourt, Brace, 1927), 146.

While Baudelaire is a pioneer of modernism, Yeats, who has been influenced by his French contemporaries, sums up the ethos of the fin-de-siècle with the same set of man-and-sea metaphors charged with mythical and metaphysical valance. In the 1899 edition of his collected poems, under the volume titled "Crossways," W. B. Yeats announces even more explicitly that the idealist aesthetics is only an anthropocentric illusion. The two poems that lead off the volume are titled "The Song of the Happy Shepherd" and "The Sad Shepherd,"[4] which lay out two contrasting attitudes: one smugly imagines that the poetic object will echo back the human thought, though only for a while, the other realizes in a twinge that the material thing is an alien Other, indifferent to the burdensome thoughts that the shepherd is eager to let out. "The Song of the Happy Shepherd" clues us into a historical understanding that we can no longer enjoy an idyllic union with nature—"The woods of Arcady are dead, / And over is their antique joy"—presumably because, after Kant, we realize that the material world is reduced to the image of our thoughts: "The wandering earth herself may be / Only a sudden flaming word." The happy shepherd, however, persists in the idealist pride that we humans are entitled to define the world with our own words: "There is no truth / Saving in thine own heart." His new motto now, repeating as a refrain several times throughout the poem, is a perfectly rhymed couplet whose fluid sounds suggest self-sufficiency:

> For words alone are certain good:
> Sing, then, for this is also sooth.

The poet equates "words" with ethical superiority ("good") and scientific certainty ("sooth," "truth"), and with the O sound that evokes an enclosed circle of self-sufficiency—he with his poetic power indeed builds an idealist edifice in which one might cling to words as truth.

The shepherd's tone is however defensive and belies a lurking anxiety. When he says "words alone are certain good," he is eager to prohibit us from exploring other possibilities. Words must be separated from deeds that might follow it, and one must protect our "human truth" by consciously renouncing our desire to search for the truth as it is, or to explore the vast and unknown universe.

> Then nowise worship dusty deeds,
> Nor seek, for this is also sooth,
> To hunger fiercely after truth,

---

[4] William Butler Yeats, *Poems* (London: T. Fisher, 1899), 185–89.

> Lest all thy toiling only breeds
> New dreams, new dreams; there is no truth
> Saving in thine own heart. Seek then,
> No learning from the starry men,
> Who follow with the optic glass
> The whirling ways of stars that pass—
> Seek, then, for this is also sooth,
> No word of theirs—the cold star-bane
> Has cloven and rent their hearts in twain,
> And dead is all their human truth.

For the shepherd, the astronomers who dedicate themselves to explore the universe would not be rewarded with happiness, for the cold stars would puncture the fragile illusion of "the human truth" and thus rent their heart. Here the shepherd seems to be entirely conscious of the sacrifices that an idealist must make in order to sustain the truth value of human words—by dissociating words from the world, the signifier from the signified, and enclosing one's vision in a familiar and protective shell.

What the shepherd advises us to seek, then, is a docile object that would unconditionally corroborate our human truth. That is, one can go to seashore to pick a "twisted, echo-harbouring shell," which seems to speak to us but in effect only echoes back our own voice for a little while.

> Go gather by the humming sea
> Some twisted, echo-harbouring shell,
> And to its lips thy story tell,
> And they thy comforters will be,
> Rewarding in melodious guile,
> Thy fretful words a little while,
> Till they shall singing fade in ruth
> And die a pearly brotherhood;
> For words alone are certain good:
> Sing, then, for this is also sooth.

Even as the shepherd only wants to hear his own words, it is strangely comforting to have a natural object external to himself, solid and concrete, to echo back to himself. The seashell's echoes of the shepherd's story, however, in a little while "fade in ruth," undo in rhyme the promise that words alone are a certain "truth."

But what exactly is untrue, and who is lying here? The seashell has a twisted shape, but its "melodious guile" is precisely the echoes of the shepherd's own words. This is a mirror structure that is prevalent in all poems of spurious correspondence, whose most faithful reflection is also considered an illusion, as the reflection has no physical substance; that is, the self-same image is not a genuine, conversational correspondent that presupposes alterity.[5] Yeats's beguiling seashell changes our structure of desire from an arrogant self-sufficiency to Narcissus's frustration: the dilemma that the lover desires only himself, yet finds his mirror image or echoing device incapable of correspondence—for correspondence in the first place presumes alterity, an independent beloved. As Yeats captures it, the fin-de-siècle is an age where the poet began to find the idealist Narcissus frustrated, because he is now in love, love that necessarily points to correspondence with an Other.

Then we must ask: is the seashell really an echoing device? No. It could have hummed or sung. The seashells are reduced to an echoing device because they are gathered out of water and "die a pearly brotherhood." For Yeats, this appropriation of natural object for self-expression is a violence that kills the maiden earth, in his phallic metaphors that the poet's songs "pierced" the earth and deflowered her garden of poppies so as to decorate his own brows.

> Pierced by my glad singing through,
> My songs of old earth's dreamy youth:
> But ah! she dreams not now; dream thou!
> For fair are poppies on the brow:
> Dream, dream, for this is also sooth.

The world used to be sentient and used to dream, but now her dream is assimilated into and mediated by the shepherd's songs. Yeats seems to be implying—though the causation of the consecutive sentences is not entirely clear—that the earth ceases to dream because the shepherd's singing has pierced through her. The defensive exclamation—"she dreams not *now*, dream thou!"—betrays the modernist awareness of our relationship with the world: words do not speak for the world or reveal it; it rather replaces and compensates for its death. To live in our own world of human truth means that we must forsake the starry universe external to us.

---

[5] A most famous instance of calling a mirror of self-image "deceiving" would be Ovid's Narcissus who for a moment considers his mirror image to be an object of love: "How often in vain he kissed the cheating pool/ And in the water sank his arms to clasp/ The neck he saw, but could not clasp himself! / Now knowing what he sees, he adores the sight;/ That false face fools and fuels his delight." Ovid, *Metamorphoses*, trans. A. D. Melville (Oxford: Oxford University Press, 2008), 64.

Introduction xvii

"The Happy Shepherd" tells Yeats' satirical comments on the idealist self-sufficiency, but "The Sad Shepherd" has us confronts directly with the modernist awareness that the world is an ultimate other, indifferent to our desire for correspondence. The sad shepherd demands vehemently that nature listens to his story, yet is poignantly aware that nature is perfectly self-absorbed as humans are, like Baudelaire's sea which hides its intimate wealth beneath its glassy surface, or Graham Harman's percept "object is withdrawn."[6]

> And then the man whom Sorrow named his friend
> Cried out, Dim sea, hear my most piteous story!
> The sea swept on and cried her old cry still,
> Rolling along in dreams from hill to hill.
> He fled the persecution of her glory.
> And, in a far-off, gentle valley stopping,
> Cried all his story to the dewdrops glistening.
> But naught they heard, for they are always listening,
> The dewdrops, for the sound of their own dropping.
> (emphasis original)

The O sound in "The Song of the Happy Shepherd" that suggests self-sufficiency—"For words alone are certain good: / Sing, then, for this is also sooth"—now becomes, on the shepherd's part, the vowels for "sorrow," whose dawdling sound bespeaks the shepherd's open desire that cannot be assuaged without the understanding and response of another. The O sound, on the part of nature however, indeed makes it clear that it is only preoccupied with itself: the sea "rolling," the dewdrops listening to themselves "dropping."[7] The sad shepherd now turns to the last resort, the seashell, for it is supposed to have a "*hollow, pearly heart*" that would echo back his story:

> I will my heavy story tell
> Till my own words, re-echoing, shall send
> Their sadness through a hollow, pearly heart;

---

[6] Graham Harman, *Tool-being: Heidegger and the Metaphysics of Objects* (Open Court Publishing, 2002), 5.
[7] Paul de Man's reading of Yeats' two poems differs squarely from that of my own. For de Man, the dewdrop is a metaphor of the poet himself: "the poet is no longer contemplating a thing in nature, but the workings of his own mind; the outside world is used as a pretext and a mirror, and loses all its substance." Paul de Man, *The Rhetoric of Romanticism* (Columbia University Press, 2000), 154.

> And my own tale again for me shall sing,
> And my own whispering words be comforting,
> And lo! my ancient burden may depart.
> (emphasis original)

But this time, the nautilus is alive and its shell is not hollow. The sea creature is not picked up by the shepherd; it rather dwells by the sea, moves about in "wildering whirls" and "changed all he sang to inarticulate moan," "forgetting him."

> Then he sang softly nigh the pearly rim;
> But the sad dweller by the sea-ways lone
> Changed all he sang to inarticulate moan
> Among her wildering whirls, forgetting him.

By exposing that the material object would not conform to our desire of reducing the ultimate Other to an echoing device, Yeats's "Sad Shepherd" poem sums up the modernist consciousness that clearly denounces the idealist aesthetics as an anthropocentric dream.

Baudelaire's poem "L'Homme et la mer" and Yeats's two shepherd poems are explicit and specific pronouncement of one of the central themes of modernism: that the superiority of idealist imagination no longer holds, if only we take a moment to recognize that the object is an Other of solid, stubborn, and opaque materiality, which would not submit to our anthropocentric transfiguration. Modernism is an age where the artists become aware of the plenitude of the material powers, and as this book will go on to discuss, began to ardently search for new ways to experience them.

II. The Fields of Conversation, and My Approach to De-anthropocentricism

The material turn and de-anthropocentrism are two of the most invigorating values in the 21st century, and inspire exciting scholarship across different disciplines, including literary studies and philosophy. These include Graham Harman's Object-Oriented Ontology, Bill Brown's Thing Theory, and a rich array of related scholarship such as Speculative Realism, New Materialisms, Ecocritical Criticism, Posthumanism, etc. This is a time where thinkers recognize that human beings are no longer at the center of the cosmos, and therefore turn attentions to things and objects; to body, sensation, and material powers; to animals, machine, and cyborgs; to the ecological system and network; and to the fact that humans are not rational, unified beings as the Enlightenment ideology dictates. Since the year of 2020, as the covid pandemic and extreme weather have threatened our survival, we come to experience the unknown material powers far exceeding our technological control.

Modernist defamiliarization—specifically Heidegger's notion that art functions to unfetter an object from its everyday context and to induce us to see the thing in a new light—plays an important role in the inquiries of contemporary scholars, most notably for Harman and Brown. Whereas Kant has simply prohibited us any access to the thing-in-itself by announcing that all that we see is but human appearance, Heidegger asks persistently "what in the thing is thingly? What is the thing in itself"?[8] For Heidegger, "the task of ontology is to set in relief the being of beings and to explicate being itself."[9] In his *Being and Time*, Heidegger explicates his method of "phenomenology" as a method that considers beings to have *an inexhaustible depth*—much beyond Kantian appearance, our perceptual gaze, and scientific abstraction—and that what is manifest is only our specific access to them in a certain context: "Beings can show themselves from themselves in various ways, depending on the mode of access to them."[10] A *phenomenon* is then what grants us a privileged access to being—"the self-showing in itself"—for example, as an artwork shows us the inner being of the thing.[11]

In Heidegger's famous tool analysis, our specific access to the being of things is circumscribed according to the ways in which we habitually live. Our gaze of the hammer would only grant us the contour of its outward appearance, but our living experience with it would provide us with an understanding its "handiness." Most often, our habitual world would guide our approach and understanding of the thing: "our association with useful things is subordinate to the manifold of references of the 'in-order-to.' The kind of seeing of this accommodation to things is called *circumspection*."[12] A useful hammer—one that becomes irreplaceable for a craftsman as he has muscular memory of its weight—is thus a "being-in-the-world," and we must understand the craftsman, the hammer, and his work as a "*unified* phenomenon."[13] Things constitute our world, making it coherent, complete, and when we are accustomed to them, we take them for granted. But when a thing goes wrong, such as when a hammer

---

[8] Martin Heidegger, "The Thing," in *Poetry, Language, Thought*, trans. Albert Hofstadter, Perennial Classics (New York: HarperCollins, 2001), 165.
[9] Martin Heidegger, *Being and Time: A Translation of Sein Und Zeit*, trans. Joan Stambaugh (State University of New York Press, 1996). Intro. II. 7. a; p.24.
[10] Heidegger, *Being and Time*. Intro. II. 7. a; p.25.
[11] Heidegger, *Being and Time*. Intro. II. 7. a; p.27.
[12] Heidegger, *Being and Time*. I. III. 16; p.65. Emphasis original.
[13] Heidegger, *Being and Time*. I. II. 12; p.49. Emphasis original.

breaks, when it slips our hand and breaks our toe, or when a toilet is put on exhibition in a museum, it disturbs our world and asserts its presence: "what is at hand becomes deprived of its worldliness so that it appears as something merely objectively present."[14] We bump into things as they are broken, breaking both our expectations and our world.

Central to Heidegger's philosophy is the dialectic of building and breaking the context of things in order to explore their plenitude and possibilities. Art—similar to a useful or a broken tool—for Heidegger functions to either build a world in which the thing may disclose some of its powers, or to deconstruct its familiar world so that the thing again becomes conspicuous and unknown. While a tool gives familiar structure to our daily life, an artwork is entitled to give conscious and creative framing to things so as to draw from them novel presentations and powers. In his famous essay "The Origin of the Work of Art," Heidegger illustrates how a Greek temple draws powers from the rock it stands upon and the sky it embraces, as the architecture gives an accessible frame to what would be otherwise infinite.

> Standing there, the building rests on the rocky ground. This resting of the work draws up out of the rock the mystery of that rock's clumsy yet spontaneous support. Standing there, the building holds its ground against the storm raging above it and so first makes the storm itself manifest in its violence. The luster and gleam of the stone, though itself apparently glowing only by the grace of the sun, yet first brings to light the light of day, the breadth of the sky, the darkness of the night. The temple's firm towering makes visible the invisible space of the air. The steadfastness of the work contrasts with the surge of the surf, and its own repose brings out the raging of the sea. Tree and grass, eagle and bull, snake and cricket first enter into their distinctive shapes and thus come to appear as what they are.[15]

In addition to the architecture, a painting or a poem likewise bring us a new perspective of the thing, drawing out its hidden features and novel powers.

Bill Brown's Thing Theory is built upon his reading of Heidegger and Lacan.[16] Brown focuses on Heidegger's distinction between object and thing in his 1950 lecture "The Thing." Whereas *an object* is what we capture in

---

[14] Heidegger, *Being and Time*. I. III. 16; p.70.
[15] Martin Heidegger, "The Origin of the Work of Art," in *Poetry, Language, Thought*, trans. Albert Hofstadter, Perennial Classics (HarperCollins, 2001), 41.
[16] Bill Brown, *Other Things* (Chicago: The University of Chicago Press, 2015), 17–48.

perceptual, cultural, or scientific representation, a *thing* in Heidegger's vocabulary is the actual being hidden beneath the representational surface: "objects are things as they appear."[17] Lacan reads Heidegger's "The Thing" essay in his *The Ethics of Psychoanalysis*, as the first part of the book is titled "Introduction to the Thing."[18] Lacan is particularly interested in how signification compensates for what is inaccessible, or how an object stands for the thing, as Brown puts it: "the Thing is a gap at the center of the real to which the subject has no access and against which it develops the signifying process itself...for the Thing, eluding representation, gets represented nonetheless."[19] Lacan speaks of "the Other as a *Ding*," which gets represented as "the inaccessible Lady within courtly poetry."[20] Building upon his reading of Heidegger and Lacan, Brown argues that we may gain a glimpse of the thing in the process of it getting re-objectified in different contexts,[21] for example, when a piece of glass is being washed upon the beach and then pickup up by a man, who then sets on the mantle as a paperweight on the table, as Virginia Woolf's short story "Solid Objects" goes.[22] Works of art function to "make of the object some *other thing*," and raises our awareness of "how media give us access to materiality"—so that we may unfetter ourselves from the habitual perception and see other aspects of the thing.

Graham Harman likewise draws upon Heidegger's tool analysis to build his Object-Oriented Ontology. His terminology that corresponds to Brown's distinction between things and objects are "real objects" and "sensual objects." A real object is forever withdrawn in the sense that it is an existence that is never exhaustible, whereas a sensual object is how it presents itself in a certain context to a certain perceiver.[23] As with Heidegger and Brown, the central axiom of OOO is that an object reveals a new facet of itself when it is re-contextualized and de-familiarized. In addition to this, Harman's philosophy has a strong ethical value of de-anthropocentrism, or "flat

---

[17] Martin Heidegger, *The Question Concerning the Thing: On Kant's Doctrine of the Transcendental Principles*, trans. James D. Reid and Benjamin D. Crowe (London: Rowman & Littlefield International, 2018), 147.Qtd. In Brown, *Other Things*, 26.
[18] Jacques Lacan, *The Ethics of Psychoanalysis, 1959-1960*, trans. Dennis Porter, Norton Paperback, The Seminar of Jacques Lacan, Book VII (New York: W. W. Norton & Company, 1997), 56. Qtd. In Brown, 33.
[19] Brown, *Other Things*, 33.
[20] Brown, *Other Things*, 33.
[21] Brown, *Other Things*, 51.
[22] Brown, *Other Things*, 55.
[23] Graham Harman, *Object-Oriented Ontology: A New Theory of Everything* (Landon: Penguin Random House, 2017), 9.

ontology" as his jargon goes: that we human is just one kind of entity that enjoys no ontological priority over other things.[24] Thus Harman emphasizes tirelessly that de-familiarization occurs not only when we humans gain a new perspective of the object, but also when one object encounters another. Following Harman's lead, Ian Bogost calls his project "alien phenomenology"[25] as the philosopher seeks to speculate the inwardness and experience of other things, such as that of a plant, an animal, an artificial intelligence, or an aerolite from the universe. Alien phenomenology is "a philosophy *claiming that things speculate* and, furthermore, one *that speculates about how things speculate.*"[26] Harman's technique to speculate the experience of the thing is, more specifically, a theatrical metaphor. Art functions to give us an aesthetic pleasure in which an object seems to execute its powers *for us to experience it,* as if we were playing its role. A metaphor such as "A cypress is a flame" gives us a new perspective of the cypress that departs from its habitual (viz. anthropocentric) outlook, and draws us in the storm of its inner powers yet alien: wild, untamed, and passionate.[27] Another effective metaphor can be found in *Zhuangzi*: a person who is enlightened would rejoice in a wide vision as that of a legendary bird, which sees the mountains and seas as it glides on the high sky.[28]

A most surprising upshot of Harman's OOO is that he does not discredit the reality of our subjective experience or imagination, insofar as we firmly understand that the existence of the object always exceeds our experience of it. If an aesthetic experience has an impact on us, it is of course real—it unpacks the powers of the object and our sensitivity, eliminating the perceptual distance and confronting us with a direct exposure. In an aesthetic experience where we see cypress inflamed, *we* are in effect the only real object who witness and recognize a facet of the executant reality of the cypress. Harman argues that a metaphor such as "the cypress is a flame" is capable of making us experience the object as if we become the inflamed cypress ourselves, of alluring us to "step in and attempt the electrifying work of becoming the cypress-substance for the flame-qualities."[29] If it is true that an aesthetic experience can be so powerful, then *we are transformed by the*

---

[24] Harman, *Object-Oriented Ontology*, 54.
[25] Ian Bogost, *Alien Phenomenology, or What It's Like to Be a Thing* (University of Minnesota Press, 2012), 34.
[26] Bogost, *Alien Phenomenology*, 31. Emphasis original.
[27] Harman, *Object-Oriented Ontology*, 82.
[28] Burton Watson, trans., "Free and Easy Wandering," in *The Complete Works of Zhuangzi* (New York: Columbia University Press, 2013), 1.
[29] Ibid., 87.

aesthetic experience in order that we touch the real, just as a cotton ball cannot experience the fire unless it is burned to ashes. In Harman's OOO, our subjective experience is still the anchor of reality, for the simple reason that we are the only real objects accessible to ourselves, while all real objects of the world are withdrawn. To explicate Harman's philosophy in my own words, Harman successfully avoids anthropocentrism not because we can achieve a worldview inhumanly objective, but because we have the capacity to go beyond the given perception—to be carried away by an aesthetic experience, to see a cypress inflamed and to see space and time in a way other than what is dictated by the *a priori* reason, to be other than ourselves in order to approach the ultimate otherness of the world.

In addition to turning the object under human gaze into a thing of inexhaustible depth and potentials, another completely different route to deconstruct the transcendental tradition is explored by New Materialism, which embraces a monist vision in which the world is composed of some kind of ultimate constituent that does not distinguish between thoughts and things. In 1996, Manuel DeLanda proposes on a digital forum "Future Non Stop":

> A new form of materialist philosophy in which raw matter-energy through a variety of self-organizing processes and an intense power of morphogenesis, generates all the structures that surround us. Furthermore, the structures generated cease to be the primary reality, and matter-energy flows now acquire this special status.[30]

Although the term "neo-materialism" or "new materialism" is coined by Manuel DeLanda and Rosi Braidotti in the second half of the 1990s,[31] as I will further document in Part Two, this monist vision was already quite influential in the fin-de-siècle and early twentieth century, and was embraced by philosophers and empirical psychologists such as Ernst Mach, Bertrand Russell, William James, as well as by modernist writers including Walter Pater and Virginal Woolf. Similar to the "flat ontology" proposed by Speculative Realists, in which humans receive no privileged ontological statues among all objects such as pebbles and basketballs, New Materialists refuse to grant the human mind any special functions such as creating and endowing for the world structures and meanings. Rather, the Kantian space and time is only a

---

[30] Manuel de Landa, "The Geology of Morals - A Neomaterialist Interpretation," Future Non Stop: A Living Archive for Digital Culture in Theory and Practice, 1996.
[31] Rick Dolphijn and Iris van der Tuin, eds., *New Materialism: Interviews and Cartographies* (Ann Arbor: Open Humanities Press, 2012), 93.

human illusion that the New Materialists seek to deconstruct, which can hardly encase the vibrant matter-energy in a perpetual flux. By wider application, New Materialists defy any dualist structures such as culture and nature, form and matter, signifier and signified: "biology is culturally mediated as much as culture is materialistically constructed."[32]

A third route to de-anthropocentrism is Posthumanism, which problematizes the assumption that humans have a transcendental and universal consciousness as Kant defines, sometimes by showing that our cognition is always already embodied and embedded in the material world. In Rosi Braidotti's preface to Francesca Ferrando's book *Philosophical Posthumanism*, he thus defines the branch of thought:

> Thinking for Ferrando is not the exclusive prerogative of Man/Anthropos, but is rather distributed across a wide spectrum of human and nonhuman entities. This produces also a new understanding of the human, not as an autonomous agent endowed with transcendental consciousness, but rather an immanent—embodied and embedded relational—entity that thinks with and through multiple connections to others, both human and nonhuman, organic and inorganic others.[33]

This understanding of our embodied subjectivity is a powerful way to defy the Cartesian cogito and Kantian consciousness, by showing that our cognition is neither a brain in a vacuum, nor universal and *a priori*, but rather shaped by our sensuous habits and material habituation. In addition to questioning the Enlightenment notion of universal human reason, Posthumanists are equally interested in exploring the consciousness and experience of other species, similar to that of Bogost's project of alien phenomenology.

This book engages in depth the three routes to de-anthropocentrism discussed above, in the milieu of modernist literature from 1860s-1920s: to recognize that the thing is forever withdrawn while the art might reveal a hidden facet of it (Object-Oriented Ontology and Thing Theory); to defy the hierarchy between thought and thing by embracing a monist vision, in which the world is primary made of a kind of matter-energy in a perpetual flux (New Materialism); and to conceptualize a new picture of subjectivity that is embodied and embedded in the material world (Posthumanism). But my

---

[32] Francesca Ferrando, *Philosophical Posthumanism* (London: Bloomsbury Academic, 2019), 159.
[33] Rosi Braidotti, "Preface: The Posthuman as Exuberant Excess," in *Philosophical Posthumanism* (London: Bloomsbury Academic, 2019), xii.

book focuses on yet another dimension that is often overlooked: *the efforts to be made to achieve de-anthropocentrism, as well as the effects of embracing it.* While we often misunderstand de-anthropocentrism as simply immersing ourselves in alien philosophical visions and forgetting about humanity, my project seeks to go back to the first meaning of the term: *to check our narcissist impulses and to unfetter ourselves from the given structures of perception, through astute and continual self-cultivation.* That is, with the recourses to modernist literature, my purpose is to demonstrate that de-anthropocentrism cannot be achieved simply by constructing a philosophical vision and then by acquiring it as a piece of knowledge: it rather has to fundamentally change a part of ourselves so that we may atone for our anthropocentric hubris and escape our perceptual trap. The ethical effects of de-anthropocentrism likewise deserve our investigation: *That is, what does it mean that our vision is no longer limited to the human finitude or, to ask the question negatively, what price to be paid and what would happen if we insisted on transgressing the bounds of reason that Kant so carefully circumscribes for the human race?* In short, this book explicates de-anthropocentrism as resolute attempts to bring fundamental changes onto the self so as to deliver ourselves from the given and the normative, and also to live by the consequences of departing from the comfortable human domain. De-anthropocentrism in this book is defined as an aesthetics of the self.

As shown in the first section, "the Moderns at the Crossways," modernist poets began to realize that idealist appropriation is as superficial and ignorant as the man mistakes the unfathomable sea for a faithful mirror that serves to only reflect our self-image, and thus reduces the immeasurable sea to its surface. And as I will go on to argue, the path that the moderns choose to liberate themselves from this narcissism is often a kind of ascetism, a kind of austere work on the self. Part One, "Artificiality," would be of interest to scholars of Object-Oriented Ontology and Thing Theory. It is built upon a central metaphor in which Baudelaire renders the image of the "La Beauté" as a stony sphinx, terribly inaccessible and incomprehensible, and prohibits poetic manipulation. The poets who love the stone thus must inhibit their innate desire to appropriate and possess the stone, and live with the mute and indifferent stone in a paradoxical relationship of *unrequited love and perpetual quest.* This is not a path for the faint-hearted: for the knight thereby can only take pride in the process, and never in the purpose. Part Two, "Autophilosophical Fiction," contributes to the scholarship of New Materialisms and Posthumanism. It introduces the empiricist psychology of the early twentieth century, which reconceptualizes the transcendental ego—no longer as a universal, *a priori* reason—but as a habitual tendency that filters in perspectival perceptions and organizes them as familiar objects. The transcendental ego thus impedes us from immersing in the stream of sensation, the ultimate constituent of the monist reality. More importantly, the philosophical visions would immediately compel the artists to explore and experiment with programs of self-cultivation so as to live up to their aesthetic ideals: Pater to seize precious sensation in the perpetual flux, and Woolf to undo the boundary of her consciousness so as be part of the sensation.

Methodologically, my discussion on the genre of auto-philosophical fiction further seeks to introduce a paradigm of thought different from that of Kantian philosophy. While Kant, following the model of science, asks what is the universal law of human reason, auto-philosophical fiction asks how to attain one's own chosen philosophical vision through an individual regime. In an auto-philosophical fiction, the artist experiments with a philosophical vision in the laboratory of lived life, and in doing so often finds that one would not be able to attain the ideal unless one aspect of life—aesthetic faculty, the practice of writing, remembrance of one's personal history—enters into the domain of self-cultivation and willed transformation. This capacity to subjective transformation, to escape the given human constitution so as to see other aspects of the thing, I submit, is the path to de-anthropocentrism.

The thread of my argument is mainly philosophical—I respond to contemporary de-anthropocentric discussions with my own solutions. But the literature I draw upon is historically circumscribed with my intention to make genuine contributions to modernist studies: in my response to contemporary inquiries, I explicate faithfully how modernist artists and thinkers began to reflect upon the anthropocentric hubris and seek to escape the Kantian perceptual trap. To avoid putting modernist literature under the straitjacket of contemporary theories, I opt to instead cite philosophy of the time in my narrative, even as the two often bear obvious resonance. That is, I will be discussing how Baudelaire responds to German Idealism rather than constructing a conversation between Baudelaire and OOO, and I will show that the monist philosophies that fascinate New Materialists today was already fashionable in the early twentieth century, and that Walter Pater has developed a radical theory of embodied subjectivity, in which our perception and predilections are in the first place shaped by our material habituation and habitation.

Where it is relevant, I also draw on Benjamin and discuss how the material culture of the modern time has facilitated their thoughts—the rapid change of the sensory environment that has incited Baudelaire and Pater to seize the fleeting sensation, the collection of global commodities in the arcade that has inspired Huysmans's design of the artificial paradise, as well as how the numbing effect of urban phantasmagoria—which turns reality into dream-like representation—figures as an ironic metaphor for Woolf's critique of her own writing. But the set of material conditions is just the premise to the intensively willed artistic endeavors to carry out the transformation of the self—while the latter remain to be the focus of my inquiry. In my research, I mean to show that the relationship between the material conditions and the artistic efforts are not one of determinism. Under the same set of material conditions—such as the modernist awareness of fleeting sensations—each artist would frame it as different questions and design different programs of self-cultivation: Baudelaire and Pater still choose to grapple with the fleeting sensation and crystalize it with concentrated energy, while Woolf would rather relax the boundary of her consciousness so as to lose herself in the stream.

Here I once again specify the usage of the terminology in this book and thus sum up this project with a conceptual roadmap. The term modernism refers to the artist endeavors from the 1860s-1920s and encompasses entirely different artist characters, but my focus is on how the artists awake with the painful realization that idealist appropriation is but a kind of infantile wistful thinking, and that one must depart from this comfortable narcissism as well as the given perceptual barrier in order to recognize the alterity of the thing. In other words, modernism is understood as a conscious breakage from its previous age, in that the artists find themselves to be painfully decentered, while at the same time they feel compelled to explore the alien world. The title of the book, "In Search of the Lost World," thematizes this modernist awakening to break free from Kant's precept—to search for the lost material world outside of the solipsist prison. The subtitle of the book is "the modernist quest for the thing, matter, and body," which refers to the main fields I engage with: the thing for Brown and Harman who, following Heidegger's lead, theorize the thing or the real object as an entity of inexhaustible depth and potentials; matter for New Materialism, which seeks to deconstruct the dualist structure by conceptualizing a monist world, in which both thoughts and things are made of a kind of atomic constituent in a perpetual flux; body for Pater's, Proust's, and Woolf's respective quests for sensuous memory or stream of consciousness, which is yet another way to repudiate the transcendental metaphysics with the understanding that our cognition is neither universal nor *a priori*, but is in the first place shaped by the material world through our sensuous habits and corporeal habituation. Conversing with three different de-anthropocentric attempts, my book rather focuses on discussing the artistic efforts *to recreate themselves* so as to live up to the metaphysical visions: Baudelaire to live with an unrequited love and perpetual quest for the thing, Woolf to relinquish her individual consciousness so as to be part of the universal sensation, and Pater's and Proust's attempts to include in their consciousness their forgotten sensuous memory.

III. The Ethical Significance of Subjective Transformation

While it is a common misconception that a de-anthropocentric project should not talk about humans, my book would show that the only real path is to piously work on the self. The problem of anthropocentrism begins with Kant, who points out that our perception of objects is in the first place conditioned by our own perceptual constitution. In the conclusion to his *Prolegomena*,[34] titled "On the Determination of the Bounds of Pure Reason," Kant suggests that there are *many other possible ways of relating to things, besides that of human experience.*

> But it would be on the other hand *a still greater absurdity* if we conceded no things in themselves, or set up our experience for the only possible mode of knowing things, our way of beholding (*Anschauung*) them in space and in time for the only possible way, and our discursive understanding for the archetype of every possible understanding; in fact if we wished to have the principles of the possibility of experience considered universal conditions of things in themselves.[35]

Kant argues that his project aims to avoid "dogmatic anthropomorphism" by, first, preventing us from transferring properties of reason to the thing-in-itself, and, second, by rigorously separating between appearance and its unknown substratum. Nonetheless, he allows a "symbolical anthropomorphism," "which in fact concerns language only," language with which we conceive and describe things—"and not the object itself."[36] That is, Kant urges us to understand that what we perceive is never the thing-in-itself, but rather *our relationship with the world*. In other words, Kant's Copernican Turn originally means to avoid anthropocentrism, by preventing us from passing human perception for the thing-in-itself.

Kant's solution to avoid anthropocentrism is however now considered dissatisfactory: for the unknown thing-in-itself is liable to be entirely engulfed again by the human relation to it. Quentin Meillassoux in his *After Finitude*[37]

---

[34] Michel Foucault, "What Is Enlightenment?," in *The Foucault Reader* (New York: Pantheon Books, 1984), 42.
[35] Immanuel Kant, *Kant's Prolegomena to Any Future Metaphysics*, ed. Paul Carus (Chicago: The Open Court Publishing Company, 1912), § 57, p. 120.
[36] Kant, *Prolegomena*, § 57, p. 129.
[37] Quentin Meillassoux, *After Finitude: An Essay on the Necessity of Contingency*, trans. Ray Brassier (London: Continuum, 2010), 5.

coins the influential term "correlationism" to thematize it as the most salient characteristic of modern philosophy, and laments that our interest in the human relation and its constitutive powers has superseded our attention to the thing. While correlationism is a shackle that we moderns cannot easily throw off, thinkers as led by Heidegger begin to rework correlationism in their burning desire to approach the unknown thing-in-itself. Despite their various stances, contemporary scholars generally emerge from the Kantian premise that our experience of the world always implies the structure of human perception, share Kant's paradoxical rigor in separating the world and the thought—but with an even stronger interest to approach the unknown thing-in-itself.

Speculative Realism as a philosophical movement engages directly with the Kantian heritage, as well as the important contemporary values, including the material turn and de-anthropocentrism. Within the Kantian framework, Speculative Realists juggle between two variables in their attempt to approach the thing: the thing-in-itself and the relations between things. Meillassoux sits at one extreme with his attempt to find the inhuman absolute despite our correlational condition, and thereby seeks to transgress the Kantian boundary of reason—at a great cost because once we depart from the human structure of space and time, what we see is only a *hyper-Chaos*.[38] Graham Harman at the other end argues that objects-in-themselves are forever withdrawn, but then he shows us how each relation between things, outside of the domain of the human perception, reveals a facet of the material reality. That is, Harman seeks to include in his metaphysical view "every possible understanding" that Kant suggests by the end of *Prolegomena*.

My project however puts a new emphasis on a third veritable: our subjective constitution. *My project explores how we may escape anthropocentrism through aesthetic cultivation and transformation of the self, in order to see the world in ways different from the given human perspective.* The seed of subjective constitution is already buried in both Harman's and Meillassoux's thoughts. Harman's theatrical metaphor is a specific kind of subjective transformation, for we may imagine a journey into the perceptual structures of a stone, an ant, a cat, or a coca-cola can—and thus escape Kantian reason through such an imaginative power. Meillassoux achieves his vision of hyper-Chaos through the most daring act of *relinquishing the principle of reason*, though without explaining how one can ever attain this:

---

[38] Meillassoux, *After Finitude*, 64.

> Speculation proceeds by accentuating *thought's relinquishment of the principle of reason* to the point where this relinquishment is converted into a principle, which alone allows us to grasp the fact that *there* is absolutely no ultimate Reason, whether thinkable or unthinkable. *There* is nothing beneath or beyond the manifest gratuitousness of the given—nothing but the limitless and lawless power of its destruction, emergence, or persistence.[39]

In one sentence, Meillassoux surreptitiously passes from the action of subjective transformation ("*thought's* relinquishment of the principle of reason") to a vision of his great outdoors (his statements that "*there* is no ultimate Reason").[40] But how can one relinquish the principle of reason? If Meillassoux has done this daring thought experiment on himself, why would he never discuss it in the first-person narrative, such as when Descartes begins his meditations by telling us that he now sits by his fireplace, overexerting his brainpower?[41] Is it that we are now forbidden to talk about ourselves in the age of de-anthropocentrism? But to escape from Kantian reason is an attempt that modern artists have indeed experimented with, which, as I will go on to discuss, can be achieved only through intense attention on the self—such as Arthur Rimbaud purposefully disorients his senses, impressionist painters who relinquish their habitual perception of the object in order to capture the primal light that changes from hour to hour, and J.K. Huysmans who confuses the conceptual categories between the natural and artificial.

My project reads Harman's philosophy in reverse and completes his metaphysical picture—we experience the plenitude of the world by taking into consideration not only all different encounters between objects in different contexts, but also the possibilities of *us* actively seeking to encounter the objects in different selves—by cultivating and expanding our perceptual field, by creating affective bonds with the thing, by being other than ourselves for the thing. To cast my thesis in concrete terms, *I argue that art is an arena to create subject-object relations, while true de-anthropocentrism happens when we are transformed in our quest of the material world.* Central to my

---

[39] Meillassoux, *After Finitude*, 63.
[40] Tsaiyi Wu, "A Dream of a Stone: The Ethics of De-Anthropocentrism," *Open Philosophy*, no. 3 (2020): 417.
[41] René Descartes, *Meditations on First Philosophy: With Selections from the Objections and Replies*, ed. John Cottingham (Cambridge: Cambridge University Press, 1996), 12.

project is the notion that *this capacity to be other than oneself is the key to de-anthropocentrism.*

What motivates me to emphasize the element of subjective transformation is that this emphasis allows me to duly foreground *the ethical responsibility* that is always, tautologically, implied in our quest of de-anthropocentrism: *to step out of the human center and to be other than ourselves!* In Foucault's *Hermeneutics of the Subject*,[42] he argues that this connection between subjective transformation and truth is presupposed in ancient Greek philosophy, although lost in modern epistemology. In Plato's myth, we humans are born to be trapped in our perceptual finitude as if we were chained in a cave and saw only the shadows of the world (*Republic* 514a-520a).[43] But to see the real world we must fall in love and be thoroughly transformed by the power of love—in the metaphor of regrowth of the wings on our soul (*Phaedrus* 245c-267d). Foucault calls this ancient mode of thinking "spirituality," for spirituality presupposes the possibility of a fundamental transformation of the self beyond the given perception—and the prize of the transformation, the real world. Spirituality for Foucault means an intimate connection between self-cultivation and one's elevated vision—the creation of the self in one's attempt to approach truth.

We might argue that even for Kant, the subject is not capable of truth, for we are trapped in subjective perception and have no access to the thing-in-itself. But then Kant seeks to still give certainty to knowledge by singling out a portion of human reason as universal, on which our science is built. In section 19 of his *Prolegomena*:

> Therefore object validity and necessary universality are equivalent terms, and though we do not know the object in itself, yet when we consider a judgment as universal, and also necessary, we understand it to have objective validity.
>
> The object always remains unknown in itself; but when by the concept of the understanding the connexion of the representations of the object, which are given to our sensibility, is determined as universally valid, the object is determined by this relation, and it is the judgment that is objective. (56)

---

[42] Michel Foucault, *The Hermeneutics of the Subject: Lectures at the Collège de France, 1981-82*, ed. Frédéric Gros, trans. Graham Burchell, 1st ed (New York: Palgrave Macmillan, 2005).
[43] Plato and Benjamin Jowett, *The Dialogues of Plato* (New York: Random House, 1937).

This universality of human reason plays an important role in the Kantian system in that it guarantees the foundation to knowledge. But this mandate in universality also effectively prohibits the possibility of self-cultivation and aesthetic transformation. Kant thereby sets up the framework in modern philosophy that the condition of our access to truth is universal rather than individual, while the philosopher's task is to discover this universal law.[44]

My project however aims to explore how our access to the world is a question not epistemological, but ethical: might it be a difficult question not for philosophers, but for ourselves; might it be that our subjective constitution is not to be interpreted, but to be cultivated; might it be that we carry with ourselves the responsibility to know the world as Plato's lover does, to be open to the world, seeking the world, revealed by the world? Just as the first meaning of de-anthropocentrism is to go beyond the universal, given human perception, I argue that any inquiry in de-anthropocentrism should be built upon a methodology in which metaphysics is not a matter of universal application, but rather of individual creation. To emphasize this element of self-creation, I explicate through the course of the book that art is the arena where the artist may create subject-object relations, while true de-anthropocentrism happens when the artist creates a new way to relate to the world—through the transformation of the self.

This book seeks to explicate de-anthropocentrism in light of Foucault's late ethics of "the aesthetics of existence," one who conceives the self as "a work of art," and asserts one's free will by choosing for the self an ideal form of existence.[45] Foucault argues that modern epistemology, as established by Cartesian and Kantian critiques, begins with defining "the conditions and limits of the subject's access to the truth."[46] But by defining our universal structure of reason, Kant has also effectively prohibited any possibility of subjective transformation. Once Kant is able to define what is knowledge as it is circumscribed by the conditions of a universal human reason, then "knowledge itself and knowledge alone gives access to the truth,"[47] and our knowledge of the thing is then reduced to a simple act of human gaze which transports and appropriates the thing into the *a priori* structure of space and time. Heidegger, Brown, and Harman are unsatisfied with Kant's prohibition and set out to explore the plenitude of the thing by continuously reframing it,

---

[44] Part of the discussion on Kant has been published on Wu, "A Dream of a Stone," 413–18.
[45] Michel Foucault, *Politics, Philosophy, Culture: Interviews and Other Writings of Michel Foucult*, ed. Lawrence D. Kritzman, paperback (New York: Routledge, 1990), 47.
[46] Foucault, *The Hermeneutics of the Subject*, 15.
[47] Foucault, *The Hermeneutics of the Subject*, 17.

but they mostly leave untouched the Kantian presumption of universal human perception. But working on the framings of the thing is only half of the job to achieve de-anthropocentrism, this book argues—while the other half is to work on the self so as to escape the given perceptual structure, and to see the thing in a new light. Foucault urges us to rethink whether subjectivity must be pre-defined, in his discussion of an alternative modality that he calls spirituality:

> Spirituality postulates that the subject as such does not have right of access to the truth and is not capable of having access to the truth. It postulates that the truth is not given to the subject by a simple act of knowledge (*connaissance*), which would be founded and justified simply by the fact that he is the subject and because he possesses this or that structure of subjectivity. It postulates that for the subject to have right of access to the truth he must be changed, transformed, shifted, and become, to some extend and up to a certain point, other than himself. The truth is only given to the subject at a price that brings the subject's being into play.[48]

While Foucault is famous for his study of how systematic power constitutes the subject, in his late books, he began to study Greco-Roman antiquity to explore the possibility that morality does not mean obedience to a code of conduct, but rather assertion of one's free will to construct oneself as an ethical being.[49] Besides antiquity, Foucault in his discussion on Baudelaire notes that modern artists are likewise conscious of the possibility of self-creation, but perhaps only in the domain of art.

> Modern man, for Baudelaire, is not the man who goes off to discover himself, his secrets and his hidden truth; he is the man who tries to invent himself. This modernity does not "liberate man in his own being"; it compels him to face the task of producing himself.[50]

Following Foucault's lead, this book explores how modernist artists might escape the Kantian mandate of universal perception, through their regimes of subjective transformation: regimes that are intensively willed, often painful, and more often failed. As opposed to the common impression that de-

---

[48] Foucault, *The Hermeneutics of the Subject*, 15.
[49] Michel Foucault, *Politics, Philosophy, Culture*, 49.
[50] Foucault, "What is Enlightenment," 42.

anthropocentrism means to avoid paying attention to humans and to immerse ourselves in all mundane yet mysterious things, my project shows that precisely this heightened attention to the self—to check our habitual impulse to appropriate the thing, to expand beyond our human ken to see the thing—in short, to be other than ourselves, is the prerequisite to de-anthropocentrism.

ONE
Artificiality

> En effet, la décadence d'une littérature,
> irréparablement atteinte dans son organisme,
> affaiblie par l'âge des idées, épuisée par les excès
> de la syntaxe, sensible seulement aux curiosités
> qui enfièvrent les malades et cependant pressée
> de tout exprimer à son déclin, acharnée à vouloir
> réparer toutes les omissions de jouissance, à
> léguer les plus subtils souvenirs de douleur, à son
> lit de mort...
>
> --Huysmans, *Á rebours*, XIV, 261[1]

As a professional critic and journalist, Baudelaire discusses a broad array of ideas, and takes pride in his cosmopolitan horizon. With a dramatic persona, partial and political, Baudelaire intends to explore each different definition of beauty in its own right, rather than to make himself a hardcore disciple of a single system. Already in "The Salon 1846" and at the age of 25, Baudelaire develops his idea of *modernity*: that each age has its own aesthetic ideal, and that as the critic and the poet of the age his task is to express *the beauty of his own time*. In that year of 1846, Baudelaire recognizes the beauty *à la mode* as Romanticism.

> Chaque siècle, chaque peuple ayant possédé l'expression de sa beauté et de sa morale, — si l'on veut entendre par romantisme l'expression la plus récente et la plus moderne de la beauté, — le grand artiste sera donc, — pour le critique raisonnable et passionné, — celui qui unira à la condition demandée ci-dessus, la naïveté, — le plus de romantisme possible. (Œuvres II, 84)

Baudelaire's commendation of Romanticism is here subordinate under his criterion of modernity: if we want to see in Romanticism what is the most recent and most modern idea of beauty, the Romantic artist must keep to the

---

[1] Joris-Karl Huysmans, *À Rebours* (Georges Crès, 1922).

standard of naivety, viz., his faith to his individuality. Romanticism is here a specific expression of the time, rather than a universalized truth. By the year 1857, where Baudelaire publishes his "Notes nouvelles sur Edgar Poe," however, Baudelaire announces his sentiment that the glory of Romanticism is declining, like the sun setting: "Ce soleil qui, il y a quelques heures, écrasait toutes choses de sa lumière droite et blanche, va bientôt inonder l'horizon occidental de couleurs variées."[2] This is when Baudelaire has reached his mature poetic power, and aspires to discover—indeed to author—the new joys of his own time, as opposed to the received tradition of Romanticism: "Dans les jeux de ce soleil agonisant, certains esprits poétiques trouveront des délices nouvelles" (ibid., ii). With the sun setting, Decadence takes the place of Romanticism to be the expression of time—Decadence is modern. While the term modernity refers to the formal requirement that art must reflect the spirit of time, the term Decadence by 1860s came to embody Baudelaire's sense of his own time—that Romanticism is in decline.

Of course, there is no clear dividing line between Romanticism and Decadence, as we know that Baudelaire still comments with conventional Romantic dictions on Wagner in the year of 1861 and Delacroix in 1863,[3] while Nietzsche calls Wagner "*the artist of Decadence.*"[4] Moreover, as Romanticism is itself already a very complicated movement, it is also impossible to assert that what Baudelaire calls new Decadent joys are unprecedented in Romanticism. Critics generally agree, as Charles Bernheimer writes, that "the content of Decadence was so multifaceted that no clear outline was discernible."[5] But if we will want to use the term Decadence productively, it might be sufficient to recognize that the very premise that motivates the movement is the artists' historical awareness and their intention to upset the old Romantic decorum. Part One of the book will dedicate itself to unraveling the Decadent joys with reference to the Romantic yardstick, especially that of the idealist dictum that theorizes Romantic art as a vision of the immaterial inwardness.

---

[2] "Notes nouvelles sur Edgar Poe" is the preface to Baudelaire's French translation of Poe's short stories. Charles Baudelaire, "Notes nouvelles sur Edgar Poe," in *Nouvelles Histoires Extraordinaires* (A. Quantin, 1884), ii.
[3] Baudelaire's essays referred here are "Richard Wagner et Tannhäuser à Paris" (Œuvres III, 207-265) and "L'Œuvre et la vie d'Eugène Delacroix" (Œuvres III, 1-44).
[4] Friedrich Nietzsche, "The Case of Wagner," in *The Complete Works of Friedrich Nietzsche, Vol. Eight*, trans. M. Anthony Ludovici (New York: Macmillan, 1911), 11.
[5] Charles Bernheimer, *Decadent Subject: The Idea of Decadence in Art, Literature, Philosophy, and Culture of the Fin de Siècle in Europe* (Baltimore: The John Hopkins University Press, 2002), 2.

For Huysmans, as cited in the epigraphs to this chapter, Decadent literature refuses a substantial definition precisely because the poet is now eager to taste every pleasure and to experiment with all possible kinds of expression. Gautier makes a similar comment in his preface to the third edition of *Les Fleurs du mal* (1868), that Baudelaire is devoted to what might be called "a style of decadence," a style so complicated and refined that it takes colors from every palette and notes from every keyboard: "Le poëte des *Fleurs du mal* aimait ce qu'on appelle improprement le style de décadence...prenant des couleurs à toutes les palettes, des notes à tous les claviers."[6] For both Huysmans and Gautier, the term Decadence refers to a historical awareness in a formal sense: a feeling that one is satiated with the old tradition and yet is too weary to start a new epoch—therefore one searches for every new pleasure with the purpose to subvert the aging tradition, rather than to establish a new one. Decadence is a paradox between ennui and curiosity— their weariness toward the long-honored ideas now provokes the artists to seek whatever upsets the decorum of the old tradition. Decadence is an even stranger paradox between novelty and decay: a Decadent idea by definition is not revolutionary, anticipates not a new epoch; it rather is a historical awareness that constantly refers itself to the golden age of Romanticism in order to shock, to subvert, and to subtly ironize the aging aesthetic yardstick. The purpose of Decadence is to turn back upon the old glory and to taunt it, where the poets re-approach their cherished aesthetic ideas with a delicate languor and a decisive mischief. Precisely as Gautier comments, we find in *Les Fleurs du mal* all different kinds of pleasures, all exotic flowers—a nostalgic evocation of the Romantic ideal in "Élévation", a dangerous, enervating sensuality in "Hymne à la Beauté", but also a strange sonnet "La Beauté", where Beauty appears to be incarnated as a stony sphinx that redefines art, no longer as immaterial imagination, but as the poet's love toward a inaccessible stone. With their grand titles, many poems such as "Hymne à la Beauté" and "La Beauté" in *Les Fleurs du mal* gesture as an aesthetic manifesto, envisioning "les faces diverses de l'absolu."[7] Baudelaire inaugurates a new epoch in which what is decadent is modern, and this desire of "dégageant de nouveaux fumets, de nouvelles ivresses"[8] is the essential feature of the fin-de-siècle literature.

Admirable scholarly efforts have been made to place Decadent literature in the collective psychological state of fin-de-siècle Europe. Yet in Part One, I

---

[6] Charles Baudelaire, *Œuvres Complètes de Charles Baudelaire* (Michel Lévy frères, 1868), Vol. I, 17.
[7] *Œuvres Complètes de Charles Baudelaire*, Vol. II, 84.
[8] Huysmans, *À rebours*, 261.

propose specifically a philosophical approach to read fin-de-siècle literature: each of these new joys is a new concept of art, many of which in turn draw new relations between matter and imagination. Such an approach means that I would not always repeat the sentiment of degeneration and depravity in my discussion of fin-de-siècle literature. Rather, fin-de-siècle literature is inductive to my project because it consciously unfetters itself from the Romantic norm, and therefore creates new relations of how imagination can relate to materiality in works of art. A fashionable theme of Decadence that Part One will focus on discussing is *artificiality*, vaguely defined as that art is superior to nature. Yet, artificiality in all its various expressions operates in opposition to its predecessor of Romanticism. A. E. Carter focuses on the notion of artificiality in his discussion on Decadence: "it was in revolt against of Romantic theory on two essential points—the cult of Nature and the cult of ideal love. Its artificiality contradicts both."[9] For the purpose of my project, however, I focus more specifically on *how artificiality operates against the idealist cult of imaginative, inward, immaterial art*. Hegel defines Romantic art, superior to nature, as an "absolute inwardness."[10] With the banner of artificiality, however, the fin-de-siècle artists draw every possible ally between imagination and materiality that often turns art inside out: all of these nevertheless keep to the maxim that art is superior to nature, now changing the flavor from Romantic pride to Decadent perversity. Art is superior to nature as Beauty incarnated as a stony sphinx is inaccessible to the feeling heart, as we will read in Baudelaire's sonnet "La Beauté." Art is superior to nature as we find Beauty conceptualized as impassive and impressive sensuous surface that is dissociated from, and in turn, subjugates the inwardness—which we find in Baudelaire's praise of dandyism and cosmetics, Gustave Moreau's jeweled surface, and Mallarmé's "Hérodiade." Finally, art is superior to nature not because imagination is immaterial, but because imagination allies itself with inorganic materiality, as we read in Baudelaire's "Rêve parisien" and Moreau's theorization of painting. All of these tropes are, in themselves, art manifestos of how imagination can be related to materiality in radically new ways.

But the artist creates new subject-object relations at great costs. The idealist tradition allows the artist to create an autonomous realm of imagination, narcissistic and self-sufficient: idealist art is an invitation to an otherworldly land that resembles ourselves. To create relationships with matter, in the

---

[9] A. E. Carter, *The Idea of Decadence in French Literature, 1830-1900* (University of Toronto Press, 1958), 150.
[10] G. W. F. Hegel, *Aesthetics,* Vol. I, p.519. Emphasis original.

Western tradition of the irreparable subject-object divide, however, always presupposes *self-alienation*. As I will discuss in the Section I, The Parnassian school which self-consciously challenges the Romantic motto of emotional expression, chooses the marble statue of Venus as the symbol of their poetic ideal of impassivity. To love the Venus statue means to honor the material form over inward expression, and the Parnassians thus redefine art, not as a pure realm of immaterial imagination, but as a relation between poetic mind and resistant matter. But the Parnassians were still idealist in their bones: for them matter is to be conquered by poetic prowess however resistant it is, just as the Venus statue will eventually be transformed into a living mistress by virtue of omnipotent imagination. This re-enactment of the Pygmalion myth is only for the faint-hearted. Compared to the Parnassian poems, Baudelaire's sonnet "La Beauté" as discussed in Section II is an allegory that pushes this self-alienation to the extreme, where the stony sphinx announces a structure of the poetic quest as a desirous poet who loves, unrequitedly, the mute stone. Baudelaire's "La Beauté" in this sense truly subverts the idealist tradition, and therefore announces the coming of the fin-de-siècle by giving us a taste of new pleasures at the sunset of German Idealism. Following the formula laid out in the sonnet "La Beauté," in Section III, I will discuss Baudelaire's theorization of artificiality: that dandies or women who wear cosmetics adorn an artificial appearance in order to subjugate their emotional expression, which Baudelaire explicitly comments on as the heroism of Decadence. In Section IV, I will further discuss the aesthetic effect of artificial appearances—articulations of why an incomprehensible jeweled surface is beautiful—through Baudelaire's "Avec ses vêtements ondoyants et nacrés," and the Salome figure painted by Moreau and Mallarmé. Section V discusses yet another facet of artificiality, where Huysmans conceptualizes matter not as mute and inaccessible stone, but as a powerhouse of unknown sensations hidden behind our conventional concepts, while art functions to unpack such sensations to the point of deranging one's senses and conceptual scheme. This difficult love of matter's insensible appearance as well its innate powers—this courageous self-alienation—testifies to my thesis that the poet creates a relation with the stone through creation of the self.

I. Pygmalion's Statue

Baudelaire's report on Romanticism in his salon essays has its closest affinity to German Idealism: in addition to his emphasis on Delacroix's naïve passion and his expressive power, Baudelaire also theorizes that art is superior to nature by virtue of its inwardness and immateriality. In one of his 1846 salon essays, "Pourquoi la sculpture est ennuyeuse," Baudelaire echoes Hegel in his argument that painting is superior to sculpture as an artistic medium, because painting is composed only of colors, free from the obscure materiality of stone or wood. At the apex of idealism, Hegel's argument is formal, regardless of the contents of the painting:

> The visibility and the making visible which belongs to painting have their differences in a more ideal way, i.e. in the particular colours, and they free art from the *complete* sensuous spatiality of material things by being restricted to the dimensions of a *plane* surface.[11]

Baudelaire renders this argument with his signature pungent style, which, however, belies a heightened anxiety—that the idealist cannot tolerate materiality because matter never entirely submits itself to the authorial control. This anxiety originates from the idealist obsession with artistic superiority over untamed nature:

> Il y a là un mystère singulier qui ne se touche pas avec les doigts.
>
> La sculpture a plusieurs inconvénients qui sont la conséquence nécessaire de ses moyens. Brutale et positive comme la nature, elle est en même temps vague et insaisissable, parce qu'elle montre trop de faces à la fois. C'est en vain que le sculpteur s'efforce de se mettre à un point de vue unique ; le spectateur, qui tourne autour de la figure, peut choisir cent points de vue différents, excepté le bon, et il arrive souvent, ce qui est humiliant pour l'artiste, qu'un hasard de lumière, un effet de lampe, découvrent une beauté qui n'est pas celle à laquelle il avait songé. Un tableau n'est que ce qu'il veut ; il n'y a pas moyen de le regarder autrement que dans son jour. La peinture n'a qu'un point de vue ; elle est exclusive et despotique : aussi l'expression du peintre est-elle bien plus forte. (Œuvres II, 185)

P. E. Charvet translates the title of this essay "Pourquoi la sculpture est ennuyeuse" as "Why Sculpture is a Bore,"[12] although the word "ennuyeuse" can also mean "annoying" or "awkward." In the quoted passage here, a sculpture is certainly not boring or monotonous; it is rather mysterious, and annoying to a tyrannical idealist who cannot allow a work of art its own life. Baudelaire here stands by the idealist stance that immaterial art is superior, although the passage betrays an

---

[11] Hegel, *Aesthetics*, Vol. 1, p. 87.
[12] Charles Baudelaire, *Selected Writings on Art and Literature*, trans. P.E. Charvet (Penguin Books, 2006), 98.

unspoken anxiety of the idealist who cannot tolerate any foreignness of materiality that does not submit itself to authorial control.

This idealist insistence on immateriality often becomes the target of parody in Decadent literature. The presence of sculpture in fin-de-siècle literature therefore evokes not merely the classical ideal, but also a streak of perverse pleasure that aims precisely to irritate the stubborn disciples of idealism. For a quick reference before I proceed with the main line of argument, the hero in Huysmans' *Á rebours* tastes his decadent pleasure by introducing in his living room "un petit sphinx, en marbre noir" and "une chimère, en terre polychrome"— and, precisely as the idealist Baudelaire forbids it, des Esseintes baths the mystic creatures in obscure shadows. Under the quivering light, the small statues were magnified and even more mysterious:

> Il plaça chacune de ces bêtes à un bout de la chambre, éteignit les lampes, laissant les braises rougeoyer dans l'âtre et éclairer vaguement la pièce en agrandissant les objets presque noyés dans l'ombre. (IX, 138)

Des Esseintes then has his mistress, a ventriloquist, to dub the two statues with strange, guttural voices. The chimera announces the mission of Decadence, a line which he quotes from one of Flaubert's scenes in *La Tentation de saint Antoine*:

> « Je cherche des parfums nouveaux, des fleurs plus larges, des plaisirs inéprouvés. » (IX, 139)

What untried pleasure here it is? Des Esseintes shares the physical malady of the fin-de-siècle, that is to say, his impotence, which is usually a metaphor that the artist has lost his authorial control over matter. If des Esseintes's creation here feels perverse, it is due to the reason that his work of art expresses not his individual thoughts, but the mysterious effect of materiality. But then des Esseintes re-writes this sheer mystery of materiality as an expression to his thirst for the unknown, for the "idéal inassouvi," which allows him to "tâtonner sans jamais arriver à une certitude" (IX, 139). Whereas the idealist painter asserts his artist superiority by creating the artistic effect precisely as he intends it, des Esseintes's relationship with the ideal is a perpetual quest since he will never arrive at the absolute, while this quest is fueled by the excitement about mysterious materiality.

Á rebours embodies the apex of the fin-de-siècle spirit, although the edifice of idealism is certainly not overthrown in one day. The Parnassian school, for example, while challenging Hegel's esteem for immaterial art by honoring the marble statue of Venus de Milo as their muse and mistress, composes in fact a group of virile poets who believe that their genius mind can conquer the most resistant matter, just as they often imagine that they can *turn alive* the marble statue of Venus *in order to violate her.* We will begin with an introduction on the Parnassian poetics in order to gauge how radical Baudelaire's and Huysmans's quests for mysterious materiality are. In Parnassian poetry, there is still a strong emphasis on the fantasy that the poet can dominate the statue with his poetic prowess, despite of the fact that the marble statue appears aloof and resistant. For Baudelaire in the fin-de-siècle cult of artificiality, however, the stone is eternally a stone, and the poet's love of the statue will never be returned. The emphasis is however shifted to a dissociation between appearance and inwardness, to the fact that the material surface is simply unintelligible, perhaps utterly inert, while the poet's projection of the statue is ironically illusory. It is this difficult, unrequited love toward the marble statue, where the matter cannot be conquered and turned alive, that I am most interested in discussing.

Parnassian poets champion for a conscious movement that rebels against the emotional expression in Romanticism, and adopt as the symbol of their poetic ideal a white marble statue of Venus or a sphinx—which symbolizes the desired poetic qualities of impassivity, eternality, and also, autonomy of a work of art which demands the poet's disinterested love, for she is sterile, her existence serves only an aesthetic purpose, and fulfills not carnal desire.[13] Hegel already comments that the statue, as the emblem of classical art, has its spirit withdrawn into itself, as opposed to the Romantic art where the work of art has the most direct emotional connection with its viewer. The statue does not communicate; it rather reflects back the viewer's desire like a transparent mirror:

> The supreme works of beautiful sculpture are sightless, and their inner being does not look out of them.... This light of the soul falls outside them and belongs to the spectator alone; when he looks at these shapes, soul cannot meet soul nor eye to eye. But the God of Romantic art appears seeing, self-knowing, inwardly subjective, and disclosing his inner being to man's inner being.[14]

For Théophile Gautier, who develops many motifs in Parnassianism, however, the statue that is withdrawn is even more attractive than one that reveals her inner being. As early as in his novel *Mademoiselle de Maupin* (1835),[15]

---

[13] An abridged version of the discussion on Parnassian poetry has been published on Wu, "A Dream of a Stone," 422–24.
[14] Hegel, *Aesthetics,* Vol. 1, p. 520-21.
[15] Théophile Gautier, *Mademoiselle de Maupin* (Paris: G. Charpentier, 1880), 153.

Gautier's hero transforms the materiality of the work of art into a metaphor that inspires the poet's disinterested love while at the same time perpetually sustains his desire, since she is forever inaccessible:

> Il y a quelque chose de grand et de beau à aimer une statue, c'est que l'amour est parfaitement désintéressé, qu'on n'a à craindre ni la satiété ni le dégoût de la victoire, et qu'on ne peut espérer raisonnablement un second prodige pareil à l'histoire de Pygmalion.

The statue, although marble, has the sensuous form of a woman, and this sensuous form allows for transactions between subjective desire and material inaccessibility. The statue is insensible, but here her inaccessibility enters into the poet's fantasy as a quality that would forever challenge him to chase. Following the Kantian dictum, the essence of the object is withdrawn, but its appearance reflects back the viewer's projected desire. To love the inaccessible statue only for its sensuous surface and not for its inward expression is then, on the one hand, an emphasis on the materiality of a work of art, while on the other it is still a variant of idealism since what we love is only a projection of our desire.

In its cult of polished poetic form, the Parnassians re-conceptualize the creation of art—no longer as immaterial imagination—but as a relation between a triumphant mind over resistant matter. In his poem "L'Art" (1852),[16] Gautier argues that words have their resistant materiality in the same way a white marble is resistant to a sculptor's chisel. And the value of the poem depends precisely upon how resistant the matter worked upon is: "Oui, l'œuvre sort plus belle / D'une forme au travail / Rebelle, / Vers, marbre, onyx, émail." The eternality of a verse now relies not on the universal eternality of Hegelian spirit, but rather on how the thought can be externalized and etched in the lasting materiality of the poem: "L'art robuste / Seul a l'eternity."

For Gautier, words have their materiality because they have their own meanings prior to entering into the poet's creation. These values innate in words constitute a beauty of their own like that of gemstones; while a poet's task is only to arrange these beautiful words into rhymed, poetic lines, like a goldsmith arranging the gemstones into a bracelet. As Gautier argues in his preface to the 1868 edition of *Les Fleurs du mal*:

---

[16] Théophile Gautier, *Émaux et Camées*, *Œuvres de Théophile Gautier. Poésies*, volume III (Lemerre, 1890), 132-34.

> Pour le poëte, les mots ont, en eux-mêmes et en dehors du sens qu'ils expriment, une beauté et une valeur propres comme des pierres précieuses qui ne sont pas encore taillées et montées en bracelets, en colliers ou en bagues : ils charment le connaisseur qui les regarde et les trie du doigt dans la petite coupe où ils sont mis en réserve, comme ferait un orfèvre méditant un bijou. Il y a des mots diamant, saphir, rubis, émeraude, d'autres qui luisent comme du phosphore quand on les frotte, et ce n'est pas un mince travail de les choisir.[17]

But then, despite of the fact that words have their irreducible materiality like gemstones, the relation between mind and matter here is still that the intellect will give poetic form to the raw content. The poet asserts his intellect when he, like a connoisseur of gemstones, chooses the precise words and arranges them into rhymed, symmetrical lines, and thereby have the words duly express his thoughts.

The poetic form must fit perfectly well with matter, thoughts with the words chosen, like shoes that fit on feet that enable one to walk further. The poet aims at asserting his prowess by shaping the difficult stone so that it will contain his floating dream, and thereby grant his fleeting ideas eternity: "Sculpte, lime, cisèle ; / Que ton rêve flottant / Se scelle / Dans le bloc résistant !" Similarly, Leconte de Lisle compares his thoughts to hard metal, which however should be melted in the fact of poetic form: "Et fais que ma pensée en rythmes d'or ruisselle / comme un divin metal au moule harmonieux." De Lisle is here praying to the statue of Venus de Milo, which is a piece of white marble that assumes its divine identity by virtue of the artist's shaping force: "Marbre sacré, vêtu de force et de genie."[18] Recognizing that words have their materiality, for the Parnassians, this materiality exists only to be conquered by the poet's intellectual power.

At times, however, we find the poet obviously cheating, and that the material resistance is only a pretense: the material presence, in some cases, exists only as an impression or figure of speech, which then can be easily transformed at the poet's whim. In Gautier's "Symphonie en blanc majeur" (1852),[19] the poet compares a woman he loves, who in his imagination is chaste, pure, and beautiful, to a series of white substances and animals, in no logical order: marble, clouds, lily, white foam of the sea from which Venus is

---

[17] Baudelaire, *Oeuvres* Vol. 1, p. 46.
[18] Leconte de Lisle, "Vénus de Milo," in *Poèmes Antiques* (Alphonse Lemerre, 1886), 134–36.
[19] Gautier, *Émaux et Camées*, 22-24.

born, ivory, ermine, quicksilver, May hawthorn, alabaster, dove. These white substances are evoked as similes to build an impression that the woman is otherworldly and out of reach. The poet exerts his poetic prowess to convince us that her beauty is divinely pure, but then, when it comes time to conquer this divine beauty, the poet conveniently chooses the white substance that can be melted, metaphorically by the poet's passion.

> Est-ce la Madone des neiges,
> Un sphinx blanc que l'hiver sculpta;
> Sphinx enterré par l'avalanche,
> Gardien des glaciers étoilés,
> Et qui, sous sa poitrine blanche,
> Cache de blancs secrets gelés ?
>
> Sous la glace où calme il repose,
> Oh ! qui pourra fondre ce cœur !
> Oh ! qui pourra mettre un ton rose
> Dans cette implacable blancheur !

A sphinx statue may be carved out of white marble, but a *snow sphinx* is surely a creature only of poetic imagination. This snow sphinx is aloof, but she is ontologically different from the marble statue that rejects the poet by virtue of her inorganic materiality. The sphinx made of snow has a white breast, but underneath it, someone hides in it a secret love. And perhaps just because the sphinx's love is exclusive to someone, she remains icy to all other pursuers. For that special person, her heart would be melted, herself perhaps dissolved, and she can no longer hold her icy identity. Here, the snowy sphinx's existence resides no doubt in the poet's imagination, for she exists to fulfill the poet's widest fantasy: to create the most beautiful woman that is exclusive to himself. What we see here is precisely a reenactment of Pygmalion's myth in which the creator is in love with the creature shaped by his imagination, while the exchange between statue and woman serves only to prove the prowess of poetic fantasy. And the poetic prowess—insofar as the poet can evoke and then transform the white substance by his whim, insofar as he can turn inaccessible marble into ice and then melt it—is a birthright granted by idealism.

Of course, my reader may doubt the value of the argument here, since we know *in advance* that the white substances in "Symphonie en blanc majeur" are only figures of speech, evoked to adorn the object of desire, here obviously a woman. In Théodore de Banville's "À Vénus de Milo" (1842), however, the poet explicitly addresses himself to a marble statue. And once again, the statue is in danger of transformation once it enters into the realm of poetic imagination. In the poem we see an easy transference of the properties between the human and the statue, in which the Venus statue turns alive and the poet becomes "amant sculpté."

> Ô Vénus de Milo, guerrière au flanc nerveux,
> Dont le front irrité sous vos divins cheveux
> Songe, et dont une flamme embrase la paupière,
> Rêve aux plis arreêtés, grand poème de pierre,
> Débordement de vie avec art compensé,
> Vous qui depuis mille ans avez toujours pensé,
> J'adore votre bouche où le courroux flamboie
> Et vos seins frémissants d'une tranquille joie.
>
> Et vous savez si bien ces amours éperdus
> Que si vous retrouviez un jour vos bras perdus
> Et qu'à vos pieds tombât votre blanche tunique,
> Nos froideurs pâmeraient dans un combat unique,
> Et vous m'étaleriez votre ventre indompté,
> Pour y dormir un soir comme un amant sculpté ![20]

In the first eight lines of the poem, we find the Venus statue is carved so livelily that she seems to embody all human emotions: her eyelids burn with passion and her lips with anger, she looks pensive while her breasts quiver with tranquil joy. While de Banville is one of the early theorists of Parnassianism, his description here is more dynamic than static, more Romantic than Parnassian. Art here is not superior to and dissociated from Life as the Decadents often assert it: rather, the statue is so well carved that it compensates for the lack of life in the statue ("Débordement de vie avec art compensé"). In the following six lines, we find again that the poet reenacts Pygmalion's myth and that the statue turns alive—and we realize just how difficult it actually is to let the statue be statue, and to restrain from appropriating it into the realm of imagination. The rhetorical figure that de Banville here employs is *apostrophe*, "the calling out to inanimate, dead, or absent beings."[21] And, as Barbara Johnson comments, apostrophe as a poetic power often demonstrates itself as "the seemingly involuntary transformation of something material into an instrument capable of sounding the depths of

---

[20] Théodore de Banville, *Les Cariatides* (Paris: Pilout, 1842), 373–74.
[21] Barbara Johnson, *Persons and Things* (Harvard University Press, 2010), 6.

humanity."[22] The poet calls out to the Venus statue, and while he is merely counting the possibility that she may one day, somehow, regain her lost arm—the power of the poetic voice is such that he can *visualize* anything imaginative in his poem, including here of restoring Venus's lost arm, turning the statue alive, striping her of her tunic, and putting her down and spreading out her body on his bed! The poet in turn is turned into a "sculpted lover," which is supposedly a punishment for his profane fantasy. But he in fact assumes no qualities of the statue; just that he swoons out of ecstasy. Turning a Venus statue into his mistress, de Banville asserts his poetic sovereign almost shamelessly. Venus's unconquered loins ("ventre indompté") is virgin and sacred for unimaginative mortals, but it is there to be relished by the poet's omnipotent imagination.

In fin-de-siècle, however, this Parnassian cult of the statue became the target of sophisticated irony. Villiers de l'Isle-Adam's *L'Eve future* (1886)[23] begins with the idealist pride to have the perfect statue mirrors our desire. The scientist in the novel is Mr. Edison, who—as Villiers has borrowed the fame from the contemporary American inventor who lights up the world with his lightbulbs—lives in Menlo Park and avoids talking to living humans except for through his inventions, such as the phonographs or telephones. Mr. Edison asserts his tenet of artificiality, that art is superior to life, that a statue is superior to a living woman, precisely because the statue is thoughtless and will only reflect back the poet's thoughts. Lord Ewald confides to Edison his distress, that his beloved Miss Alicia has the perfect form of the marble Venus Victorious (in fact, she bears a striking similitude to her) (40), but only possesses a shallow soul who values money and fame.

> Le seul malheur dont soit frappée miss Alicia, c'est la pensée ! – Si elle était privée de toute pensée, je pourrais la comprendre. La *Vénus* de marbre, en effet, *n'a que faire de la Pensée.* La déesse est voilée de minéral et de silence. Il sort de son aspect ce Verbe-ci : – « Moi, je suis *seulement* la Beauté même. » (64, emphasis original)

Unknowingly, Ewald pronounces the dictum of artificiality, that Beauty must be skin-deep and the highest ideal form of it must be a thoughtless marble statue. Edison promises to deliver Ewald out of his distress—but then his solution is to create a metallic android who looks exactly like Alicia without

---

[22] Johnson, *Persons and Things,* 8.
[23] Auguste Villiers de L'Isle-Adam, *L'Ève Future* (Paris: Bibliothèque-Charpentier; Eugène Fasquelle, 1909).

her philistine personality. The narrative takes place as Edison gives a long lecture of the mechanical anatomy of the android, and, while Ewald would occasionally protest that he will not love a soulless substitute, Edison uses these moments to further advance his philosophy of artificiality. Their conversations vaguely follow the fashion of Plato's dialogues, while Ewald is the interlocutor who exposes the absurdity of Edison's proposals before the latter is finally initiated in the occult of a love toward the inorganic thing. Edison speaks in impeccable logic and takes advantage of a line Ewald cries out in his agitation, where he wishes Miss Alicia would just be a perfect statuesque form without her vulgar thoughts—"Qui m'ôtera cette âme de ce corps?" (80)—and reiterates this line back to Ewald whenever he raises objections (142, 224), in order to reassure Ewald that the most ideal object of desire will be a soulless statue.

Ewald has, in his description of the marble Venus, echoes Hegel's definition of statues quoted above—the "light of the soul falls outside them and belongs to the spectator alone," that the spectator will assume inward depth in the statue precisely because she is thoughtless:

> Je ne pense que par l'esprit de qui me contemple. En mon absolu, toute conception s'annule d'elle-même, puisqu'elle perd sa limite. Toutes s'y abîment, confondues, indistinctes, identiques, pareilles aux vagues des fleuves à l'entrée de la mer. Pour qui me réfléchit, je *suis* telle qu'il peut m'approfondir. (64)

While for Hegel the beautiful is defined by the inward depth of the spirit, Edison argues for a love of the android's surface appearance. But, most perversely, Edison also argues that this love of the statue fulfills exactly Hegel's definition of the Ideal, as the negation of the statue's soul will facilitate the spirit's self-same unity in the object of art: *"The Thing is 'I,'"* "the Self's pure knowledge of itself."[24] The android is named Hadlay, meaning "Ideal" in Iranian (126). And Edison explicates the Ideal as an objectification of Edison's desire, a reproduction of Edison's own soul.

> Enfin, c'est cette vision, objectivée de votre esprit, que vous appelez, que vous voyez, que vous créez en votre vivante, *et qui n'est que votre âme dédoublée en elle.* (110)

---

[24] Hegel, *Phenomenology of Spirit*, 481-82. Emphasis original.

But then, we will soon see that this ideal dream of narcissistic love is realized in the most ridiculous way.

Edison produces, on the one hand, the impression that the android will be a perfect, or sublimated, mimic of life. Replacing "spiritisme" with "l'électricité" (160), Edison claims that the android's gait is that of a "somnambule" which signifies her "extase mystique" (237). Before she assumes the flesh of Miss Alicia, Edison takes Ewald to visit her, who is then covered by a coat of elegant armor and her face heavily veiled, and has command over a flock of noisy artificial birds (158). She seems, also, able to respond to Edison's questions with subtly and gentle sophistication. When Ewald asks Edison if he will infuse into the Android "an intelligence,"

> – *Une* intelligence ? non : l'Intelligence, oui. (105, emphasis original)

On the other hand, Edison bombards Ewald with a meticulous lecture of the artificial constitution of the android in plain scientific terms, to the point that Ewald is overwhelmed: "Savez-vous...qu'il est vraiment infernal de voir les choses de l'Amour sous un jour pareil ?"(271-72, elliptical mine). We learn that the android is made of very precious substances, and thus immortal. In addition, her joints are lubricated by oil of roses, her eyes are made of precious stones (267). The android wears rings of turquoise and amethyst that are buttons with which Ewald must give commands to her actions and, above all, her voice organ is two phonographic discs of "l'or vierge," for the metal "doué d'une résonnance plus féminimement sonore, plus sensible, plus exquise" (132).

Only later (but of course!) does Edison explain that what he means by intelligent conversations are actually recorded phonographs of words, twenty hours in total length, of "les plus grands poètes, les plus subtils métaphysiciens et les romanciers les plus profonds de ce siècle," some of them unpublished but Edison has procured the copyright at extravagant cost (215). Ewald suddenly realizes that in order to interact with the android, he must learn by heart what the android's prerecorded response is—in order to ask the right question! (216). But Edison proceeds with his lecture:

> Il est tant de mots vagues, suggestifs, d'une élasticité intellectuelle si étrange ! et dont le charme et la profondeur dépendent, simplement, de *ce à quoi ils répondent !*
>
> Un exemple : je suppose qu'une parole solitaire... le mot « *déjà !* » soit le mot que *devra* prononcer, — en tel instant, — l'Andréïde. Je prends ce seul mot, au lieu de n'importe quelle phrase. Vous attendez cette

parole, qui sera dite avec la voix douce et grave de Miss Alicia Clary et accompagnée de son plus beau regard perdu en vos yeux.

Ah! songez à combien de questions ou de pensées ce seul mot peut répondre magnifiquement! Ce sera donc à vous d'en créer la profondeur et la beauté *dans votre question même*. (219, emphasis original)

The android's answers are always suggestive, Edward proudly explains. For example, she might proclaim "already!", and her lover can construct all kinds of questions to make this answer sounds wise, sophisticated, and yet detached. To Hegel's aesthetics that the work of art should be the projection of our soul, Villiers exposes that this narcissism is surely absurd, as absurd as Yeats's shepherd speaking to an echoing shell. In protest of idealism, the fin-de-siècle artists are emphatic of the simple truth that to love or to converse is essentially a desire to build a connection with an Other.

But just as Edison's lecture about the android's artificial constitution continues, the android starts to impose her individuality and strange logic of thinking. She requests donations in full eloquence on behalf of a poor widow, and Ewald is compelled to drop several bank notes into her purse (247-248). When Edison starts to laugh compulsively at the idea of being in love with a machine, the android finds a chance to laugh at Miss Alicia, echoed more loudly by her artificial bird. And the narrator comments:

Lord Ewald comprit que l'Andréïde lui montrait qu'elle savait rire aussi des vivants. (260)

More uncannily, if the android seems to show sympathy to a particular widow, she does not concern herself with the fate of the planet, as if her perspective is far beyond humanity. When Edison asks her a hypothetical question: what if there is a god who, out of whim, destroys the whole solar system with his thunderbolt?

— Eh bien ? dit Hadaly.

— Eh bien! que penseriez-vous d'un tel phénomène, s'il vous était permis d'en contempler l'effrayante performance ? acheva Edison.

— Oh! répondit l'Andréïde avec sa voix grave et en faisant monter, sur ses doigts d'argent, l'oiseau de paradis, – je crois que cet événement passerait, dans l'inévitable Infini, sans qu'il lui fût accordé beaucoup plus d'importance que vous n'en donnez aux millions d'étincelles qui pétillent et retombent dans l'âtre d'un paysan. (266-267)

The novel continues to play with the dynamic of self-same illusion and alienate alterity, and Ewald is challenged by both. The android is at once a mirror of illusion that is designed to reflect the lover's wistful desire, a replica that Ewald does not deign to fall in love with, and an ultimate Other that exposes humans' anthropocentric perspective. If the android would not even worry about the destruction of the whole planet, then Ewald's belief that he should only devote his love to another human being would be for her even far more meaningless, in fact pathetically self-pitying, than a peasant's care for the sparks at his hearth.

Towards the end of the novel, Villiers reconciles all of these challenges to humanity by giving the android an unknown soul, since she is animated by a woman in her cataleptic trance (368), and by having the android destroyed in fire in order to preclude the forbidden love (370). Still, the Decadent novel turns the idealist desire to impose one's imagination on a thing into a sophisticated formula of artificiality—which at once exposes the absurdity of this narcissistic love, and the impossibility of domesticating the mysterious thing. The fin-de-siècle cult of artificiality is often formulated as an ironic incongruity between appearance and inwardness, and in this case, the android, created as the perfect object of love so as to fulfill the human desire, serves only to highlight the Otherness of the material thing.

II. A Dream of Stone

Whereas Villiers's project is to ironize idealism by exposing the foreignness of the thing underneath the narcissistic love, Baudelaire's poem "La Beauté"[25] is to openly overthrow the idealist doctrine by loving the Otherness of the stone. Among works that pursue the Parnassian motif of the poetic love of the statue,[26] which is usually wildly conceived and badly executed, Baudelaire's poem "La Beauté" is the one that follows through its original manifesto and *does not* re-enact the myth of Pygmalion. In this sense, the poet in "La

---

[25] Charles Baudelaire, *Les Fleurs du mal* (Poulet-Malassis et De Broise, 1861), No. 17. The discussion on Baudelaire's "La Beauté" has been published on Wu, "A Dream of a Stone," 421–27.
[26] Francis Heck, however, argues that Baudelaire's "La Beauté" presents an underlying irony of the Parnassian aesthetics. See Francis S. Heck, "'La Beauté': Enigma of Irony," *Nineteenth-Century French Studies* 10, no. 1/2 (1981): 85–95.

Beauté" is the one who has truly tasted the new joy of Decadence. With the poem's grand title, I propose that the poem should be read as a philosophical treatise of how imagination should be related to matter in the process of poetic creation. Contrary to the image presented by its Parnassian contemporaries, in this poem, resistant matter no longer allows for poetic domination, despite its seemingly inviting attitude that vainly provokes the poet's desire. The poem begins with the first-person narrative from Beauty's own voice:

> Je suis belle, ô mortels! Comme un rêve de pierre,
> Et mon sein, où chacun s'est meurtri tour à tour,
> Est fait pour inspirer au poète un amour
> Éternel et muet ainsi que la matière.

The rhetorical figure here is not apostrophe, as in de Banville's "À Vénus de Milo," which is capable of transforming the object as it enters the poetic vision. It is rather *prosopopeia* in which a thing is personified and given a voice and a face, such as a monument or a tombstone that speaks through its epitaph, while its existence proves that art outlives its creator.[27] The first line of the poem is already one of extreme complexity. "Je suis belle, ô mortels!"— the first half of the first line already gives an image of Beauty, and the exclamation mark calls for a temporary pause to examine this image. This *first impression* of Beauty, although partial, counts much and gives an original point for further analysis. Beauty begins by claiming its self-sufficient existence—I am beautiful or Beauty is beautiful—which is surprisingly independent of the poet. The statement is a reversal to the maxim of German Idealism: Fichte's maxim A=A, that our perception of the object is produced by our perception; as well as Hegel's definition that art is produced by the desire of the man "represent[ing] himself to himself" by "altering external things whereon he impresses the seal of his inner being,"[28] which Gautier renders as "Que ton rêve flottant / Se scelle / Dans le bloc resistant!" Beauty for now refuses to be a mirror of the poet's image (though she is precisely so, which she will admit by the fourth stanza); she rather asserts her tautological, absolute autonomy: Beauty is beautiful. Beauty presumes the status of a goddess and addresses poets as "mortals." She appears to be Plato's singular, archetypical Idea of Beauty, which is independent of and sought after by every poet; rather than, as Baudelaire explicates Romanticism, that the beautiful is

---

[27] Johnson, *Persons and Things*, 12-13.
[28] Hegel, *Aesthetics*, Vol. I, p. 31.

the expression of the poet's inward vision colored by his individual temperament—"C'est l'invisible, c'est l'impalpable, c'est le rêve, c'est les nerfs, c'est l'*âme*" (Œuvres III, 6).

As we finish reading the first line, however, we find the absolute Beauty is qualified, "comme un rêve de pierre." "Un rêve de pierre" is ambiguous in meaning since we cannot be certain who is dreaming (the poet or the stony Beauty), and what the dream is composed of (the stone or the beautiful). This linguistic copula "de" allows "the infinite chain of tropological transformations,"[29] to borrow a phrase from Paul de Man, while a critical hypothesis is required to momentarily freeze its movement. One possible way is to read Baudelaire's usage of "un rêve de pierre" as an allusion to de Banville's "rêve aux plis arrêtés, grand poème de pierre," which—if the white marble could dream—grants thoughts and expression, and therefore aesthetic value, to the Venus statue. If the stone can dream, and dream is traditionally the power of poetic imagination, then Beauty is *indeed* self-sufficient, while the poet is perpetually exiled from her garden of Eden. Another way to read it—if we want to salvage the poet's abject status—is to assume that it is the poet implied who is dreaming, *and* the poet is masochistic in that he elevates Beauty to this inaccessible pedestal. Considering that the poem is composed in a symmetrical structure that constantly allows transference between the subject and the object, I propose to read it as the poet who is dreaming, which will then make a parallel with the end of the stanza "un amour / Éternel et muet ainsi que la matière." Reading this way, the little sonnet then gestures itself as a philosophical treatise of a work of art: a prescription of how the creative mind should relate itself to resistant matter. My hope of adopting this exclusive point of view is, to follow Baudelaire's lead, that this hypothesis would open up a broader horizon ("la critique doit être partiale, passionnée, politique, c'est-à-dire faite à un point de vue exclusif, mais au point de vue qui ouvre le plus d'horizons") (Oeuvres II, 84). The philosophical definition of "the beautiful," then, is explicated as a *relationship* between two entities—the dream of stone—that stands for the dynamic of the subject and the object. The object of love ("un rêve de pierre") here is incorporated as plain as a stone, the exemplar of mute, insensible matter itself, rather than any objects that are conventionally associated with poetic values such as gold or gem. "Je suis belle, comme un rêve de pierre": the stone is beautiful, because and precisely because it enters into a relation with the poet, and becomes the object of poetic desire.

---

[29] de Man, *The Rhetoric of Romanticism*, 241.

"Et mon sein, où chacun s'est meurtri tour à tour"—Beauty here again asserts the ultimate independence of the thing as she is impervious to the poet's love. Her breast is capable of wounding, presumably because her breast is made of stone. As opposed to the Parnassian fascination with the Venus statue, Beauty in this poem would not be transformed by the poetic love. "Est fait pour inspirer au poète un amour"—by the third line, the autonomy of Beauty is however secretly betrayed: the stone is made or created ("est fait") to be inaccessible, or it is conceptualized so by the philosophical poet—in order to sustain the poet's eternal love. "Est fait pour inspirer au poète un amour/ Éternel et muet ainsi que la matière"—finish reading the fourth line, we then realize why the transcendental status of Beauty is imperative: counter to the idealist tradition, the poet's love transforms not matter but *himself*. The poet aspires a transformation of himself toward Otherness, to assume qualities of matter in square contrast to life, as mute as eternal (Baudelaire's term for this desire, as will be further discussed, is dandyism). More radically than its Parnassian peers, the stony statue in Baudelaire's poem is resistant, not in order to be eventually conquered, transformed, and violated as in Parnassian poetry, but to sustain a perpetual poetic quest and to prompt the poet to transform himself in order to love the Other. The beautiful is then defined as the most peculiar structure of the poetic quest: It is beautiful because the poet loves the stone, and because the stone is forever inaccessible that the poetic desire is perpetual. Here mind and matter are conceptualized in sharp contrast: the poet is inspired, the stone indifferent; the poet vulnerable to wounds, the stone eternally mute. And Baudelaire metaphorizes the qualities of matter itself—mute, impassive, and eternal—as the virtues of the Ideal that inspires the poetic quest. The poem then can be read as Baudelaire's aesthetic manifesto: the beautiful is defined by the love of the poet toward mute matter, and by the disparities between the two. The poet is desirous; the stone is mute; the love will not be fulfilled—but will define *the beautiful as this structure of perpetual poetic pursuit*. This is a drastically new formulation of the beautiful compared to his idealist predecessors. Whereas Hegel defines Romantic art as that the poetic Idea becomes self-sufficient and stands independent of matter, Baudelaire in this little sonnet redefines the beautiful as the poetic love toward the ultimate Other, the inaccessible matter.

The second stanza is presumably about the poet's creative process, but it is again spoken from Beauty's point of view. Here we find Beauty usurps the power of metaphorical transference that is traditionally ascribed to the poet—for the poet's creative efforts will be redefined in the third and fourth stanza.

> Je trône dans l'azur comme un sphinx incompris ;
> J'unis un cœur de neige à la blancheur des cygnes ;
> Je hais le mouvement qui déplace les lignes,
> Et jamais je ne pleure et jamais je ne ris.

A stone is indeed mysterious for it lacks any emotions and never communicates. The incomprehensible sphinx is however an image of poetic imagination through which the poet relates himself to the stone. Beauty's essence might be simply a stone, but in order to relate itself to the poet, it still needs to assume a sensuous appearance, a figure of human meaning. The poetic quest is then predicated upon a misunderstanding—stony impassivity taken for psychological mystery—in which mind and matter exchange traits. "J'unis un cœur de neige à la blancheur des cygnes" might be a riddle that the sphinx pronounces, by virtue of which she usurps the poetic power to unit and exchange traits between subject and object, between the heart of a swan and whiteness of snow. And if we compare Baudelaire's sphinx to Gautier's sphinx in "Symphonie," we find that in Baudelaire's poem any poetic progress is strangely suspended and proactively forestalled. While Gautier's sphinx has an icy heart that awaits to be melted, Baudelaire's stone does not anticipate being shaped into a work of art—it simply hates the poet's movement that may disturb the line. Gautier's sphinx is anticipated to blush, while Baudelaire's claims that she will never cry and never laugh. The resistance of Baudelaire's stony sphinx is not a flirtatious gesture for eventual conquest; it rather serves to perpetuate the poetic desire.

The third stanza then redefines the meaning of creation: it does not aim to transform the object of desire (from a stony statue to a living woman in order to answer to the poet's carnal desire); it rather *transforms the poet himself* in his devotion to art.

> Les poètes, devant mes grandes attitudes,
> Que j'ai l'air d'emprunter aux plus fiers monuments,
> Consumeront leurs jours en d'austères études ;

In addition to the image of the sphinx, the stone assumes the second metaphorical appearance: the eternal stone has such grand attitudes that it *seems, to the poet,* to borrow from proud monuments. In contrast to de Banville, who evokes the Parnassian ideal of impassivity through the alluring appearance of the Venus statue, Baudelaire's stone monument declares a material presence that is not anthropomorphic. She is a stone, but her presence suggests some monumental significance in human history that is more than herself: this excess, this enchanting exchange between poetic imagination and Beauty's plain material existence, inspires the poet to do all his austere study. But what is it that the poet should study by the monument? He would have to study the function of the work of art: to make what is transitory, eternal, and what is personal, universal. In his "Essay on Epitaphs," William Wordsworth explicates well the style that the monumental inscription should employ:

> It is to be remembered, that to raise a Monument is a sober and a reflective act; that the inscription which it bears is intended to be permanent, and for universal perusal; and that, for this reason, the thoughts and feelings expressed should be permanent also—liberated from that weakness and anguish of sorrow which is in nature transitory, and which with instinctive decency retires from notice. The passions should be subdued, the emotions controlled; strong, indeed, but nothing ungovernable or wholly involuntary.[30]

A work of art should bear the qualities of a stony sphinx or monument, which the poet spends his days to study: eternal, universal, invulnerable and self-possessed. But then, if art should be like a stone and be devoid of emotional expression, if it is larger than human and would not allow poetic manipulation, what then should the poet works on?

The final stanza reiterates the necessity of misrecognition, where Beauty asserts her transcendental status, while the productive poetic consciousness is only implied.

> Car j'ai, pour fasciner ces dociles amants,
> De purs miroirs qui font toutes choses plus belles :
> Mes yeux, mes larges yeux aux clartés éternelles !

The poet yearns for Beauty, but Beauty's eyes are like mirrors that reflect back only the poet's self-images and deflects the poet's search for the object of love. Baudelaire here seems to repeat the Kantian dictum that we only see the appearance of things produced by our own consciousness, and not the thing-in-itself. If the sphinx's mysterious air appears to the poet like a linguistic riddle, the answer to this riddle will not capture the stone, but will be "the man" himself. Repeating the Kantian dictum, the poem is however structured in such a way that it is Beauty who raises the mirrors with her magical eyes—

---

[30] William Wordsworth, *The Complete Poetical Works of William Wordsworth* (Troutman & Hayes, 1854), 705.

thus reversing the power dynamics between the lover and the beloved, and negating the idealist pride about the poet's productive consciousness. The fact that we only see things as our own mirrors does not preclude the possibility that these things have their own eyes: it is just that we cannot see through the eyes to the souls of Others, and wrongly takes the eyes as our mirrors. The stone might indeed have its inwardness, though forever withdrawn from human understanding.

Baudelaire however translates this ultimate alienation as a structure of perpetual desire: it is possible to love the Absolute, or the stone, despite of the fact that it is forever inaccessible and conceals itself beneath our projections. The sphinx's riddle invites devotion, but never allows achievement. The poetic practice then will be forever in quest and never in rest, as the riddle will never be solved and stone never in grasp. That is, Baudelaire claims that the poetic desire is predestined to not contain the *object* of beloved. As the work of art is the stone, matter plain and incomprehensible, the beautiful is the poetic dream of the stone, the process of transformative pursuit, that never reaches the sphinx misunderstood. Although Baudelaire recognizes the power of productive consciousness, as we see that it produces images of the sphinx and the monument, in excess to the essential existence of the stone, "La Beauté" as a poem no longer grants this productive consciousness the status of the Ideal. Rather, the beautiful is defined as the poet's perpetual, doomed desire to capture the stone, the desire to come closer to the real.

Critics sometimes read the speaker of the poem, who pronounces that "Je suis belle, ô mortels! Comme un rêve de pierre," as a beautiful woman rather than as a stone. Judith Ryan, for one example, supposes that the speaker in the poem is "the courtesan Phryne posing for the sculptor Praxiteles." Ryan poses the hypothesis in order to answer to the question that why the stone has human eyes.

> This hypothesis would explain the curious shifts between statue and human being, while locating the ambiguities of the poem in the situation of the sculptor's model. Accustomed to remaining motionless during long hours of posing in the studio, she feels estranged from ordinary life, more like a statue than a person. Yet although the statues are designed to eternalize her much vaunted beauty, she claims that she herself is superior to them, both because she is their inspiration and because one

part of her cannot be petrified however long she poses: her clear, living eyes, which enhance the beauty of all they reflect.[31]

Ryan reads the poem as a woman who takes on the figure of a stone, rather than as a stone who is capable of speaking. Yet, considering that in the poem any fleshly description about Beauty is curiously absent, I disagree with Ryan's interpretation. In Gautier's "Symphonie en blanc majeur," the woman who is compared to an icy sphinx has a vivid carnal charm. Gautier names each of her body parts—her breast, her shoulder, her skin, her flesh—although these parts are then compared rather abstractly to all white substances. Théodore de Banville's "À Vénus de Milo" likewise emphasizes the sensual charm of the marble statue, and following this, the poetic fantasy to relish it, by virtue of his power of apostrophe that is capable of transforming the stony statue into a living mistress. In both cases, the desired women, either a living or a stony one, are symbols of the poetic ideal in the poets' anthropomorphic imagination, of their ambition to conquer the most difficult matter and make it the poetic object. In Baudelaire's "La Beauté," however, Beauty has no physical traits and all description that we see is about her inaccessible attitude that we can rightly expect from a real stone: Her chest is not "neige montée en globe" as we see in Gautier's "Symphonie," rather it hurts because it is figuratively, perhaps literally also, stony. Two major figures in the poems, an incomprehensible sphinx statue coupled with the attitude of proud monuments, rather presupposes the speaker's essence as a stone. In return, the poet's love toward her is not carnal but metaphysical, and is related explicitly to the kind of love that the poet imbues into a work of art: that this love inspires the poet to be in a perpetual quest for the beautiful. Another reason I am opposed to Ryan's reading is that it is an attempt to revert the poetic metaphor of the stone back to the actual referent of the woman, from the mysterious riddle to the prosaic answer, and to escape from the metaphorical realm of the poem in order to restore the historical importance of the Phryne myth (though Ryan has her own strong theoretical agenda that she unfolds through the Phryne motif). But if we may read the stone in the poem qua the stone, then we acquire an intriguing piece that fleshes out the Parnassian-Decadent leitmotif: the poet now rejects the idealist formula that the stone should be carved at his will; rather, he recognizes that the stone is forever inaccessible while he is willing to be on a perpetual quest for it.

---

[31] Judith Ryan, "More Seductive Than Phryne: Baudelaire, Gérôme, Rilke, and the Problem of Autonomous Art," *PMLA* 108, no. 5 (1993): 1134.

If we want to give philosophical weight to Baudelaire's stony Beauty, we might be reminded of the vigor of Schopenhauer, whose metaphysics (and not merely his pessimism) became influential in the fin-de-siècle. Schopenhauer lambastes German Idealism for ignoring to seek the Kantian thing-in-itself inaccessible to human reason, and rejects Idealism as a "theoretical egoism, which considers all appearances outside of the individual to be phantoms."[32] In his essay "Critique of the Kantian philosophy," Schopenhauer comments that *"Kant's greatest merit is to distinguish between appearance and thing in itself*—by proving that the *intellect* always stands between us and things, which is why we cannot have cognition of things as they may be in themselves."[33] But Schopenhauer criticizes German Idealism for equating *"a priori* certainty" with the Absolute,[34] which to Kant is not "objectively valid" and only "subjectively necessary."[35] German Idealism equates our intellectual constitution with the Absolute because it is the point of certainty that organizes our perception, but for Schopenhauer, this is only vain optimism that cannot solve the problem of the existence of the real world. For Schopenhauer, no argument made by German Idealism is convincing: and he calls the *a priori* certainty—our sense of space, time, and causality that organizes our perception of things— "the misty forms they dream up."[36] Frustrated with the convoluted rhetoric of German Idealism that elevates the human finitude to the status of the Absolute, Schopenhauer proposes to have a different Absolute after the yardsticks of Plato's Ideas: that the Absolute must be immutable and independent of the human perception. Schopenhauer models his Absolute after a synthetization of Plato's Ideas and Kant's the thing-in-itself,[37] both of which are the essence of matter as distinguished from human perception. But in a singular passage, Schopenhauer drops his philosophical terminology and merely refers to it as "matter."

> But if my dear sirs absolutely must have an Absolute, then I will supply them with one that satisfies all requirements for such a thing much

---

[32] Arthur Schopenhauer, *The World as Will and Representation*, ed. Judith Norman, Alistair Welchman, and Christopher Janaway, vol. I (Cambridge: Cambridge University Press, 2010), 129.
[33] Arthur Schopenhauer, "Appendix: Critique of the Kantian Philosophy," in *The World as Will and Representation*, vol. Vol. I (Cambridge: Cambridge University Press, 2010), 444.
[34] Schopenhauer, "Critique of the Kantian Philosophy," 513.
[35] Schopenhauer, "Critique of the Kantian Philosophy," 514.
[36] Schopenhauer, "Critique of the Kantian Philosophy," 513.
[37] Schopenhauer, *The World as Will and Representation*, Vol. I, § 25., p. 152-155.

better than the misty forms they dream up: it is matter. Matter is uncreated and imperishable, and is thus truly independent, that which is in itself and is grasped through itself, and everything emerges from its womb and everything returns to it: what more could you want in an Absolute?[38]

Whereas German Idealism raises subjectivity to the status of the Absolute because the thing-in-itself is no longer accessible to us, for Schopenhauer the thing-in-itself deserves to be called the Absolute because it is independent of the ken of human perception, *precisely because it is inaccessible*. Schopenhauer's reading of Kant, in reaction to German Idealism, helps articulate the radical revolution of the ontology of art in Baudelaire's little sonnet "La Beauté": that the Absolute is matter-in-itself outside of human ken, and—following Plato's myth that one should fall in love in order to see the real world beyond the original capacity of human perception—Baudelaire defines this quest of the Absolute as *the beautiful*.

In his famous essay "the Origin of the Work of Art," Heidegger proposes that art provides us a way to appreciate the stones that compose the Greek temple. The Greek temple as a work of art would bring us to see that "a stone presses downward and manifests its heaviness. But while this heaviness exerts an opposing pressure upon us it denies us any penetration into it."[39] Art is such a paradoxical and difficult attempt to approach the thing, for it must let the thing be the thing rather than using it up, it should allow us to see the being of the thing and, at the same time, recognize that the thing remains withdrawn: "it shows itself only when it remains undisclosed and unexplained".[40] By contrast, any "technical-scientific objectivation"[41] of the stone, such as weighing up the stone and representing it as a number, or smashing it into pieces, would only exhaust the thing, without revealing the being of it. But how can one achieve such a self-contradictory demand of seeing the mysterious thing while letting it be? Baudelaire's poem reminds us that this poetic achievement can be attained only when the poet can love the stone in a right way: only when the poet can endure the stone's tyrannous mystery, refrain from possessing it, and submit himself to it in his unrequited love.

---

[38] Schopenhauer, "Critique of the Kantian Philosophy," 513.
[39] Martin Heidegger, "The Origin of the Work of Art," in *Poetry, Language, Thought*, trans. Albert Hofstadter, Perennial Classics (HarperCollins, 2001), 45.
[40] Heidegger, "the Origin of the Work of Art", 45.
[41] Heidegger, "the Origin of the Work of Art", 46.

Reading through the ridiculous attempts of the Parnassian predecessors, we now understand how difficult Baudelaire's asceticism is.

In the second half of the nineteenth century, the idealist pride that uncritically celebrates immaterial imagination held no more. Baudelaire is again facing the greatest metaphysical predicament after Kant, that of subject-object divide. But Baudelaire's response to this predicament opens up an entirely new path as to how we might approach the metaphysical predicament: that the poet approaches—embraces and absorbs—the metaphysical conundrum through *transformation of the self*. Baudelaire seeks to transgress the irreparable abyss between the subject and the object through *his unrequited love of the stone. Baudelaire defines this perpetual, futile quest of matter as the beautiful.* The subjective love will not capture the stone, but it is nevertheless inspiring, creative, and transformative. The poet's love in the poem follows a vague Platonic structure. In *Symposium*, Socrates argues that Love, a son born of Poros (wealth) and Penia (poverty), is by definition a desire that is driven toward the Otherness (203b) for qualities that it lacks, such as that the mortal poet loves eternal matter. In *Phaedrus* (245c-267d), the poet must fall in love to be thoroughly transformed—in the metaphor of the regrowth of the wings of his soul—in order to fly up from the realm of sensuous appearance to the realm of the absolute truth,[42] or, if we recast it in modern terms, to the realm of the thing-in-itself that for Kant is inaccessible to our consciousness. And if Baudelaire here is indeed responding to the metaphysical problem of subject-object divide through the poet's transformative love, it flatly violates Kantian metaphysics. Kant seeks to grant scientific certainty to metaphysics by raising our perceptual constitution as the *a priori*, which in terms grants necessity to our sense of causality[43]—and after Kant, our subjectivity is considered as a universal given. But *Baudelaire again opens up our subjectivity as the field of transformation, and includes subject-object relation into the domain of creation.* While Foucault argues that this association between knowledge and self-transformation is the fundamental trait of ancient philosophy, my book aims to demonstrate that between the 1860s-1930s, in French and British art, many artistic attempts were made to approach the metaphysical problem of the subject-object divide through the transformation of the self. Baudelaire's love of the inaccessible stone seems futile, but it is productive in the aesthetic sense, for the poet will be inspired to create art, and more importantly to

---

[42] Plato, *The Dialogues of Plato*.
[43] Kant, *Kant's Prolegomena to Any Future Metaphysics*, 7–8.

create the self as the lover, who has the eyes to see things more beautiful than they are.

III. Spirituality of Dandyism, and of Cosmetics

In the poem "La Beauté," Beauty claims that her existence is transcendental and should not be tampered with, while the poet who cannot transform his object of desire will rather have to transform his love, whose quality is no longer a passionate and spontaneous expression, but will rather emulate the qualities of matter, mute and eternal. Beauty's stony breast "est fait pour inspirer au poète un amour / Éternel et muet ainsi que la matière." Baudelaire's dandyism is an illustration of this pious (and perverse) lover of Beauty, who disciplines his own demeanor and subjugates his natural emotions so as to maintain an impeccable material appearance. In his dandyism, Baudelaire still extols the dandy's spiritual independence and freedom, as he is capable of controlling his bodily comportment. Only that, with a cunning twist of rhetoric, Baudelaire argues that the dandy takes as the battlefield the site of the material body, rather than the immaterial realm of reverie as for the Romantics. The inner passion is not to be expressed, but subjugated under the material surface. Art, therefore, turns material, artificial, sensuous and superficial. In this section, I will discuss Baudelaire's theory of artificiality through his writings on dandyism and cosmetics, in one of his most famous essays, "Le peintre de la vie modern."

Baudelaire's discussion on fashion in his "Painter" essay—"l'homme finit par ressembler à ce qu'il voudrait être" (Oeuvre III 53)—has its idealistic root, which asserts the artistic pride to revise and spiritualize material things. However, under this dictum, Baudelaire reworks drastically the idealist definition of spirituality, and thus the ontology of art. For a point of comparison, Hegel remarks that the ego is ontologically a Concept or an Idea, whose highest purpose is to become self-conscious of its unity. He despises the organisms whose inner Idea remains inward, since the Idea for the senses would remain "indeterminate and abstract" (130). Once the ego becomes self-conscious, it must manifest itself without. This Hegel defines as "the beautiful" when the organism is capable of "displaying to sense the concrete Concept and the Idea" (129), when the physical reality of the self-conscious ego is transformed and idealized (132). Life is therefore "an inherent continual process of idealizing" in order to acquire an explicit unity between the inner and the outer (122). Baudelaire adopts a similar rhetoric that the artist should rework the appearance as a manifestation of his or her ideal.

> L'idée que l'homme se fait du beau s'imprime dans tout son ajustement, chiffonne ou raidit son habit, arrondit ou aligne son geste,

et même pénètre subtilement, à la longue, les traits de son visage. (Œuvre III, 53)

But here what Baudelaire refers to as "l'idée" of beauty is actually fashion, "la morale et l'esthétique du temps," rather than the man's individuality. The dandy desires an originality "contenu dans les limites extérieures des convenances" (93), just as Monsieur Guys always renders the dandy his "caractère historique" (96). As a cunning twist of Hegel's Idealism as we will see, the dandy who takes elegance as his sole profession shapes himself not from within, but rather assimilates the mode of his time so as to shape himself down to the within. The dandy's appearance is not ideal, but rather a material appearance dissociated from inwardness.

The section on dandyism (IX) of the "Painter" essay is very slyly staged with the preceding section on military man, whose spiritual condition is shown by his perpetual attitude of nonchalance, always ready to face death. Already Baudelaire notes here that Monsieur Guys loves to draw portraits of soldiers not just for their inward qualities, but more often for their profession's showy accessories, of "la coquetterie militaire" (88), for there is a moral sense innate in those dazzling costumes ("le sens moral de ces costumes étincelants") (ibid.). The dandy, unlike a brave solider, however, is rich and idle and fights no war, but he nevertheless keeps the same blasé appearance, and makes the keeping of this artificial appearance, forever elegant, his most rigorous pursuit. If a dandy suffers, he may still smile like the Spartan boy bitten by a fox upon his chest. The dandy's impeccable toilet and never-relaxed elegance for him is a matter of religious doctrine, most tyrannical of its kind, as it demands excessive passion and energy, as well as self-discipline, to submit oneself to the sovereign of the most punctilious, in fact trivial, regime of style. Baudelaire boosts the dandy's vocation with grandiloquence:

> Que le lecteur ne se scandalise pas de cette gravité dans le frivole, et qu'il se souvienne qu'il y a une grandeur dans toutes les folies, une force dans tous les excès. Étrange spiritualisme ! Pour ceux qui en sont à la fois les prêtres et les victimes, toutes les conditions matérielles compliquées auxquelles ils se soumettent, depuis la toilette irréprochable à toute heure du jour et de la nuit jusqu'aux tours les plus périlleux du sport, ne sont qu'une gymnastique propre à fortifier la volonté et à discipliner l'âme. (94)

The dandy is at once the priest and the victim—the self is cut into a subjective will and the objective body. The dandy's *own* body becomes the object of discipline that the will seeks to subjugate it entirely under its control, down to every minute details—to refine it, to define it, to make it a work of art like a sculptor carefully incises the stone. Baudelaire calls dandyism a strange kind of spirituality, and his usage of spirituality indeed aligns well with Foucault's aesthetics of the self. "Une force dans tous les excès" becomes for Baudelaire the justification for the new concept of art: because the pursuit is traditionally considered foolish and frivolous, and because the material surface is for the spirit forever distant and rebellious, only the artist with the strongest passion might be capable of this pursuit. Whereas for Hegel the ultimate consummation of Romantic art is achieved when spirit and matter is unified, for Baudelaire an incongruous disjoint or an alienating distance between the poet's fierce, turbulent heart and his impassive appearance is charged with the spiritual significance of self-discipline and perpetual pursuit. As Beauty pronounces it in the poem "La Beauté," the poet is himself inspired a love as mute and as eternal as matter itself, but this love, however strong, is concealed well underneath the poet's stony appearance.

> Le caractère de beauté du dandy consiste surtout dans l'air froid qui vient de l'inébranlable résolution de ne pas être ému ; on dirait un feu latent qui se fait deviner, qui pourrait mais qui ne veut pas rayonner. (96)

Baudelaire's *spirituality* is defined in opposition to Hegel's ego: *while the latter is a natural given, the unique temperament as Baudelaire depicts in his praise of Delacroix, the former is cultivated and artificially made, entirely willed by the artist.* While Hegel defines subjectivity as the ego's capacity to alter its external appearance, Baudelaire defines subjectivity as the ego's submission to the reign of the elegant material surface. This definition of spirituality, or of creation, establishes its ground not on an expression of the given inwardness, but on the material body that is at the artist's disposal. Delacroix's art shows us an inward mood; Baudelaire's dandy parades the external artifice dissociated from inwardness.

Baudelaire definition of dandyism as a material mask is indeed peculiar, if we compare it with Jules Barbey d'Aurevilly's analysis in *Du dandysme et de George Brummell* (1845),[44] whose rhetoric, while as perverse as it would be marked as that of an early Decadent, is still idealistic. D'Aurevilly idealistic heritage prompts him to elevate the dandy's given temperament or his nature above material appearance. D'Aurevilly tells us that when Brummell began to be interested in his dress, his purpose was to impress people: "il n'ignorait pas que le costume a une influence latente mais positive sur les hommes qui

---

[44] Jules Barbey d'Aurevilly, *Du dandysme et de Georges Brummell* (Lemerre, 1879).

le dédaignent le plus du haut de la majesté de leur esprit immortel" (48). But later, as Brummell grew more mature in his profession, he follows a similar Hegelian dialectic, and conceptualizes his material outfit as only a means to express his inner spirit—and the summit of art is achieved when his outfit meets his nature.

> Il resta mis d'une façon irréprochable ; mais il éteignit les couleurs de ses vêtements, en simplifia la coupe et les porta sans y penser. Il arriva ainsi au comble de l'art qui donne la main au naturel. (48-49)

D'Aurevilly's dandy bears no Baudelarian piety to his material appearance, for Brummell's beauty is less physical than intellectual, originated from within rather than without.

> Son air de tête était plus beau que son visage, et sa contenance – physionomie du corps – l'emportait jusque sur la perfection de ses formes. (49)

Although d'Aurevilly's dandy already bears the indifferent, sphinx-like attitude, this attitude originates from his inward pride, rather than deriving from his material appearance with which Baudelaire seeks to emulate the stone.

> Quelquefois, ces yeux sagaces savaient se glacer d'indifférence sans mépris, comme il convient à un dandy consommé, à un homme qui porte en lui quelque chose de supérieur au monde visible. (49)

D'Aurevilly subverts the moral system by treating a vain dandy seriously, which is enough to earn him the fame of being a Decadent, but Baudelaire's dandyism revises the Romantic aesthetics and idealist metaphysics[45] by dissociating material beauty from inwardness.

---

[45] Dandyism has rarely been regarded by critics, then in French and British societies of 1890s and now, as a positive theory of art. Baudelaire's dandyism, especially when it is read with that of Barbey d'Aurevilly, is often understood as an issue of identity construction—a defiant gesture to the opposite sex or to the mainstream bourgeois values—in the face of modernity. Very often, critics are puzzled by the split between one's pretentious appearance and controlled emotion, and resort to psychoanalysis to argue that the artificial appearance the dandy painstakingly adopts is a "protective veneer" to cover the "unstable and fragile" psyche underneath. See Christopher Lane, "The Drama of the Impostor: Dandyism and Its Double," *Cultural Critique*, no. 28 (1994); Deborah Houk, "Self-Construction and Sexual Identity in Nineteenth-Century

That Baudelaire argues for the superiority of material surface over emotional spontaneity does seem to offend his readers' sensitivity, and in the following section, Baudelaire openly confronts with their discomfort. In the section titled "Éloge du maquillage" (XI), Baudelaire in his provocative rhetoric criticizes the popular ethics in the eighteenth century, in order to further facilitate his aesthetics of artificiality: "La nature fut prise dans ce temps-là comme base, source et type de tout bien et de tout beau possibles" (100). The cult of Nature in the eighteenth century, most broadly speaking, includes all philosophers and artists who considered that sincere expression from inwardness is the foundation of one's moral edifice and hence carries aesthetic significance: Rousseau's nature that guides the inner conscience, Hegel's spirit, and Delacroix's passion in Baudelaire's salon essays. Since Rousseau, this inwardness is more often associated with the given, the feeling of heart, and emotional spontaneity. But Baudelaire argues in a sweeping assertion that nature is nothing but our animal impulses, not the inner voice of conscience but rather "la voix de notre intérêt" (100). Everything that is good and noble must rather be, Baudelaire asserts, the result of reason and of calculation, "artificielle, surnaturelle" (100). We do not need to take Baudelaire's unjustified ethical presumption seriously; what is noteworthy is rather that *Baudelaire associates self-discipline with the metaphor of the material surface that covers up the natural body*. Baudelaire argues that what Rousseau refers to as noble savages actually aspire toward "la haute spiritualité de la toilette" (101).

> Le sauvage et le baby témoignent, par leur aspiration naïve vers le brillant, vers les plumages bariolés, les étoffes chatoyantes, vers la majesté superlative des formes artificielles, de leur dégoût pour le réel, et prouvent ainsi, à leur insu, l'immatérialité de leur âme. (101)

As the soul is immaterial, Baudelaire assigns the material surface the agency to discipline our spontaneous expression and to represent our moral edifice. Negating the ethical value of inwardness and of the natural given, Baudelaire shifts the ontological weight of spirituality and imagination onto the visible material surface. Whereas in "La Beauté" the pious poet is not entitled to carve the stone, here, the poet rather shapes his soul with a disciplinary material appearance.

French Dandyism," *French Forum* 22, no. 1 (1997); Philip G. Hadlock, "The Other Other: Baudelaire, Melancholia, and the Dandy," *Nineteenth-Century French Studies* 30, no. 1/2 (2001); Elisa Glick, "The Dialectics of Dandyism," *Cultural Critique*, no. 48 (2001).

With his perverse spirit, Baudelaire remarks that the Decadent project is one in which the artist asserts her agency by consistently reforming nature. Women, therefore, must not conceal the fact that they use cosmetics. Rather, they should use black eyeliners and red blush to flaunt the material surface, to create for themselves an appearance "magique et surnaturelle" (102).

> La mode doit donc être considérée comme un symptôme du goût de l'idéal surnageant dans le cerveau humain au-dessus de tout ce que la vie naturelle y accumule de grossier, de terrestre et d'immonde, comme une déformation sublime de la nature, ou plutôt comme un essai permanent et successif de réformation de la nature. (101)

Contrary to Hegel's formula of Romantic art, this is Baudelaire's very definition of artificiality: that the sensuous appearance alone, rather than Idea, now carries artistic agency to revise nature. In contrast to Hegel, who defines the beautiful as Idea shown through sensuous material, Baudelaire here turns art inside out. That is, art is ontologically not the Idea, but the material surface that revises the given nature.

Many critics note that Decadence as an artistic movement is a sophisticated continuation rather than a decisive break from Romanticism. The pioneers of dandyism, Lord Byron and Beau Brummel, champion for the Romantic glorification of the individual and the desire for original expression. But Baudelaire twists Romantic individualism and makes the dandy's inscrutable material presentation more important than his spontaneous expression. Baudelaire's theorization of dandyism is a symbol of Decadence, an awareness that this emphasis in artificiality now best expresses the spirit of time, as opposed to Delacroix's naïve expression that epitomizes the past decade.

> Le dandysme est le dernier éclat d'héroïsme dans les décadences…Le dandysme est un soleil couchant ; comme l'astre qui décline, il est superbe, sans chaleur et plein de mélancolie. (95)

Baudelaire's dandyism, his elevation of material appearance, constitutes one of the most important motifs of Decadence, that of artificiality. Dandyism is a perverse kind of aesthetics of the self, but then by submitting his emotional spontaneity to the discipline of material surface, Baudelaire creates—indeed lives—a most innovative relation between spirituality and materiality.

IV. The Style of Inorganic Things

As opposed to his idealist predecessors who celebrate autonomous imagination, Baudelaire's poem "La Beauté," as well as his writing on dandyism and cosmetics in the "Painter" essay, outline the metaphysical rationale of this cult of incomprehensible material surface dissociated from inwardness. In the present section, I will further supplement some concrete details about the aesthetic effect of this new Decadent Beauty. As articulated by Baudelaire's poem "Avec ses vêtements ondoyants et nacrés," Gustave Moreau's Salomé, and Mallarmé's "Hérodiade," the Beauty who adorns inorganic appearance is felt to be immune from emotional vulnerability, exempted from social pressure to communicate, and therefore larger than life. In the fin-de-siècle, this insensibility of materiality replaces the Romantic spirit, and becomes a metaphor for transcendence, otherworldly and absolute.

While Baudelaire's interest in the inorganic is most famously investigated by Benjamin,[46] mainly in the context of modernity and the phantasmagoria of fashion and commodity, here, I will begin with Baudelaire's poem "Avec ses vêtements ondoyants et nacrés," in which the poet encounters the inorganic in a space traditionally belonging to Petrarchan or Romantic aesthetics, in a private room that foregrounds individuality and intimacy, in contrast to the outer social world. In the poetic description, Baudelaire transforms the woman into an incomprehensible sphinx with metallic eyes in an imaginary realm outside of social context—and what he finds alluring is precisely the inorganic qualities of diamonds, gold, and steel—for they refuse to speak or signify, and can be simply there in themselves. The poem is idealist in essence for the poet possesses his birthright to shape his object of desire in his imagination, and in this regard, much less radical than "La Beauté." Still, the poem can be read as a complement to "La Beauté" since it gives us a more concrete image of what Beauty looks like—it is not merely a metaphysical statement, but rather justifies the alluring sensuous effect of an inhuman thing. The unintelligibility of materiality subverts the conventions of courtly poetry, not only because what the poet confronts here is not a human beloved but a thing, a stony sphinx, but also because the intimate description of the inorganic sphinx concerns *its very insensibility*. This is the other half of Baudelaire's art, the eternal Ideal as opposed to a phantasmagoria of impressions.

While in the first stanza, Baudelaire seems to be depicting the woman's personal charm—that by virtue of her floating silks, we might think she is dancing when she walks, in the second stanza, the movement is compared to an unfeeling, vast nature that nevertheless rises and falls. The garments undulate like the drab sand and cloudless sky of the desert, or might roll like

---

[46] Walter Benjamin, *The Writer of Modern Life: Essays on Charles Baudelaire* (Harvard University Press, 2006), 86.

the long webs of sea waves. The woman expands herself with indifference, in the same way nature is insensible.

> Comme le sable morne et l'azur des déserts,
> Insensibles tous deux à l'humaine souffrance,
> Comme les longs réseaux de la houle des mers,
> Elle se développe avec indifférence.[47]

The unpopulated nature exists for itself; the beloved is now sublimated beyond the human relation as she ceases to please and to receive. If for Hegel the absolute is defined as the artist's sublimation and spiritualization of the otherwise inert, senseless object, Baudelaire's transformation of the pleasing woman works precisely the other way around. Baudelaire defines the transcendence with the very material qualities of nature: the woman exists for herself as nature does, for she is indifferent or better, insensible. Admittedly, the woman might appear aloof in order to cater to the poet's peculiar taste, or might be, after all, the poet who is defining the woman in terms of the inorganic. But these backstage efforts of how the human actor emulates the artifice are stories concerning the process of creation; what is presented to us is the successful transformation that delineates the Ideal. It is Baudelaire's peculiar Ideal that I am most interested in discussing here.

> Ses yeux polis sont faits de minéraux charmants,
> Et dans cette nature étrange et symbolique
> Où l'ange inviolé se mêle au sphinx antique,

If the inorganic is insensible, the human poet is not. For the poet, the mineral eyes are charming, at once strange as it is made of something simply inhuman, but also symbolic since the mind understands matter only in terms of its meaning. But if the eyes seem suggestively symbolic, one cannot fathom precisely what they mean. The eyes rather shine for the poet a light of perpetual puzzle. The mineral eyes are polished, either by human hands or natural forces—they have been worked upon, undergone a rigorous process of transformation, and now fulfill Baudelaire's cult of artificiality since the stone is now no longer a raw given. This encounter between the human projection and the inorganic thing in Baudelaire's metaphor assumes the image of an inviolable angle united with an antique sphinx—this strange creature does not lend herself to comprehension as she does not submit itself to

---

[47] Baudelaire, *Les Fleurs du mal* (1861), No. 27.

the assimilation of signs. She charms the poet precisely because she is entirely self-sufficient—she exists for herself and signals the ideal of the absolute.

In the final stanza, the poet completes transforming the object of desire. If the woman's eyes seem half symbolic, the poet now affirms that all is but gold, steel, light, and diamonds. What was a mixture between the human and matter is now revealed as diverse, but all inorganic, materials, plus shimmering light that reflects not the heart, but the metallic surface.

> Où tout n'est qu'or, acier, lumière et diamants,
> Resplendit à jamais, comme un astre inutile,
> La froide majesté de la femme stérile.

Baudelaire's ideal woman is one that extracts herself from human relations and assumes the qualities of the inorganic, but the woman might also be interpreted as a metaphorical medium that allows the poet to appreciate the qualities of the thing-in-itself beyond individuality, beyond space (as she expands herself like the sea waves), and time (as she shines externally like the star). The woman is sterile—she cannot be touched by men, and she neither reproduces nor nurtures, like a useless star. The useless star is there only for aesthetic values and for disinterested appreciation.

This sterile woman of frigid majesty, enveloped in dazzling gemstones, makes the iconic figure of fin-de-siècle, most significantly the august post of Salome created by the painter Gustave Moreau. As Pierre-Louis Mathieu documents, Moreau "nourished an exaggerated admiration for Baudelaire" and his library keeps in possession of the four-volume *Oeuvres completes de Charles Baudelaire,* the first one of which, *Les Fleurs du mal,* is dedicated by the painter's mother to her son.[48] And as Émile Zola notes, Moreau

> has disdained the Romantic fever, the easy effects of colours, the excesses of a brush seeking inspiration as it covers the canvas with contrasts of shadow and light that make your eyes sting. No! Gustave Moreau practises symbolism. He paints pictures that often remain enigmas, looks for archaic and primitive forms, takes Mantegna as an example and attaches tremendous importance to the smallest accessories in a painting…He

---

[48] Pierre-Louis Mathieu, *Gustave Moreau: The Assembler of Dreams,*1826-1898. trans. Charles Penwarden, ACR Edition ed. (Courbevoie: Poche Couleur, 2010), 11.

paints reveries—...subtle, complicated and enigmatic reveries whose meaning we cannot immediately untangle.[49]

Moreau's paintings, in which an enigmatic aura prevails the unique sphere together with his notorious preciosity, fuels the Decadent imagination about the jeweled sphinx. Many of them, in addition to the most famous cases of Huysmans and Jean Lorrain, transcribe Moreau's paintings into ekphrases of verse or prose. As recorded in his correspondences, Moreau also receives ardent admiration from Gautier, de Banville, de Montesquiou, Laforgue, Joyce, and Yeats.[50]

Moreau's close friend Ary Renan, himself a Symbolist painter and, as we will see, a critic well-versed in contemporary aesthetics and gifted with an incisive analytical force, in his book *Gustave Moreau* (1900)[51] foregrounds two paradoxical but closely related guiding principles of Moreau's creation: "le *Principe de la belle Inertie et le Principe de la Richesse necessaire*" (36). Renan cites Baudelaire's formula of artificiality, that passion is too natural and vulgar to be allowed into the superior realm of Beauty (39). In Baudelaire's original words:

> Car la passion est naturelle, trop naturelle pour ne pas introduire un ton blessant, discordant, dans le domaine de la beauté pure, trop familière et trop violente pour ne pas scandaliser les purs désirs, les gracieuses mélancolies et les nobles désespoirs qui habitent les régions surnaturelles de la poésie.[52]

Renan notes that this rule can be well applied to Moreau, as he would paint neither action, nor character, and certainly not sentiments that are immediately convincing to the audience: "volontairement, ce maître s'est interdit de rechercher l'action, le chractère, la verité immediate des sentiments" (36). As Renan notes, in Moreau's paintings, it is the rich, motionless material surface that replaces the elements of emotions and actions.

---

[49] Qtd. In Mathieu, *Gustave Moreau*, 98.
[50] Mathieu, *Gustave Moreau*, 241-44.
[51] Ary Renan, *Gustave Moreau: 1826-1898* (Paris: Gazette des Beaux-Arts, 1900; repr., PDF e-book). Emphasis and capitalization original. Though the book is currently out of print, an electronic facsimile of it can be easily downloaded from Google Books or the website of *Bibliothèque nationale de France*.
[52] Charles Baudelaire, "Notes nouvelles sur Edgar Poe," in *Nouvelles histoires extraordinaires* (A. Quantin, 1884), xvii.

> Pour remplacer ces éléments d'émotion, ces agents d'illusion consacrés, il a fait résider le prix de ses œuvres dans leur perfection intrinsèque, dans leur extrême richesse matérielle, dans l'accompagnement, pour ainsi dire, que les artifices matériels du pinceau peuvent apporter au thème le plus vulgarisé. (36)

Moreau rather situates the value of his works in the intricate perfection, their sensuous richness, their composition; in short, in the material artifices. With these, Moreau seeks to achieve the aesthetic effect of beautiful inertia.

Renan's commentary on Moreau's painting deserves to be quoted in length, because it has not yet been translated into English and rarely discussed in full by critics, and because it is, in my view, one of the most articulate accounts on the power of sheer material appearance, against the Romantic cult of intense emotions. Renan insists that Moreau paints neither emotion, nor action, and not even precise gesture. Moreau refuses any human sentiments; he paints only certain states of a stony Beauty, forever frozen and suspended.

> Il choisit un instant décisif au point de vue moral et non pas un instant pathétique au point de vue scénique. L'amour et la haine lui échappent ou, pour mieux dire, il les écarte et retourne à sa méditation sereine.
>
> Voici donc un peintre qui rejette non seulement l'agitation, mais l'action, non seulement la mimique violent, mais le geste précis. Il en a peur comme d'une trivialité; la traduction des sentiments humains par les mouvements des membres, par les flexions du corps, par les expressions du visage, lue paraît une étude inférieure. Il peint non des actes, mais des états, non des personnages en scène, mais des figures de Beauté. (39-40)

Moreau paints not drama, but disposition, not love or hatred, but serene meditation. He paints not passing and pathetic characters on the stage, but perpetual figures of Beauty. For Moreau, the still, self-possessed, introvert attitude suggests a certain superiority that belongs only to material artifice, and not to spontaneous life. This stony Beauty neither cries nor laughs. Moreau's figures are not individuals with peculiar characters; rather, Renan remarks that we should regard Moreau's inertia figures as noble archetypes.

> Mais, à l'inertie des figures de Gustave Moreau ne trouve-t-on pas de nobles archétypes? Ils se présentent d'eux-mèmes au regard, et nous n'insisterons pas sur leur profond caractère.
>
> Le demi-geste rituel, l'attitude suppléant à l'action triomphent. (40)

In Moreau's paintings, the figures' almost ritualistic attitudes substitute for triumphant actions. These figures appeal to the eyes but do not communicate with our heart, and Renan warns that we should not seek to infer from his figures any profound characters.

As Renan reports it, Moreau himself comments on Michelangelo's *Prophets and Sibyls*, as the figures exist in the work of art and not the human world, should show us only one kind of expression—that they are absorbed in a monotonous reverie. The figures of Beauty should have no desires, no emotions, no thoughts—for the simple reason that they are inhuman.

> Toutes ces figures, nous disait-il, semblent être figées dans un geste de somnambulisme idéal ; elles sont inconscientes du mouvement qu'elles exécutent, absorbées dans la rêverie au point de paraître emportées vers d'autres mondes. C'est ce seul sentiment de rêverie profonde qui les sauve de la monotonie. Quel actes accomplissent-elles? Que pensent-elles? Où vont-elles? Sous l'empire de quelles passions sont-elles? On ne se repose pas, on n'agit pas, on ne médite pas, on ne marche pas, on ne pleure pas, on ne pense pas de cette façon sur notre planète… (42)

What is "un geste de somnambulisme ideal"? Somnambulism indeed becomes an ideal expression in fin-de-siècle philosophy and art. Schopenhauer speculates two ways to escape Kantian reason and to be in touch with the essence of things, a monist force that he calls "the will": through artistic genius (especially that of music since music is not representational but express directly the material power), and through magnetic somnambulism: "the composer reveals the innermost essence of the world and expresses the deepest wisdom in a language that his reason does not understand, just as magnetic somnambulist explains things that he has no idea about when awake."[53] Somnambulism thus fascinates the fin-de-siècle imagination with some vague impression of metaphysical significance. In June 1881, a knowledgeable and eloquent doctor, M. Regnard, delivered two lectures to *Association Scientifique de France*, with a crowd of two thousand people. His lectures testify how the physiological abnormality acquires cultural significance in the fin-de-siècle. Regnard refers to

---

[53] Arthur Schopenhauer, *The World as Will and Representation, Vol. I*, trans. Judith Norman, Alistair Welchman, and Christopher Janaway, vol. 1, 2 vols. (Cambridge: Cambridge University Press, 2010).

somnambulism as "this celebrated malady,"[54] and assumes the audience "will probably ask if this terrible disease, so much talked of at the present day, is new—if it is a production of this 'nervous century,' if I may so express myself, or whether it is of ancient date."[55] Artificial somnambulism elicited by the doctor is then defined as "sleep is produced, real sleep accompanied by total loss of sensibility."[56]

As Henri Dorra rightly notes, somnambulism also prevails over Pre-Raphaelite and Symbolist paintings, including that of Burne-Jones, Gauguin, Puvis de Chavannes, D.G. Rossetti, and Rodin's sculptures.[57] Moreau's figures, most famously Salome, are often in somnambulism, and with a stony composure. Critics, in their efforts to contextualize Moreau as a transitional figure from Romanticism to Symbolism, often compare Moreau's somnambulism to the trance-like attitudes of J. E. Millais's *Ophelia* (1852) or D. G. Rossetti's *Beata Beatrix* (1863) and argue that Moreau likewise aims to depict a contemplative attitude that bespeaks a psychological depth, as if his figures are absorbed in their own intense feelings.[58] But I hope to draw attention to the fact that—compared to Rossetti's Beatrice, who is humanly vulnerable—Moreau's lotus-holding Salome is strangely statuesque, an attitude that only a stony sphinx can pose. Moreau associates transcendence with artifice, for the other world to which the painted figures are transported is not the world of inward emotions, but of reveries carved out of marble and stone.

The principle of beautiful inertia gives Moreau's figures "one only sentiment of profound reverie" that is at once enigmatic, suggestive, and intriguing, but Renan surprisingly remarks that this is only *an effect* of Moreau's dazzling material surface, under which the inwardness of the painted figures is forever withdrawn. As Renan remarks, Moreau conceives that a painting should be enhanced by all kinds of ornaments that suggest an ineffable significance, though such significance is only an illusion of the dazzled sight: he "pensait qu'un tableau doit être rehaussé de tous les ornements auxquels on peut rattacher une signification, paré de toutes les beautés qui tombent sous le sens de la vue" (42-43). This suggestive, indefinite significance generated out of pure decorative surface is, we remember, precisely the argument

---

[54] M. Regnard and Clara Lanza, "Sleep and Somnambulism. I," *Science* 2, no. 49 (1881), 260.
[55] M. Regnard, "Sleep and Somnambulism. II," *Science* 2, no. 50, 272.
[56] M. Regnard, "Sleep and Somnambulism. II," 272.
[57] Henri Dorra, *Symbolist Art Theories: A Critical Anthology* (University of California Press, 1994), 23.
[58] Jean Paladilhe and José Pierre, *Gustave Moreau* (New York: Praeger Publishers, 1972), 83.

Baudelaire raises in the poem "Avec ses vêtements": after remarking that his sphinx has strange and symbolic eyes, he immediately reveals that but all there is a glittering array of gold, steel, reflected lights and diamonds. What is strange and symbolic is nothing but the sensuous powers of metal and precious stones, terribly incommunicable and incomprehensible. Moreau explicates in length, as Renan reports, his theory that materiality in itself generates an indefinable significance—but actually, he cannot quite articulate this intuition except for noting that the Renaissance masters have been adopting these decorative formulas to ennoble their framed subjects and to solicit from the audience a religious sentiment. The Renaissance masters, Moreau argues, employ the same technique to "ennoblir le sujet que de l'encadrer dans une profusion de formules décoratives," and to verify the principle one only needs to look at the Virgin Mary, for her noble saintliness is an effect of her accessories, crown, jewelry, the embroidery at the rim of her mantle, and her chiseled throne! (43). In Moreau's paintings, the rich material surface—artificial, inhuman, and superior to organic nature—now substitutes Hegel's immaterial inwardness to claim the transcendental power of imagination. As Renan reports it, Moreau exclaims that these decorative arabesques, if they seem enticing, it is only because they point us to "un univers dépassant le reel." The paintings are "de fenêtres ouvertes sur des mondes artificiels qui semblent taillés dans le marbre et l'or et sur des espaces *nnécessairement* chimériques!" (43, emphasis original).

For Moreau, imagination is no longer inward and immaterial, but an artificial world carved out of metal and stone. This vision of art is already proposed by Baudelaire in his poem "Rêve parisien,"[59] where the painter paints a dream of heavy, inorganic materiality, which is an escape from the painter's sordid life in the city.

> Et, peintre fier de mon génie,
> Je savourais dans mon tableau
> L'enivrante monotonie
> Du métal, du marbre et de l'eau.
>
> Babel d'escaliers et d'arcades,
> C'était un palais infini,
> Plein de bassins et de cascades
> Tombant dans l'or mat ou bruni ;

---

[59] Baudelaire, *Les Fleurs du mal* (Poulet-Malassis et De Broise, 1861), No. 102.

> Et des cataractes pesantes,
> Comme des rideaux de cristal,
> Se suspendaient, éblouissantes,
> À des murailles de métal.

The poem depicts an imaginative vision in which the irregular vegetation ("le végétal irrégulier") is banished, and the poet sings of intoxicating monotony. There are no trees, but stands instead rows of marble columns ("Non d'arbres, mais de colonnades"). Baudelaire's artificiality is one in which he admires monotonous metals and crystals because with them, time is arrested, unlike plants that must grow, bloom, and wither. Metals and stones are also insensible and therefore invincible, unlike vegetation that is sensitive to environmental elements such as climate changes, and reacts accordingly. Baudelaire mentions monotonous water, but then he replaces them with cascades of molten gold, waterfalls so heavy that they look like suspended curtains of crystals. In other words, Baudelaire replaces malleable water with heavy and motionless materiality, and in the same vein substitutes the immaterial Ideal with oppressively magnificent, metallic landscape. Everything is still and polished: the poem concludes that this is a novel Ideal of "un silence d'éternité."

Renan theorizes Moreau's paintings as sumptuous, purely decorative material surface, without signifying explicit meaning and human emotions. But the decors, as Renan notes, are indeed powerfully affective, only that the effects are communicated in a way beyond reasoned or linguistic means, and is not owned by an individual and her eloquent expression. The effect is bodily, of the signification of sight. Renan describes Moreau's iconic painting *Salome Dancing before Herod* in a way that is perhaps more incisive than what Huysmans renders in *À rebours* (though the two accounts bear some semblance). Renan begins the ekphrasis with a description of the architecture, and its atmosphere that anticipates Salome's dance.

> Le harem, en son abside la plus reculée, prison d'onyx incrustée d'émaux, crypte monumentale aux portiques emplis de silence, baigne dans une religieuse pénombre et dans l'*aura* qui glace les moelles et prépare aux pires hallucinations les esprits vacillants. Émanée de baies lointaines, la poudre d'or du couchant flotte bien entre les fortes colonnes, comme pour rattacher à la terre des vivants cette architecture sépulcrale; mais des lampes luisent, des parfums brûlent, d'insaisissables richesses scintillent à la façon des cristaux et des stalactites dans les abîmes; et des être animent cette immense caverne : les sons étouffés d'une mandore s'égrènent, on entend un cliquetis de joyaux, unfroissement de soies et d'orfrois. Quels acteurs suppose

Artificiality 43

> donc un décor où suinte la peur mystique, où la mort plane, sinon de merveilleux automates, des spectres engendrés par la fièvre, des créatures pâlies, énervées et déchues? (63).

Renan does not immediately set his eyes on the human figure of Salome. Rather, he notes how powerfully the architecture is capable of setting up the aura, before Salome has stepped on the stage. The whole paragraph has no reference to a living life, since the characters— Hérode, the eunuchs, the musician and the guard—all blend into the vapor of the oriental sphere. The silent harem is a prison of onyx encrusted with enamel. It is the most remote apse of the architecture, a monumental crypt with vaulted porticos. The space is bathed in a religious dusk and in a special aura of long minutes waiting for something dramatic, an aura which freezes the marrow of the weakened spirits and prepares them for their worst hallucinations. From the distant windows, the golden stream of the setting sun shines into the strong columns, as if to reconnect the sepulchral architecture with the living earth. But the lamps are shining, the perfume is burning, the imperceptible treasures hidden at the background scintillate as if they were crystals and stalactites in the abyss. But some beings animate this immense cavern: the stifled sounds of a mandore now chime out; we hear the jingles of gemstones, the rustling of silk and of golden folds. Now Salome is walking toward the stage. But Renan is unsure of that. He hears rather the chiming of the instrument (as if it were not played by a musician), the rustling of silk and jiggling of gemstones (as if it is not necessarily worn by Salome). He still asks who would be coming, as anticipated by the sphere? Implicitly, however, Renan argues that it is the architecture, not the human, that is defining the aura of the space.

Then comes in Salome. When Salome comes in, Renan's French suddenly switches from present to past tense, as if this human character gives the eternal oriental sphere a sense of time.

> Dans le champ d'un décor surabondant en richesse arbitraire, Salomé lui apparut magnifique et presque sacrée. Si rien ne devait rappeler la débauche vulgaire, tout devait concourir à exalter la sensualité supérieure que la danse orientale éveille. Blanche de fard, grasse et le visage atone, la docile esclave, formée pour le plaisir au fond du gynécée, ignore encore quel prix paiera son triomphe. (64)

In a sphere of a décor overabundant in arbitrary richness, Salomé appeared magnificent and almost sacred. Though no ornamentation should remind us of vulgar debauch, all should compete to exalt the sensuality superior to the stimulating oriental dance. Her maquillage white and oily, her face emotionless, the docile slave, trained to give pleasure in the depth of the gynaeceum, was still ignorant of what price her triumph would entail.

Salome is pure, upright, solemn. Her muscles tense, her post rigid, she assumes the burden of precious stones and the strain of her hair coiffed for the religious occasion. She walks in the somnambulistic attitude and to Schopenhauer, it's the moment of aesthetic contemplation in which she is free from the bondage of carnal desires.[60] If she is powerful, it is not because, as des Esseintes inaccurately imagines, she is lascivious and she has wielded her sultry charm, with thrusts of her breast, undulations of her belly, and quiverings of her thighs: "par des remous de seins, des secousses de ventre, des frissons de cuisse"(71). Rather, it is because Salome is as self-possessed as a high priestess, her movement almost liturgical:

> Dressée sur les orteils, rigide et crispée sous la charge des pierreries qui constellent ses écharpes, ses ceintures, ses robes traînantes, un sommeil magnétique la possède et la ravit toute; et ce glissement à menus pas, c'est un exercice solennel, vaguement liturgique, pour lequel l'officiante a revête des atours qui emprisonnent ses membres et coiffé la haute tiare ovoïde qui raidit sa nuque. Telles les hiérodules des temples dansant devant le Saint des Saints. (64)

Standing upon her toes, rigid and tense under the gems that constellate upon her sash, her belt, her shuffling robes, a magnetic slumber possessed her and truly delighted her. And her glide in small steps was a solemn exercise, vaguely liturgical, for which the priestess has assumed these fineries that confine her limbs and coifed the tall, ovoid tiara that stiffened her nape. In the same way the sacred prostitute enslaved in a temple would dance in front of the Saint of Saints.

Then finally, Renan switches to the present tense and comments on the terrible destiny that Salome facilitates, but she is only half conscious of it.

> Elle entre, et le vent du Désir la suit; dans les plis de ses voiles l'iniquité réside; et sa face est pure.

> Sa chair se fond en tièdes effluves; mais son corps reste droit, sans fléchir, tant est grave le rite qu'on lue apprit pour se faire aimer.

---

[60] Schopenhauer, *The World as Will and Representation*, Vol. I, p. 201.

Son geste ordonne déjà; son bras tendu désigne sans doute un emblème terrible; mais elle élève aussi la fleur dans ses doigts nonchalants. (64)

Her face is pure, but the wind of Desire follows her. Her gesture already commands; her tightened arm without doubt designates a terrible emblem, but she also raises a flower in her nonchalant fingers. Despite the horrible power Salome possesses, she assumes the attitude of a stony sphinx, still, rigid, indifferent, in a withdrawn and insensible somnambulism.

Moreau's Salome is as pure as her scintillating gems; her sexuality is subdued by her steadfast pose. By contrast, des Esseintes' interpretation of the painting, one that is "accessible seulement aux cervelles ébranlées, aiguisées, comme rendues visionnaires par la névrose" (70), as famous as it is, concerns only a crude passion—a monstrous beast—that Baudelaire would banish outside of the realm of beauty:

> la Bête monstrueuse, indifférente, irresponsable, insensible, empoisonnant, de même que l'Hélène antique, tout ce qui l'approche, tout ce qui la voit, tout ce qu'elle touche. (71)

Following Baudelaire's poem "La Beauté," Moreau's interpretation of Salome articulates well why a stony, incomprehensible statue—even before the moment she exercises her venereal charm—is as beautiful, powerful, and fatal.

This cult of artificial worlds carved of marble and gold—purely sensuous, rejecting signification and masking life—makes a unique fin-de-siècle fashion. Mostly famously, the aesthete in Huysmans's novel *À rebours*, before appreciating Moreau's paintings (Ch. V), creates his own emblem that realizes the dual principles of beautiful inertia and necessary richness—it is a tortoise (Ch. IV) gilded in gold and encrusted with gemstones arranged in a delicate bouquet of flowers, designed to crawl on his carpet and to subdue its garnish colors. The tortoise survives gilding, but dies of the burden of the dazzling, religious receptacle of "ciboire" (66). Huysmans in the preface to *À rebours* argues that his aim is to write about signifying minerals and talkative substance that are themselves symbols: "l'on peut très bien dire qu'elles sont des minéraux significatifs, de substances loquaces, qu'elles sont, en un mot, des symboles" (xii-xiii). The gemstones speak, however, not through meaning, but merely through their sensuous forces. What Huysmans aims to offer in the book, as he notes it, is not jewelry of a meaning beyond itself ("une joaillerie de l'au-delà"), but merely jewelry well described, well arranged, well displayed: "Il se compose d'écrins plus ou moins bien décrits, plus ou moins bien rangés en une montre" (iii). The chapter on gemstones is merely as superficial as jewelry arrayed into a flower: "Le chapitre d'*À Rebours* n'est donc que superficiel et à fleur de chaton" (iii). And the chapter on flowers discusses only their shapes and colors, not their significance; as des Esseintes chooses orchids that are bizarre yet silent : "*À rebours* ne les [fleurs] considère qu'au point de vue des contours et des teintes, nullement au point de vue des significations qu'elles décèlent ; des Esseintes n'a choisi que des orchidées bizarres, mais taciturnes" (xv). For Huysmans, jeweled surfaces and grotesque flowers, with their foreign materiality, have their sheer sensuous effect, precisely because they refuse to signify and symbolize.

While des Esseintes dwells on the femme fatale's destructive, lascivious passion, Mallarmé is with Moreau to imagine a sterile image of "Hérodiade."[61] The poem is traditionally read in terms of the Symbolist motif that the artist wishes to remain in her autonomous reverie, and to disengage from the coarse bourgeois society. Most singularly, however, Herodias is capable of extracting herself from human relations by virtue of her hair, the part of our organic body that nerves do not reach and thus does not feel pain. Herodias claims that she is immortal when her solitary body, the ice of horror, is bathed in her hair, enclosed by light—as if she would be suddenly ossified when the condition of a certain material presentation is met.

> Le blond torrent de mes cheveux immaculés,
> Quand il baigne mon corps solitaire le glace
> D'horreur, et mes cheveux que la lumière enlace
> Sont immortels (56).

In this pronouncement, Herodias refers to herself as if from an external perspective—that she notes how the hair covers her body with the light shining on it—as if she is an object of art that a painter comments on. Herodias proclaims her wish to transform herself into a sterile passive object of art, mirroring not the world, however, but the objects in her nursery room.

> Je veux que mes cheveux qui ne sont pas des fleurs
> À répandre l'oubli des humaines douleurs,
>
> Mais de l'or, à jamais vierge des aromates,
> Dans leurs éclairs cruels et dans leurs pâleurs mates,
> Observent la froideur stérile du métal,
> Vous ayant reflétés, joyaux du mur natal,
> Armes, vases, depuis ma solitaire enfance (57-58).

---

[61] Stéphane Mallarmé, *Poésies*, 8 ed. (Paris: Nouvelle Revue française, 1914), 55-70.

Herodias can be a sterile woman of frigid majesty by virtue of her hair, which emulates metal that is mostly pale, and only occasionally glints, in a way that is cruel because its glint is transitory, and never responds to human wishes. With her hair as her prop, she is, like Baudelaire's dandy and women wearing cosmetics, a living life that assumes a statuesque attitude. Herodias is detached, somnambulist, sculpturesque and self-absorbed, as she, longing for nothing human but rather embodies the ideal of art.

>Mais qui me toucherait, des lions respectée ?
>Du reste, je ne veux rien d'humain et, sculptée,
>Si tu me vois les yeux perdus au paradis,
>C'est quand je me souviens de ton lait bu jadis (62-63).

When the nurse asks Herodias for whom does she keep her unknown splendor and vain mystery, Herodias answers that, art for art's sake, she keeps that for herself—art is withdrawn from the spectator, thus sterile. But most curiously, Herodias then addresses, in apostrophe, to gold and crystal mines that buried underneath the ground, which she cannot see but calls to presence—in order to share her feelings, as if she considers herself to be part of the inorganic world.

>Oui, c'est pour moi, pour moi, que je fleuris, déserte !
>Vous le savez, jardins d'améthyste, enfouis
>Sans fin dans de savants abîmes éblouis,
>Ors ignorés, gardant votre antique lumière
>Sous le sombre sommeil d'une terre première,
>Vous, pierres où mes yeux comme de purs bijoux
>Empruntent leur clarté mélodieuse, et vous
>Métaux qui donnez à ma jeune chevelure
>Une splendeur fatale et sa massive allure (63)!

Herodias is a deserted flower, blooming for herself, in the same way crystal buried underground shines since the primeval time. Herodias borrows from crystals the inorganic, purple light in her eyes, and from gold the metallic glint for her hair—a glint of fatal splendor and massive allure! Art is self-enclosed, here not by imagination distinct from reality, not by dint of relations between signs, but rather through material objects that refuse to signify.

This interest in materiality as a pure sensuous surface, in its contrast with life as it is terribly insensible and incomprehensible, is a unique fin-de-siècle invention, and perhaps a facet least explored in our recent theoretical interest in materiality. Though I cannot mention all related schools here, for a diametrical example Jane Bennett in her book *Vibrant Matter*[62] theorizes a "vital materiality" (vii) in order to blur the distinctions between humans and inorganic things, and to strengthen our empathetic bond and ethical concerns toward the material world (ix). Her project is mainly inspired by Deleuze and Félix Guattari's "material vitalism" (x) that looks for theorizing motionless matter for what it does not look like: for its life-like capriciousness and "self-transformations" (59) on the atomic level of vibratory energy.

> The aim is to articulate the elusive idea of a materiality that is *itself* heterogeneous, itself a differential of intensities, itself a life. In this strange, *vital* materialism, there is no point of pure stillness, no indivisible atom that is not itself aquiver with virtual force. (57, emphasis original)

In the Chapter "A Life of Metal," Bennett thus negates the idea that Prometheus's impregnable chain is made of a homogeneous substance. Rather, citing a scientific account, Bennett observes that metals "consist of hosts of very tiny crystals...and they differ in size and shape," and argues that "a metallic *vitality*, a (impersonal) life, can be seen in the quivering of these free atoms at the edges between the grains of the polycrystalline edifice" (59). But Baudelaire, Moreau, and Mallarmé, as discussed above, appreciate metal and precious stone precisely for their inorganic, inanimate qualities: that it does not quiver, that it is still in its grandeur. The fin-de-siècle artists conceptualize matter in square contrast to life, and appreciate its beauty because it is inhuman. Their capacity to appreciate the otherness of matter, in contrast, is truly remarkable.

The fin-de-siècle creates a notion of artificial appearance that remains forever a veil that defies penetration. Baudelaire defines beauty strictly as an appearance that will never reveal its inwardness, or better, it has no inwardness, as in the poem "L'Amour du mensonge"[63] the poet confesses that he knows eyes that are most melancholic when it holds no precious secret, like the sky (which he calls to presence) that is most profound when it is empty: "Plus vides, plus profonds que vous-même, ô Cieux!" He then calls out in apostrophe to masks and decorations, and claims that he loves the artificial appearance in itself, without a predisposition of inwardness.

---

[62] Jane Bennett, *Vibrant Matter: A Political Ecology of Things* (Duke University Press, 2009).
[63] Baudelaire, *Les Fleurs du mal*, No. 98.

> Mais ne suffit-il pas que tu sois l'apparence,
> Pour réjouir un cœur qui fuit la vérité ?
> Qu'importe ta bêtise ou ton indifférence ?
> Masque ou décor, salut ! J'adore ta beauté.

Baudelaire concedes to the Kantian trap that we only see the appearance of things and never the thing-in-itself, but for Baudelaire this appearance is not comfortably anthropocentric. It is rather superficial, insensible, and incomprehensible. With Baudelaire's peculiar taste of alienation, he elevates the foreign appearance of things as the site of Beauty. While Jane Bennett's vibrant matter brings us closer to the material world by fulfilling our human desire of knowing the essence and of intimate connection, a prominent trend in the fin-de-siècle demands a *difficult love* toward the stony sphinx, a love of appearance without inwardness. This strange amalgam of imagination and materiality is the reward of the fin-de-siècle artist's honest love of metal and stone, which does not harbor a secret desire to re-enact the myth of Pygmalion and to transform the stone into something alive and familiar. In other words, the fin-de-siècle artist creates a relation with things through a difficult transformation of the self and discipline of one's desire—by loving, unrequitedly, the insensible stone.

V. Huysmans's Artificial Paradise

So far, we have discussed the fin-de-siècle leitmotif, artificiality, as a philosophical enterprise of how art might relate in ingenious ways with matter. While for the idealists art functions to transfigure nature so as to transfer it to the immaterial realm of imagination, the Decadents reinterpret the formula—art is superior to nature—by creating manifestos where art figures as a stony sphinx, a marble statue, or jeweled surface, that may allure, injure, and discipline the subject. Art is the arena where the artist may create subject-object relations, and we have discussed two of such relations that purposefully subvert the idealist dictum. First, the poet may perversely choose to love the Venus statue, stony sphinx, or an android machine, while claiming that the inhuman beloved is superior to a living woman—for she is insensible and forever inaccessible, thus capable of sustaining the poetic desire in a perpetual quest. Second, the poet praises instances where a material surface covers up the living body, as in the cases of dandyism, cosmetics, and Salome's jeweled regalia, so the poet or the ideal woman may emulate the material qualities such as invulnerability and transform themselves into a mysterious sphinx. In both cases, materiality, stony or dazzling, fascinates the fin-de-siècle for all its inhuman qualities. In the present section, I will discuss the third formula of artificiality (and creative subject-object relation) as experimented in Joris-Karl Huysmans's *À rebour*: it is the poet's endeavor to unpack foreign sensations innate in materiality, to the point of deranging one's own senses, of sacrificing the conceptual power of intellect and to allow its disorientation. Huysmans's project of artificiality can be summarized by Arthur Rimbaud declaration: "Je est un autre": "Il s'agit d'arriver a l'inconnu par le dérèglement de *tout les sens*."[64] Huysmans's hero is dedicated to deranging his own senses, by substituting the contents of anthropocentric concepts with novel sensations, by forsaking the Kantian anchor in this foreign world and welcoming its outlandish assaults. While Meillassoux speculates that we may cut the correlationist tie through "thought's relinquishment of the principle of reason,"[65] without asking how this can be done, Huysmans indeed carries out the project, and shows us what can be achieved is not mere a *"hyper-Chaos,"*[66] but rather rich manifestations of material powers hidden behind the order of our habitual perception. The difference between Meillassoux and Huysmans is that the philosopher postulates for a universal condition, while the artist includes himself in his individual experiments and practices—Huysmans seeks, first of all, to derange his own senses and reasons in his artistic endeavors. In all three formulas of artificiality, the poet creates new relations with materiality only through *a willed creation of the self.*

Baudelaire has two homonym poems called "L'Invitation au voyage": the famous one is written in verse and cumulated in *Les Fleurs du mal*,[67] while the other prose poem is published in *Petits poèmes en prose* (the poetry album is otherwise named or *Le Spleen de Paris*) (1869).[68] In the prose poem, the pleasure is not one of calm and narcissistic, self-same and self-sufficient union between the soul and the land as in the verse counterpart; rather, it is a land which allows the artist to dream and prolong the hours through an infinity of heterogeneous sensations ("rêver et allonger les heures par l'infini des sensations"). Unity is replaced by diversity. Whereas in the verse poem all is but order, beauty, and pleasure ("La, tout n'est qu'order et beauté,/Luxe,

---

[64] Arthur Rimbaud, "[Lettre] À G. Izambard--13 Mai [1871]," in Rimbaud: Complete Works, Selected Letters, ed. Seth Whidden (Chicago: The University of Chicago Press, 2005), 371 (emphasis and capitalization original). As Huysmans indicates in his Preface to *À rebours*, composed in 1903, 8 years after the novel has been written, he is not aware of Rimbaud's work at the time when he composes the novel.
[65] Meillassoux, *After Finitude*, 63.
[66] Meillassoux, *After Finitude*, 64.
[67] *Les Fleurs du mal*, No. 53.
[68] Charles Baudelaire, "Petits Poèmes en prose," in *Œuvres complètes de Charles Baudelaire*, IV. (Michel Lévy frères, 1869), No. XVIII.

calme, et volupté"), in the prose poem the pieces of furniture are large, curious, bizarre, armed with locks and secrets like refined souls of their own ("Les meubles sont vastes, curieux, bizarres, armés de serrures et de secrets comme des âmes raffinées"). The mirrors, metals, fabrics, well-wrought wares of gold, silver, and ceramic, speak to the eyes not in the sweet native tongue ("douce langue natale") as in the verse poem, but rather a mute and mysterious symphony ("une symphonie muette et mystérieuse") perhaps incomprehensible but nevertheless intrigues the soul.

In the prose poem, the land still resembles the soul of the artist, and it is even more explicit to emphasize the creative process that Nature is first refashioned by the artist so as to correspond with his dream:

> Pays singulier, supérieur aux autres, comme l'Art l'est à la Nature, où celle-ci est réformée par le rêve, où elle est corrigée, embellie, refondue. (51)

The aphorism sounds traditionally idealist, but here, rather than remolding Nature so as to express one's temperament and innermost feelings, Baudelaire's exemplar artist here is a horticulturalist who can manipulate materiality and to manufacture novel sensations, to devise exotic "*tulipe noire*" and "*blue dahlia*"[69] that embodies the artist's imagination:

> Fleur incomparable, tulipe retrouvée, allégorique dahlia, c'est là, n'est-ce pas, dans ce beau pays si calme et si rêveur, qu'il faudrait aller vivre et fleurir ? Ne serais-tu pas encadrée dans ton analogie, et ne pourrais-tu pas te mirer, pour parler comme les mystiques, dans ta propre *correspondance* ? (51)

The correspondence here is not anchored in one's essence; it rather aims toward endless diversity. In Barbara Johnson's words, the difference in the correspondences between verse and prose poems lies with that the former offers the land as a mirror of the self, whereas in the latter "the poet in fact

---

[69] Emphasis Baudelaire's. It alludes to Alexander Dumas's historical novel *La Tulipe Noire* (1850) in which the city of Haarlem, Netherlands sets a high monetary prize for the horticulturist who can grow a black tulip. The novel is set at 1672, 30 years after the tulip mania. The tulip mania is the first recorded economic bubble in which the price of the tulip bulb was feverishly inflated but then collapsed dramatically in February 1637. See Anne Goldgar, *Tulipmania: Money, Honor, and Knowledge in the Dutch Golden Age* (University of Chicago Press, 2008).

transforms that self into an empty hall of mirrors,"[70] fulfilling Rimbaud's dictum "Je est un autre." The "allegorical flower" in the prose "L'Invitation," Johnson forcefully argues,

> is no longer the point of primal convergence, of metaphorical fusion, where metaphor and metonymy, signified and signifier, harmoniously unite, but the very locus of substitution and of dissemination, a mere linguistic constant in an infinitely extensible equation. (32)

This new correspondence in the prose "L'Invitation," which in fact compels the poet to empty out the self and to embrace all unknown sensations, which endlessly substitutes in linguistic metaphors the familiar with the foreign, as I will go on to argue, is further developed by Huysmans.

In Baudelaire's other writings, he associates this artistic aptitude to welcome indiscriminately all kinds of sensations with *modernity*, and the flâneur is the one who practices this spirituality by actively savoring all novel sensations the modern city brings. As Baudelaire claims in his prose poem "Les Foules":[71] the flâneur must cultivate his openness to absorb unknown urban sensations, "vastes voluptés, changeantes, inconnues," to give himself "à l'imprévu qui se montre, à l'inconnu qui passe,"[72] and enjoys an immense spiritual reward which almost verges on "mystérieuses ivresses."[73] This openness comes however with a heavy price: the flâneur sacrifices his personality, or humanity indeed, for a fit of vitality.[74] The flâneur enjoys the universal communion in the same way the lady may sacrifice her chastity, so that the flâneur can join the "ineffable orgie," "cette sainte prostitution de l'âme tout entire." Baudelaire's sacred spiritual prostitution is his perverse metaphor which argues forcefully that chaste love is small, limited, and weak.

Baudelaire's perception of modernity, of a spiritual quest of novel sensations, can be performed not only on the streets, but also in an artificial interior where aesthetic experience is carefully choreographed. Baudelaire's

---

[70] Barbara Johnson, "Poetry and Its Double: Two Invitations au Voyage" in *The Critical Difference: Essays in the Contemporary Rhetoric of Reading* (Johns Hopkins University Press, 1985), 33.
[71] Baudelaire, *Petits Poèmes en prose*, No. XII.
[72] "Le Voyage" in *Les Fleurs du mal*.
[73] "Les Foules."
[74] "Les Foules." "Il n'est pas donné à chacun de prendre un bain de multitude: jouir de la foule est un art; et celui-là seul peut faire, aux dépens du genre humain, une ribote de vitalité."

prose poem of "L'Invitation au voyage" thus inspires Huysmans's hero in *À rebour*, a rich, cultured, emancipated and oversensitive Duc des Esseintes, to retreat from Paris to his country house at Fontenay, and there build his own ideal abode. Huysmans imagines that the private poet can *own* the world perhaps by virtue of his cultivated spirituality, as Baudelaire compares the poet to a hard-working man who collects all treasures from the world in his ideal room:

> Les trésors du monde y affluent, comme dans la maison d'un homme laborieux et qui a bien mérité du monde entier.

In des Esseintes's artificial paradise he curates decadent artworks, collects strange flowers, manufacts perfumes, arranges jewelry bouquets, and seeks to generate all kinds of sense experience such as constructing an artificial sea voyage in his own dining room.

Walter Benjamin argues that the arcade is a guiding metaphor of the consciousness of modernity in nineteenth-century Paris.[75] The arcade is an iron architecture that collects luxury items and images from around the world, "a world in miniature."[76] At the same time, painting and literature are also inspired to depict nature and society in panoramic views[77]: "One sought tirelessly, through technical devices, to make panoramas the scenes of a perfect imitation of nature."[78] And the interior design of private houses likewise echoes the spirit of the arcade.[79] Benjamin's depiction of the interior space here seems applicable to Huysmans's ideal room:

> From this arise the phantasmagorias of the interior—which, for the private man, represents the universe. In the interior, he brings together the far away and long ago. His living room is a box in the theater of the world.[80]

The flâneur is a denizen of modernity, who enters into the phantasmagoric arcade just to be enchanted and distracted: "He surrenders to its manipulation

---

[75] Walter Benjamin, *The Writer of Modern Life: Essays on Charles Baudelaire*, trans. Howard Eiland et al. (Cambridge, Massachusetts: Harvard University Press, 2016).
[76] Benjamin, *The Writer of Modern Life*, 31.
[77] Benjamin, *The Writer of Modern Life*, 33.
[78] Benjamin, *The Writer of Modern Life*, 33.
[79] Benjamin, *The Writer of Modern Life*, 41.
[80] Benjamin, *The Writer of Modern Life*, 38.

while enjoying his alienation from himself and others."[81] But the collector who has the world in possession is the true artist, for the latter transfigures things and paints his or her own ideal world, creating an artificial paradise, with intense concentration. Here the artist again transfigures commodities with the stamp of his creative impulse, thus again takes possession of them:

> The interior is the asylum of art. The collector is the true resident of the interior. He makes his concern the transfiguration of things. To him falls the Sisyphean task of divesting things of their commodity character by taking possession of them. But he bestows on him only connoisseur value, rather than use value. The collector dreams his way not only into a distant or bygone world but also into a better one.[82]

Benjamin's distinction between the flâneur and the collector might have been derived from Baudelaire's writing on the painter Guys, who as an artist, has a loftier aim than the flâneur who lets things pass by. For Baudelaire, Guys's childlike receptivity of modern impression is only the first step—at night, the painter will paint from his memory everything that he so eagerly absorbs during the day. For Baudelaire, the true artist must passionately transform the fleeting impression into the poetic and the eternal: "de dégager de la mode ce qu'elle peut contenir de poétique dans l'historique, de tirer l'éternel du transitoire." This process of internalization that transforms sensation into creation might be a way to interpret why Baudelaire, Huysmans, and Benjamin put the artist not in the streets but in a room: the modern artist is a collector who *own* novel sensations from around the world.

An obvious difference between the flâneur and the artist in the room is that the former roam about the bustling streets, whereas the latter is more likely a hermitic misanthrope; another is that the flâneur welcomes any sensations as the chance circumstances bring, whereas the latter carefully controls and choreographs his material experience. But for Baudelaire, the common ground between the two—the common ground which he defines as the artistic spirit—is an aptitude to savor all different kinds of impressions or sensuous experience. Baudelaire dictates that this "the alchemist of horticulture" must ceaselessly search for and postpone the limits of their happiness, as his artistic stature is defined by whether he can be receptive and stay desirous to sensations of any kind.

---

[81] Benjamin, *The Writer of Modern Life*, 36.
[82] Benjamin, *The Writer of Modern Life*, 39.

Artificiality 55

Qu'ils cherchent, qu'ils cherchent encore, qu'ils reculent sans cesse les limites de leur bonheur, ces alchimistes de l'horticulture !

Central to Baudelaire's particolored banner that combines at once the leitmotifs of decadence, artificiality, and modernity is this spirit of perpetual quest and spacious receptivity. Susan Buck-Morss explicates Benjamin's phantasmagorias as "technoaesthetics...the goal is manipulation of the synaesthetic system by control of environmental stimuli"[83]—and such technoaesthetics, of creating an artificial environment in which all novel sensations are carefully searched and generated, is precisely Huysmans's project.

Huysmans's *À rebours*[84] is a literal (and literary) reenactment of Baudelaire's prose poem "L'Invitation au voyage." Baudelaire's prose poem writes "tant la chaude et capricieuse fantaisie s'y est donné carrière, tant elle l'a patiemment et opiniâtrement illustré de ses savantes et délicates végétations" and, as Baudelaire dictates, Huysmans's hero in the novel is transported to a singular room, so superb as that des Esseintes's hot and capricious fantasy takes on the mission to patiently and persistently illustrate the room with learned and delicate vegetation. Reversing the Romantic poetic convention about flowers—mostly the organic symbol of nature in which William Black sees a universe—des Esseintes searches not for the harmony of natural order, but rather for monstrosity created out of intersections between the boundaries of the natural and the artificial. Des Esseintes used to like artificial flowers that impeccably copy nature's creation in every detail. But Chapter 8 of the novel narrates that des Esseintes now collects rather strange flowers produced by nature that violate our concepts of them, as they look like being crafted out of man-made materials—"l'étoffe, le papier, la porcelaine, le métal, paraissaient avoir été prêtés par l'homme à la nature pour lui permettre de créer ses monstres" (120). Des Esseintes compares leaves and flowers to animal organs and metal, examining their singular materiality, which monstrously offends our concepts of them. With this collection or better, production, of strange flowers as his aesthetic enterprise, des Esseintes pronounces: "décidément, par le temps qui court, les horticulteurs sont les seuls et les vrais artistes" (122).

But what is the aesthetics of horticulture? In what way does Huysmans interpret Baudelaire's alchemy of horticulture? Nietzsche argues that our conventional truth is but an abstract Idea, a protecting shield of the intellect,

---

[83] Susan Buck-Morss, "Aesthetics and Anaesthetics: Walter Benjamin's Artwork Essay Reconsidered," *October* 62 (1992): 22.
[84] *À rebours* (Paris: Georges Crès, 1922).

that scaffolds the raw material powers of the object and prevents us from their assaults.

> As creatures of *reason*, human beings now make their actions subject to the rule of abstractions; they no longer tolerate being swept away by sudden impressions and sensuous perceptions; they now generalize all these impressions first, turning them into cooler, less colourful concepts in order to harness the vehicle of their lives and actions to them. Everything which distinguishes human beings from animals depends on this ability to sublimate sensuous metaphor into a schema, in other words, to dissolve an image into a concept.[85]

To defy what Nietzsche calls anthropomorphism that reduces things of sensuous powers to abstract concepts, the horticulturalist manipulates at once the flesh of flowers and our concepts of them, while his alchemy releases from matter the unknown sensuous forces imprisoned by conventional ideas.

While Kant dictates that we cannot see the thing-in-itself as our perception is already structured by our a priori conception, the unknown sensation sought in fin-de-siècle often exceeds our conceptual scheme. The fin-de-siècle *inconnu* is an inversion of the Kantian sublime. For Kant,[86] a sublime object that overwhelms our senses will rather "awakens the feeling of a supersensible faculty" in us, a "reflective judgement" (134) or "subjective purposiveness" (137) that functions independent of the object and prompts a satisfactory emotion that celebrates our *a priori* independence or our conceptual relation to "the infinite" (138)—in short, a pleasurable emotion that our reason is superior to our inadequate senses, which for Kant is part of our aesthetic "vocation" (141).

> Thus sublimity is not contained in anything in nature, but only in our mind, insofar as we can become conscious of being superior to nature within us and thus also to nature outside us (insofar as it influences us). (147)

But the fin-de-siècle *inconnu* is precisely a quest to court novel sensations that violate our conceptual scheme, leaving ourselves helpless at their

---

[85] Friedrich Nietzsche, "On Truth and Lying in a Non-Moral Sense," in *The Birth of Tragedy and Other Writings* (Cambridge: Cambridge University Press, 1999), 146.
[86] Immanuel Kant, *Critique of the Power of Judgement*. trans. Paul Guyer (Cambridge of University Press, 2000).

assaults. Des Esseintes's grotesque flowers can be classified as what Kant defines as the monstrous: "an object is *monstrous* if by its magnitude it annihilates the ends which its concepts constitute" (136, emphasis original). This disorientation of our conceptual scheme, this masochistic pleasure of receiving unknown sensations innate in materiality, this banner of artificiality, is part of the modernist project to escape the Kantian reason that scaffolds our everyday perception. And this escape of Kantian reason would be for Meillassoux the most astonishing feat of de-anthropocentrism.

In addition to seeking monstrous sensations that disorient our conceptual schemes, Huysmans's hero also rejoices in unsettling our most banal yet lyrical concepts with what is humorously artificial. Des Esseintes pursues Baudelaire's leitmotif of sea voyage, as in chapter four of the novel he conducts his (ridiculously) imaginary cruise in a ship cabin that he builds inside his own dining room, with a vaulted ceiling and semicircular beams, and its paneling cut into the shape of a porthole (25). Des Esseintes then puts an aquarium between the porthole and the window of the actual dining room, and places in the aquarium mechanical fish and imitation seaweed. As his moods fit it, he would drip dye into the water in order to imitate the changing colors of the sea, such as that of various rivers—green, greyish or silvery—flowing into it, of the glint of the sunlight in different seasons and hours, as well as the atmospheric qualities of the impeding rain (25-26). Having set up the vistas of variable water and mechanical marine creatures, and pumping into his artificial cabin the smell of tar, des Esseintes on his imaginary cruise also contemplate upon a huge collection of voyage-related items—timetables of steamship lines, measuring devices such as compasses and maps, fishing rods and nets, and even a fake anchor made not of raw iron but of cork, painted black—which des Esseintes refers to as "un léger subterfuge, par une approximative sophistication de l'objet poursuivi par ces désirs mêmes" (28). A prevalent motif of des Esseintes's aesthetics consists of this spurious, artificial imitation of nature through his approximate objects and his manipulative setup, as well as the employment of imagination that substitutes and correlates the natural and the artificial—together creating the most unique sense experience.

In addition to his collection of exotic flowers and construction of artificial sea voyage, des Esseintes with his theory of sensory correspondence, in which the sensation of sight, sound, smell, and taste are interchangeable, likewise seeks to challenge our normative correlation between concepts and sensations. Notably, to see the correspondence between the senses, one must cultivate at once one's susceptibility as well as one's knowledge in the respective arts. The novel impressions he receives might be in fact minute, but the true artist would have to magnify them ten folds, and then to coordinate and combine them into a work of art.

> Il pensait que l'odorat pouvait éprouver des jouissances égales à celles de l'ouïe et de la vue, chaque sens étant susceptible, par suite d'une disposition naturelle et d'une érudite culture, de percevoir des impressions nouvelles, de les décupler, de les coordonner, d'en composer ce tout qui constitue une œuvre. (145)

Des Esseintes then experiments with how each taste of liquors might correspond to different musical notes and the sound qualities of different instruments—for example the violin may be represented by old brandy, "fumeuse et fine, aiguë et frêle" (61)—so that he can play a symphony on his palate by inventing a machine, a "orgue à bouche" that carefully drips one drop of liquor in his mouth at a time (60). Des Esseintes's expertise with the perfume likewise demonstrates his aesthetics to confuse the categories between the natural and the artificial. Des Esseintes explains that the architect of the scent cannot possibly reproduce the aroma of the living flowers by distilling the essence from the smashed petals. Rather, perfumes that bear the names of any flower—with one exception of jasmine, which cannot be imitated by any artistry—are adept combinations between alcoholates and essences (146). The consummate artist, an alchemist indeed, is one who is capable of befitting to the evocative name of the perfume by knowing faultlessly the hidden and manifest powers of each ingredient, and bringing them to the orchestrated performance by blending them in precise ratio, together with one's creative and personal touch. With des Esseintes's theory of correspondence, he compares the art of perfumery to that of a jeweler who polishes precise stones (146), and to that of a poet who can decipher an exotic language of concise grammar and suggestive beauty: "des Esseintes qui déchiffrait maintenant cette langue, variée, aussi insinuante que celle de la littérature, ce style d'une concision inouïe, sous son apparence flottante et vague" (147).

Des Esseintes's aesthetics might be articulated by what Nietzsche calls "a mobile army of metaphors, metonymies, anthropomorphisms,"[87] which, through endless interplays of the categories between the natural and the artificial, set our conventional ideas into a rich metamorphosis so as to unleash the sensuous powers innate in materiality that are usually locked up in abstract and universal concepts. Under the general, much poeticized and

---

[87] Nietzsche, "On Truth and Lying in a Non-Moral Sense," 146.

therefore conventionalized concept, des Esseintes musters an otherwise improbable assemblage of objects that are used to generate sensations that he casually names as sea voyage, which only somehow make comprehensible, but not quite, the sensation of his uncanny, clumsy mechanical fish swimming in the tank, entangled with the imitation seaweed, driven by clockwork. Des Esseintes's enemy, Nature, is to a great extent equated with our naturalized sense of how things are, whereas his artificiality aligns with his virtuoso manipulation of materials in the quest for incomparable sensations that parodies the real. Our ideas of what an object is—which Nietzsche refers to as the conventional truth, an abstract Idea scaffolding its material power—is then mobilized into an imaginative metaphor, a forged analogy, a porthole facing a colored aquarium, dreaming sea voyage.

Reading Nietzsche's *On Truth and Lie,* Paul de Man points out that metaphor and metonymy allow endless Ovidian metamorphosis, whereas the third term of this enumeration, anthropomorphism, freezes the chain of artistic translation as it assumes a given human standard, the point of "truth."[88] But for des Esseintes his aquarium that reflects actual sunlight with colored water, his artificial sea that he looks through the porthole, is precisely the most self-consciously fatuous object, a simulacrum that aims to mock "the real" and reveals it as conventional concepts that hardly designate unknown materiality. For Nietzsche as well as for des Esseintes, for whom truth is only convention, conspicuous artificiality is the weapon against anthropomorphism: it sets our rigid concepts in motion while unleashing unknown sensations.

VI. Summary of Part One

Artificiality—or the concept that art is superior to nature—is the leitmotif in the fin-de-siècle artists: Baudelaire, the Parnassians, Villiers de L'Isle-Adam, Moreau, and Huysmans. Part One of the book argues that artificiality is a purposeful and perverse twist of the idealist dictum. In idealism, art is superior to nature as it theorizes art as the imaginative power that transforms and therefore transfers nature to the immaterial realm, whereas the banner of artificiality always subverts the power relations between materiality and subjectivity. Part One discusses three formulas of artificiality. First, the poet willingly loves the marble statue and stony sphinx, and recasts the qualities of the stone: insensible, incomprehensible, and inaccessible, as qualities of the

---

[88] Paul de Man, "Anthropomorphism and Trope in Lyric," in *The Rhetoric of Romanticism* (New York: Columbia University Press, 1984), 240-41.

ideal that can sustain the poet's perpetual quest. Second, as in the case of dandyism, cosmetics, and Salome's regalia of gemstones, the artist assumes impassive masks of materiality, so as to subjugate the feeling heart and discipline the soul. Third, as in the case of Rimbaud and Huysmans, the artist seeks to unpack novel sensations hoarded in matter, to the point of deranging one's senses and unsettling one's conceptual scheme. In all of these three cases, the poet creates ingenious relations with the thing only through recreations of the self.

Part One of the book thus argues that the work of art in fin-de-siècle undergoes an interesting ontological reconceptualization whose identity is no longer Hegel's free, immaterial dream, but more often this strange association of artificiality with incomprehensible materiality, this ally of imagination and inert matter that is dissociated from inwardness, an ideal of Beauty made with metal and marble that is eternal, immovable, and insensible—which together creates new imagination-material dynamics and negotiates the long-honored hierarchy of mind and matter. The relation between the poetic imagination and the artistic medium of materiality, as Baudelaire conceptualizes in the poem "La Beauté," still aligns well with the abysmal subject-object divide cut by Kant. But what Baudelaire inspires in fin-de-siècle artists, most peculiarly, is at once *a heightened desire and escalated alienation of the feeling heart toward insensible matter.* This doomed yearning and impossible quest will be the first paragon to the thesis of the book that charts, historically, the plethora of creative *subject-object relations* sprouting up by the wane of German Idealism, and that evinces, theoretically, art provides such an arena to experiment with new subject-object relations, while the poet often creates new relations with things through creation of the self.

TWO
Auto-Philosophical Fiction

In Part One, I have discussed the actual *practices* of how the artists cultivate their unique forms of love—Baudelaire's unrequited love toward the stone, for example—as creative approaches to respond to the Kantian conundrum that matter is inaccessible. In Part Two, I will further investigate the *literary form* that self-reflectively and explicitly responds to the metaphysical question. My purpose is to discuss literature as a mode of thought different from philosophy in that it does not merely seek to maintain an aesthetic ideal or to champion for a universal truth, but rather to investigate how one should achieve the ideal through the cultivation of the self, as well as how the ideal should shape life—as such will show the ethical and aesthetic implications of embracing the ideal. Recent scholarship is enthusiastic about exploring how modernist literature is being influenced by the most advanced science and psychology of the time.[1] But other than carefully documenting how art is being influenced by quantum physics and empiricist psychology, scholars however have not developed a systematic approach as to how art can otherwise relate itself to claims of truth. Another approach is to read literature itself as a kind of philosophical work, for example as Joshua Landy proclaims in his book *Philosophy as Fiction* that "it is one of the primary aims of my book to show that…we can in fact extract a consistent, powerful, and original philosophical system from *A la recherche du temps perdu*" (8). Part Two of the book however argues that literature differs from philosophy as a mode of reasoning in that literature sets aesthetic ideals in the laboratory of life, and examines these ideals through the medium of life. Walter Pater does exactly so through a genre he developed and called *imaginary portrait*. But I would like to call the genre, more explicitly, *auto-philosophical fiction,* and include Marcel Proust's *Recherche* and Virginia Woolf's experimental novel *The Waves* in the same category.

Pater claims that his genre imaginary portrait, following the Romantic tradition of sympathy, allows us a privileged access to the hero's sensations and ideas (Pater rarely depicts heroines). Through the genre, philosophy is no

---

[1] See, for one example, Benjamin Morgan, *The Outward Mind: Materialist Aesthetics in Victorian Science and Literature* (Chicago: The University of Chicago Press, 2017).

longer an absolute and objective truth. Rather, ideas are adopted because of one's temperament, and it is a matter of aesthetic choice. In such a genre, Pater shows us how an ideal may be lived; what then would be the flavor of life if we adopt a certain philosophical doctrine as our spiritual precept; and, most importantly, how might we live up to an ideal through aesthetic education and cultivation. *While metaphysics after Kant inherits a framework in which subjectivity is a universal given, literature allows the artist to create the self and thus creates relationships with the world.* By this subjective creation, literature is the mode of thinking that allows us to depart from the universal reason that for Kant separates humans from things, and thus achieves de-anthropocentrism.

While philosophy asks what truth is, art asks how we should respond to truth. All three writers discussed in Part Two—Pater, Proust and Woolf—operate within an empiricist predicament similar to what I will further outline in Section I: that our consciousness or transcendental ego has very limited access to our sensuous experience which at every moment is fleeting and irrevocable. In Section II, I discuss how this metaphysical conundrum poses a paradox that cannot be easily smoothed out by simply choosing a coherent, universally applicable stance. Rather, the nature of the question as such requires: first, cultivation of the self, such as expansion of one's consciousness and elevation of one's passion for embracing the fleeting sensations; and second, a negotiation between one's receptivity and one's artistic agency, which creates subject-object relations on the battleground of the work of art. Both tasks demand that the artist translates an aesthetic ideal into rigorous practices, and to bear with the ramifications of these ideals with their own life. Auto-philosophical fiction is the genre where the artist may test if they have lived up to their aesthetic ideals and, more importantly, to test if their ideals truly answer the metaphysical conundrums. The following sections discuss how each individual artist chooses to respond to the metaphysical predicament: Pater's hero vows to expand his powers of perception so as the register the fleeting sensations; Proust's protagonist wishes to transcend time by claiming to have possession of the past sensuous memory; Woolf's characters dream of completely relinquishing their individual consciousness so as to immerse themselves in the universal sensation. There is, of course, always an ambiguous relation between the fictions and the writers' biological life. But my emphasis is not so much on the autobiographical elements of these fictions, but rather on a *method* of relating our life to ideas—the term "auto" refers to this self-reflection where the artist examines the conflicts between practice and theory, as well as the consequences of applying a certain idea to life.

By putting the idea into practice, literature presumes individual subjectivity rather than universal applicability: it acknowledges what can be created rather than what is. This book argues that art is the mode of thinking with which we can answer to the call to de-anthropocentrism, the call to escape Kantian universal reason: for the first meaning of de-anthropocentrism is that we depart from the universal given, and create ourselves so as to create new relationships with the world. My argument here aims to square the general stereotype that modernist de-anthropocentrism aims to achieve an inhuman vision by simply eliminating the human presence in the discourse or artistic representation. Rather, *how* the artist may achieve de-anthropocentrism through *aesthetic cultivation* remains the central question and, for this very reason, the self for the modernist writers receives attention intense and anew. As Aaron Jaffe puts it, "in this sense, Woolf isn't writing about a thing or an object *per se* but an inhumanist literary laboratory."[2] Writing is an experimental laboratory in the sense that the artists must put theories into practice, and test the ideas with their own lives. As I will go on to argue, receptivity and memory are chosen sites of aesthetic cultivation for the artists to achieve a visual alternative to the habitual perception.

To foretell what follows upfront, Proust's narrator in *À la recherche du temps perdu* (hereafter Marcel) claims that, through his famous mechanism of involuntary memory, he has found a means to sublimate transitory and mysterious sensations and to take full possession of them in his mind. But then, juxtaposing Marcel's artistic pursuit with his romantic fiasco, we find that Marcel's idealist appropriation can never compensate for what he really desires—intimacy with an elusive woman, an ultimate Other at the present moment. Although Marcel openly professes his idealist affinity, it is ironically clear to the reader that this idealist appropriation leads to the most painful isolation for the artist. For Woolf, this idealist concept of art is simply contradictory to her aesthetic goal to relinquish her individual consciousness so as to embrace indiscriminately all passing thoughts and sensations. Despite her best efforts to register the stream of thoughts then, in Woolf's self-estimation the act of writing will always involve the exertion of individual consciousness—and this recognition amounts to a confession of her ultimate failure. The most mature concept of art, in my view, is offered by Pater in one of his imaginary portraits, an essay titled "the Child in the House." Sharing a similar view with empiricist psychology that our selective consciousness is shaped by our habits, Pater here offers a valuation of habits different from

---

[2] Aaron Jaffe, "Introduction: Who's Afraid of the Inhuman Woolf?," *Modernism/Modernity* 23, no. 3 (2016): 495.

what he maintains in his famous "Conclusion" to the *Renaissance*. In "the Child in the House," Pater traces the formation of these habits back to our material habituation. The exertion of our consciousness therefore does not transport nature to the immaterial realm of imagination, but rather demonstrates our unique tastes and predilections that have been in the first place shaped by the material world. The mission of art, Pater suggests, lies with this remembrance of our material formation.

I. Empiricist Psychology

As Judith Ryan carefully documents in her book *The Vanishing Subject: Early Psychology and Literary Modernism*, the term empiricist psychology may denote early psychology of late nineteenth century, whose central figures were Ernst Mach and William James.[3] As Ryan patiently teased it out, a broad array of modernist writers were intrigued by empiricist psychology, including Pater, Huysmans, Rilke, Alice James, Henry James, Gertrude Stein, Kafka, Joyce, Proust, Woolf, Robert Musil,[4] and I would add, impressionist painters. The premise of empiricist psychology begins with a problematization of Kantian transcendental ego, as well as its privileged status of organizing experience so as to give certainty to knowledge. As part of the modernist critique of the underserved central place of the human in the universe, the champions of empiricist psychology challenge the legitimacy of Kantian *a priori* reason and reconceptualize it as an anthropomorphic structure that prevents us from having a direct contact with the phenomenal world. As William James summarizes it, Kantian transcendental consciousness is not an inescapable prison completely independent of and prior to our experience. Rather, it is merely a psychological function that allows us to be aware of the contents of experience, "our habits of attention" that selects certain sensations which notify us the existence of a certain object, and overlooks what falls outside of our attention.[5] Our consciousness as such does not organize experience by virtue of an innate structure of universal validity. Rather, for James, our habit of attention is a tenacious tendency that is however negotiable, and it is in fact possible to expand our perceptual attention through cultivated efforts, if we are interested in doing so:

---

[3] Judith Ryan, *The Vanishing Subject: Early Psychology and Literary Modernism* (Chicago: University of Chicago Press, 1991), 2.
[4] Ryan, *The Vanishing Subject*, vii-viii.
[5] William James, *Psychology: The Briefer Course* (Dover Publications, 2001), 39.

We notice only those sensations which are signs to us of *things* which happen practically or aesthetically to interest us, to which we therefore give substantive names, and which we exalt to this exclusive status of independence and dignity. But in itself, apart from my interest, a particular dust-wreath on a windy day is just as much of an individual *thing*, and just as much or as little deserves an individual name, as my own body does.[6]

Our body might have felt the dust-wreath, only that this dust wreath does not invade our awareness. But the artist can purposefully cultivate and expand his attention to include the dust-wreath in our perception domain.

Instead of the Kantian hierarchy between the transcendental ego and the shaped and verified experience, James proposes a different dualism between *our awareness of our experience* and *our stream of thoughts*, or the knower *I* and the experiential *me*. The stream of thoughts, the sum of our subjective life, William James argues, "consists in these rapid premonitory perspective views"[7] before our consciousness recognizes them as objects, as well as an incessant flow of sensations, emotions, and unarticulated thoughts. However, our awareness of experience, "the Knower I," can only capture a fraction of this stream of thoughts as it cuts the flow and consolidates it into the so-called reality, through a certain habitual filter— "The attempt at introspective analysis on these cases is in fact like seizing a spinning top to catch its motion, or trying to turn up the gas quickly enough to see how the darkness looks."[8] Challenging the notion of the Kantian transcendental ego, the purpose of James' attention to the stream of thoughts is to find a field accessible to us prior to the subject-object divide:

> The instant field of the present is at all times what I call the 'pure' experience. It is only virtually or potentially either object or subject as yet. For the time being, it is plain, unqualified actuality, or existence, a simple *that*. In this *naif* immediacy it is of course *valid*; it is *there*, we *act* upon it; and the doubling of it in retrospection into a state of mind and a reality intended thereby, is just one of the acts. ...the immediate

---

[6] James, *Psychology*, 38 (emphasis original).
[7] Ibid., 31.
[8] Ibid., 28.

experience in its passing is always 'truth,' practical truth, *something to act on*, at its own movement.⁹

In other words, for James, what is called reality no longer needs to be sanctioned by our *a priori* reason, but rather exists before our consciousness, *in the contact zone between our body and the sensuous world*. In his book *Essays in Radical Empiricism,* James "blots out the notion of consciousness from his list of first principles" and challenges the Kantian subject-object divide by means of granting the "pure experience" before our consciousness the highest ontological status. At his most radical, James negates the subject-object divide for he thinks consciousness as an entity is "fictitious," and proposes a monism that the world is made of "pure experience": "But thoughts in the concrete are made of the same stuff as things are," that the stream of thinking is as physiological as "the stream of my breathing."¹⁰ As I will further account for in Section V, Woolf's project of writing the characters' stream of consciousness bears the strongest similarity to James' philosophy: she indeed transcribes all these passing thoughts and minute emotions so as to stay at the preconscious level, prior to the subject-object divide.

James's monism summarizes the collective philosophical efforts at the turn of the nineteenth century—to break free from the idealist prison. Most of these efforts are gathered in the journal *The Monist*, which was founded in the year 1888 and is still run by Oxford University Press today. The thesis of this journal is indeed radical, but is nevertheless discussed and corroborated by many leading thinkers for two decades—that the world is composed of sensations before it enters into our consciousness, and that these fleeting sensations instead of our *a priori* reason deserve the highest ontological status. Ernst Mach in his article published at *The Monist*, "The Analysis of Sensations" (1890), for example, argues that the entire inner and outer world is composed of sensations, although he prefers to call sensations "elements"—because for Mach sensation is not what is perceived by humans, but *is real and exists in the objective world.*

> Thus perceptions, as well as ideas, volition, and feelings, in short the entire inner and outer world, are composed of a small number of homologous elements united in relations now more evanescent and now more lasting. These elements are commonly called sensations.

---

⁹ William James, *Essays in Radical Empiricism* (Longmans, 1912), 23–24.
¹⁰ Ibid., 37.

But since vestiges of a one-sided theory now inhere in this term, we prefer to speak simply of elements, as we have already done.[11]

Twenty-five years later, Bertrand Russell repeats the same thesis in his article "The Ultimate Constituents of Matter," likewise published at *The Monist*: "I believe that the actual data in sensation, the immediate objects of sight or touch or hearing, are extra-mental, purely physical, and among the ultimate constituents of matter."[12] As I will further discuss in Section V, both Walter Pater and Virginia Woolf are champions of this monist concept of universal sensation, that we are part of this sensation that envelops us all, that our transcendental ego which debars us from immersing in the entirety of the universal sensation is almost our original sin, and that a true artist should seek to forestall the activities of our transcendental ego.

The three writers discussed in Part II of the book—Pater, Proust, and Woolf—all concern themselves with questions left by empiricism. Recent scholarship has conducted extensive intertextual readings that set the writings of Pater, Proust, and Woolf in the context of the contemporary philosophical-scientific findings, mainly that of empiricist psychology.[13] Yet I think for the purpose of the present chapter the above-cited ideas are sufficient to summarize the general background the three writers engage themselves with. In the next section, I will briefly outline how the modernist artists engage with empiricism on the sites of two major aesthetic media: receptivity and memory.

---

[11] Ernst Mach, "The Analysis of the Sensations. Antimetaphysical," *The Monist* 1, no. 1 (1890): 61 (emphasis original).

[12] Bertrand Russell, "The Ultimate Constituents of Matter," *The Monist* 25, no. 3 (1915): 402.

[13] For studies of how modernist writers respond to the empiricist psychology of the time, see Judith Ryan, *The Vanishing Subject: Early Psychology and Literary Modernism* (Chicago: University of Chicago Press, 1991); Benjamin Morgan, *The Outward Mind: Materialist Aesthetics in Victorian Science and Literature* (Chicago: The University of Chicago Press, 2017); Marilyn M. Sachs, *Marcel Proust in the Light of William James: In Search of a Lost Source* (Lanham, Maryland: Lexington Books, 2014); Rosa Slegers, *Courageous Vulnerability: Ethics and Knowledge in Proust, Bergson, Marcel, and James*, (Leiden; Boston: Brill, 2010). Many books that study the intersection of empiricist tradition and modernist literature place Woolf at the final chapter, presumably because her thinking is the most radical one that takes self-dissolution as the aim of self-cultivation. This includes Ryan's *The Vanishing Subject*, Jesse Matz, *Literary Impressionism and Modernist Aesthetics* (Cambridge University Press, 2003); Finn Fordham, *I Do, I Undo, I Redo: The Textual Genesis of Modernist Selves in Hopkins, Yeats, Conrad, Forster, Joyce, and Woolf* (Oxford: Oxford University Press, 2010).

II. Receptivity and Memory

Against the general intellectual milieu, Part Two of the book however focuses more on *the aesthetic and ethical implications* that the artists explore. In this section, I will briefly outline how the modernist artists in general, including Baudelaire and Roger Fry on impressionist paintings, as well as Pater, Proust, and Woolf, who are the main figures of the discussion, in the face of the metaphysical conundrum left by empiricist psychology formulate their specific questions and aesthetic responses. The questions that concern the modernist artists are, simply put: First, how our consciousness (or intellect, as Proust puts it) can be aware of all sensations, emotions, and passing thoughts? Second, how might the artists participate in the passing sensation with their memory, i.e., to make *the-self-remembering-the-sensation* an aesthetic object? Receptivity and memory become the site of self-cultivation in which the artists relate to fleeting sensations through the media of *their own selves*. But we will also see that each writer conceptualizes memory differently, which embodies their aesthetic relationships with the world: memory is the site of idealization for Baudelaire, a way to retrieve the lost past for Marcel, for Pater, the gem of life that survives the all-devouring flame of the passing time, and for Woolf the porous sieve where the past interacts with the present, the body with the world.

For modernist writers, *receptivity* generally becomes a thorny aesthetic polemics, when the given human perception is now conceived to be inadequate in the face of fleeting sensations. Pater articulates the empiricist worldview in the image of the all-sweeping Heraclius stream which our consciousness can hardly catch up with, as in his famous "Conclusion" to the *Renaissance* (1868)[14]: "all that is actual in it being a single moment, gone while we try to apprehend it, of which it may ever be more truly said that it has ceased to be than that it is" (249). This empiricist view is also seen in a passage in Pater's novel *Marius the Epicurean*:

> The swift passage of things, the still swifter passage of those modes of our conscious being which seemed to reflect them, might indeed be the burning of the divine fire: but what was ascertained was that they did pass away like a devouring flame, or like the race of water in the mid-stream—too swiftly for any real knowledge of them to be attainable. (Chp. 8, p. 131-32)

---

[14] Walter Pater, *The Renaissance: Studies in Art and Poetry* (Landon: Macmillan, 1888). The book can be downloaded on Google Books.

This sense of epistemological crisis is likewise poignantly expressed by Proust, whose hero Marcel laments that his intellect cannot comprehend, let along retain, much of his sensuous experience. When Marcel discovered the mechanism of involuntary memory, his reaction is marked with a curious self-aggrandization.

> Une minute affranchie de l'ordre du temps a recréé en nous pour la sentir l'homme affranchi de l'ordre du temps. Et celui-là on comprend qu'il soit confiant dans sa joie, même si le simple goût d'une madeleine ne semble pas contenir logiquement les raisons de cette joie, on comprend que le mot de « mort » n'ait pas de sens pour lui ; situé hors du temps, que pourrait-il craindre de l'avenir ? (V15. p. 15).[15]

Here, Marcel's ecstatic joy is not sensuous but rather metaphysical. The joy belongs not to the present sensation, not to his savoring of the madeleine cake soaked in the tea on a rainy day, but to the fact that Marcel can summon up a piece of memory from the past, with all its strength and vividness, and thus effectively prevents time from being irrevocably lost. But then, as I will further discuss it in Section IV, Marcel's involuntary memory differs radically from the conscious cultivation of Pater, as he has not actively trained his receptive faculty to capture the present, but rather relies on his magical gimmick to retrieve what he has not consciously lived. Marcel's approach will provide us with a negative example that serves to illuminate what genuine self-cultivation requires.

While aesthetic receptivity is already a prevalent theme in Romanticism, for Baudelaire receptivity becomes an even more important site of self-cultivation in the modern age, when urban sensation is vast and ever-changing. Regarding the choices between aesthetic receptivity and agency, Baudelaire carefully and gracefully balances between the two contradictory demands that it almost seems unproblematic. In his famous "Peintre" essay,[16] Baudelaire praises the painter Constantin Guys for his passion toward fleeting urban sensations, and comments on Guys's cultivated curiosity toward sheer appearances of the crowds, their movements and fashionable dresses, as "l'enfance retrouvée à volonté" (62). However, for Baudelaire true art must undergo the process of idealization, and thus the painter Guys must paint from memory and not from the model: "En fait, tous les bons et vrais dessinateurs dessinent d'après l'image

---

[15] Marcel Proust, À La Recherche Du Temps Perdu, 15 vols. (Gallimard, 1946).
[16] Baudelaire, Œuvres Complètes de Charles Baudelaire, III:51–114.

écrite dans leur cerveau, et non d'après la nature" (75). Guys's art is "L'art mnémonique" (73):

> Et les choses renaissent sur le papier, naturelles et plus que naturelles, belles et plus que belles, singulières et douées d'une vie enthousiaste comme l'âme de l'auteur. La fantasmagorie a été extraite de la nature. Tous les matériaux dont la mémoire s'est encombrée se classent, se rangent, s'harmonisent et subissent cette idéalisation forcée qui est le résultat d'une perception enfantine, c'est-à-dire d'une perception aiguë, magique à force d'ingénuité! (67)

However innocent Guys's childlike perspective is, Baudelaire insists that it is the artist's perspective that is shaping the natural material. Although Guys indeed passionately cultivates his receptive faculty so as to welcome the fleeting sensations of modernity, the human artist here remains comfortably the Creator of his work of art.

As with Baudelaire, Pater advocates for a cultivation of one's receptive faculty, but Pater's exhortation is built upon his psychological understanding that our consciousness is very narrow and can hardly be aware of all that passes by. While Pater's "Conclusion" to *Renaissance* well predates James's work,[17] the argument here shows a strong affinity to empiricist psychology. Pater laments the selective and narrowing effect of consciousness that prevents our direct contact with the world:

> And if we continue to dwell in thoughts on this world, not of objects in the solidity with which language invests them, but of impressions unstable, flickering, inconsistent, which burn and are extinguished with our consciousness of them, it contracts still further; the whole scope of observation is dwarfed to the narrow chamber of the individual mind. ("Conclusion," 248)

In order to imbibe in the fleeting sensation, Pater seeks to undo our cognitive propensity, which sees only what we habitually see and overlook the plenitude of the phenomenal world.

As with Baudelaire, who defines modernity as this childlike curiosity that perpetually thirsts for fleeting sensation, Pater has various regimes of self-cultivation, one of which is articulated in the formula of "sharp and eager observation," in order to be "present always at the focus" when some perfect

---

[17] For possible sources of Pater's empiricist psychology, see Ryan, *The Vanishing Subject*, 26.

moment strikes us: "Every moment some form grows perfect in hand or face; some tone on the hills or the sea is choicer than the rest; some mood of passion or insight or intellectual excitement is irresistibly real and attractive for us—for the moments only" ("Conclusion," 249). More radically however, unlike Baudelaire's painter who sublimates the fleeting sensation with artistic agency, for Pater, it is the beauty of the sensations that redeems us from our mortality. The following passage is frequently quoted, but its nuanced meaning is often missed:

> To such a tremulous wisp constantly reforming itself on the stream, to a single sharp impression, with a sense in it, a relic more or less fleeting, of such moments gone by, what is real in our life fines itself down. It is with this movement, with the passage and dissolution of impressions, images, sensations, that analysis leaves off—that continual vanishing away, that strange, perpetual, weaving and unweaving of ourselves. (249)

With his strong empiricist affinity, Pater here however is not presenting an image of the self that is, as Judith Ryan argues, merely vanishing away without any remains.[18] Rather, when all vanishes away, the single sharp impression is like a tremulous wisp still lingering and floating on our stream of sensations— the sharp impression stays with us longer as it impresses itself on our memory. This sharp impression constantly reforms itself as it interacts with our current experience, but then as it continues to be polished by time, what is most precious to us will eventually *fine itself down*. This is the process of how the sharp impression continually unweaves and reweaves ourselves. In other words, in the flux of time where everything passes by, our only salvation is to seize upon sharp, gem-like impressions that will stay with us for longer, that we can remember and cherish, in order to have truly lived.

Roger Fry theorizes impressionist paintings as the artistic efforts to capture the fleeting sensation precisely as it presents itself to our eyes, before our transcendental ego—in fact our habitual perceptual tendency—reifies the raw sensation into everyday objects. To truly see a sunset on the field requires us to pay attention to the colors of the sunlight and the shapes of the clouds that exist only for the unique, passing, irrevocable moment.

> In the direction, that is, of preventing the mind from making the step from sensations to things—a step so natural, and, owing to the needs of

---

[18] Ryan, *The Vanishing Subject*, 28.

everyday life, so necessary as to have become quite instinctive. Painting then, tends more and more to rest on the solid basis of appearances, which are for its purposes the only ultimate realities, and refuses to become entangled in the hypothetical abstractions of ordinary life. It is ceasing in fact to attempt the impossible feat of eliminating the human factor in experience.[19]

Fry's theorization of impressionism is philosophically rigorous, and shows a strong affinity to empirical psychology. For Fry, the impressionist painters seek to stay at the level of perspective appearance before our consciousness organizes it into objects. Such is the way to escape the Kantian trap, and for this very reason, Fry valorizes the pure sensuous appearance of things, before it enters our intellect, as "the only ultimate realities." By contrast, it is our intellectual recognition of everyday objects that is rather "hypothetical abstractions." While our preconscious perception of sensuous appearance and our intellectual organization of it into objects are both human experience, Fry grants the former the highest ontological status of "the only ultimate realities" because it has not been filtered through the Kantian ego. Notably, Fry also considers the act of observing and of painting the primal sensuous appearance an act of aesthetic cultivation—what is important here is not so much the artwork, but the transformation of *the painter*: by the act of painting the painter can train the self to *rest* more on sensuous appearance and to *refuse* transcendental cognition. We may read Fry's words again to get his sense of imperative here: "*Painting* then, *tends* more and more to *rest on* the solid basis of appearances, which are for its purposes the only ultimate realities, and *refuses to* become entangled in the hypothetical abstractions of ordinary life." Through the act of observing and of painting the passing sensuous experience, the painter will eventually be transformed into an artist who can *live* at the level of the primal sensation. Fry elevates receptivity over the artist's organizing agency, and such a radical self-creation is one of the posthumanist ways the artist chooses to relate to the world.

Woolf's ultimate aesthetic ideal is very similar to what Roger presents here: to stay entirely on the preconscious level prior to subject-object divide, to stay with the stream of thoughts and sensations. Woolf's stream of thoughts favors the characters' subjective world at the cost of the traditional organizing structure of the novel, such as the chronology and the plot. But Woolf is not an idealist or a writer of psychological inwardness. The stream of thoughts of her characters is occasioned by the present scenes and flows freely between

---

[19] Roger Fry, *A Roger Fry Reader* (University of Chicago Press, 1996), 14, emphasis mine.

memory and retrospection, and, just as the memory is also involuntary, it serves to register the preconscious psychological activities before and beyond the transcendental reason. In her novel *Mrs. Dalloway*, Clarissa Dalloway muses about her old lover as she walks on the London streets:

> For they might be parted for hundreds of years, she and Peter; she never wrote a letter and his were dry sticks; but suddenly it would come over her, if he were with me now what would he say?—some days, some sights bringing him back to her calmly, without the old bitterness; which perhaps was the reward of having cared for people; they came back in the middle of St. James's Park on a fine morning— indeed they did.[20]

Clarissa is a passive medium, registering thoughts and memory as they come to her. This faithful description of Clarissa's stream of thoughts makes a sharp contrast to Baudelaire's painter, who asserts his agency by organizing the raw materials with the authorial perspective. Here Peter's personality is presented in the context of Clarissa's stream of thoughts, which is composed of a tapestry that weaves together different physiological layers: of the scene that would trigger the old memory, of the present emotion accompanying and interpreting the memory, of the deep connection between Pater and Clarissa that still exists. For Woolf, writing the stream of impression is a way to understand how the embodied self is porous and part of the world—where the present sensations and moods might evoke and reinterpret the past memory, while she allows her consciousness to follow and flow with all these.

From Baudelaire who asserts the artist's individual perspective, to Woolf who passively observes the self as the medium that at every moment responds to the surrounding, the modernist artists proffer a rich array of responses to a modernity of fleeting sensations, and often through cultivation of one's aesthetic faculty. In what follows, I will discuss how literature, different from philosophy, provides a unique mode of reasoning to respond to the metaphysical conundrum: while philosophy presumes a universal truth, literature emphasizes that how one responds to the existential conditions is rather an individual choice.

III. Pater's Imaginary Portrait

The genre which Pater specifically designs to explore how the hero might contemplate on different philosophical ideas, to deduce from ideas their

---

[20] Virginia Woolf, *Mrs. Dalloway* (London: The Hogarth Press, 1947), 9.

implications, and, most importantly, to set the ideas into practices through the cultivation of the self, is called imaginary portraits. This genre encompasses all his major fictional works, including "The Child in the House: An Imaginary Portrait" (1878),[21] his novella collection *Imaginary Portraits* (1887), his two-volume novel *Marius the Epicurean* (1885), and his unfinished novel *Gaston de Latour* (1896). Recent studies on this genre of imaginary portrait focus primarily on the "artistic hybridization" or "interplay of the sister arts, literature and painting" in the context of the fin-de-siècle total art or Victorian novels, for example, as Eliza Bizzotto comments that "the imaginary portrait…should have enabled the audience to perceive or, even better, to 'see' its protagonist as if in a pictorial portrait".[22] But my discussion pursues along with William E. Buckler's direction that the *portrait* refers not so much to the pictorial as to "the storytelling dimension of painting by drawing out the psychic lineaments of a persona"; while the adjective *imaginative* refers to "the particular or relative conditions of the fiction" to which the hero responds with feelings and thoughts (183).[23] Imaginary portrait as a genre is a laboratory in which human experience is being tested and transcribed in response to imaginative circumstances, just as Pater famously notes in a letter to George Grove, dated 17 April 1878, after he submits the manuscript of "The Child in the House": "I call the M.S. a portrait, and mean readers, as they might do on seeing a portrait, to begin speculating—what came of him"?[24]

As Buckler notes, the "ultimate purpose" of imaginary portraits is "the application of ideas to life."[25] More specifically, in Pater's *Marius the Epicurean*,[26] the hero is the one who embarks on a spiritual exploration, who contemplates, feels through, and tests all philosophical ideas in his search, and asks what the consequential experience is if one adopts these ideas.

---

[21] Walter Pater, *A Child in the House: An Imaginary Portrait* (Oxford: H. Daniel at his Private Press, 1894).
[22] Eliza Bizzotto, "The Imaginary Portrait: Pater's Contribution to a Literary Genre," in *Walter Pater: Transparencies of Desires*, ed. Laurel Brake, Lesley Higgins, and Carolyn Williams (ELT Press, 2002), 213–14. For arguments along the line, see, Martine Lambert-Charbonnier, "Poetics of Ekphrasis in Pater's 'Imaginary Portraits'," ibid.; Lene Østermark-Johansen, "Pater and the Painterly: Imaginary Portraits," *English Literature in Transition, 1880-1920* 56, no. 3 (2013), E. Clements and L. Higgins, *Victorian Aesthetic Conditions: Pater Across the Arts* (Springer, 2010).
[23] William E. Buckler, *Walter Pater: The Critic as Artist of Ideas* (New York: New York University Press, 1987), 183.
[24] Walter Pater, *Letters of Walter Pater*, ed. Lawrence Evans (Oxford: Clarendon Press, 1970), 30.
[25] Buckler, *Walter Pater*, 181.
[26] Walter Pater, *Marius the Epicurean: His Sensations and Ideas* (Macmillan, 1913).

During the time when Pater was composing his *Marius the Epicurean,* Pater writes to Vernon Lee and discusses the purpose of this singular genre: "to make, viz. *intellectual theorems* seems like the life's essence of the concrete, sensuous objects, from which they have been abstracted."[27] Pater aims to set abstract theories in concrete life for the reason that he believes the meaning of philosophy lies not with "absolute or transcendental knowledge," but functions by "suggesting questions which help one to detect the passion, and strangeness, and dramatic contrasts of life."[28] The genre of imaginary portraits also allows Pater's various personas to contemplate upon contradictory philosophical stances, as prompted by dramatic contrasts of life. For a modern artist, it is more important to court new theories and taste new experiences than to be faithful to a certain coherent system of thought.

As a modernist novel, *Marius the Epicurean* departs from the mimetic tradition toward an inward self-reflexivity. In an almost metafictional passage, Pater grants Marius a consciousness of what would come of him as he can intuit the meaning and consequences of all experiences that he has been through: "And if you can imagine how, once in a way, an impressible boy might have an *inkling,* an inward mystic intimation, of the meaning and consequences of all that, what was implied in it becoming explicit for him, you conceive aright the mind of Marius" (Ch. 1, p. 16). Marius contemplates upon all thoughts and events that he has experienced, articulates their philosophical implications implied in "all that"—and this fictional persona is Pater's mechanism to test philosophy in the sphere of life. The purpose of the spiritual journey is not to find the absolute, universal truth but rather to open up the being-in-the-world as a field of creation and constant transformation. Pater's aesthetics might indeed be defined as a creation of the self, embodied "in the form of a tale the radical self-awareness of the soul's becoming."[29] That is, in Pater's mind, the contribution of *Marius* is formal or methodological, which serves to test any intellectual ideas through the experience of life, rather than, as Matthew Kaiser argues, to present the charming, seductive contents with deceptive reasoning.[30] Scholars have amply discussed the philosophical

---

[27] Walter Pater, *Letters of Walter Pater,* ed. Lawrence Evans (Oxford: Clarendon Press, 1970), 54, emphasis original.
[28] Pater, *The Renaissance: Studies in Art and Poetry,* 242.
[29] Buckler, *Walter Pater: The Critic as Artist of Ideas,* 249.
[30] Matthew Kaiser, "Marius at Oxford: Paterian Pedagogy and the Ethics of Seduction," in *Walter Pater: Transparencies of Desire,* ed. Laurel Brake, Lesley Higgins, and Carolyn Williams (ELT Press, 2002), 189.

underpinnings of Pater,[31] but Pater's unique approach to philosophy, what David Carrier calls "the art of living"[32] or Hext refers to as "self-culture,"[33] have not yet been thoroughly explored.

The purposes of the genre are to show us the affective motivation and personal responsibility in affiliating oneself to a metaphysical belief and, further, the aesthetic cultivation necessary to live up to an idea. Two interrelated motifs are important to Pater's project that aims to translate metaphysical stances into ethical choices and aesthetic cultivation. First, in setting ideas into the laboratory of human life, Pater emphasizes how our temperament factors in our reception of ideas, "their admission into the house of thought" (Chapter 8, 136), as well as the role of sentiment that translates "a precept as to how it were best to feel and act" (ibid., 135). That is, an idea matters to *us* not merely because it is true, but because it attracts a certain personality and will consequently shape for us a mode of life, as well as a way of looking at and feeling through life. Second, an aesthetic education is always necessary for one to truly live up to an idea. If one chooses to adhere oneself to an idea, what follows is not that this idea is universally applicable, but that the idea calls for its true disciple through a transformation of the self.

For Pater, our attraction to and reception of philosophical ideas is a subjective process, having to do with our temperament and affective experience. Pater rejects the Kantian ethics which holds that a true ethical imperative must be universally applicable, effective even on the most disinterested subject. Rather, through the genre of imaginary portrait Pater aims to emphasize the affective conditions of any metaphysical belief. After the death of his dear friend Flavian, Marius learns to test the ideas he inherits against his experience of life, and, like his author Pater, for Marius concrete experience feels always more real than any metaphysical theory. Here Marius finds "the religion of his childhood"—the belief in the eternal soul—"seemed wholly untenable" when he experiences the actual reality of Flavian's death.

---

[31] For scholars who take Pater's philosophy seriously, see Carolyn Williams, *Transfigured World: Walter Pater's Aesthetic Historicism* (Cornell University Press, 1989); Hext, *Walter Pater: Individualism and Aesthetic Philosophy*. I do not agree with Gabriel Roberts's assessment that "Pater's writing, having been crafted primarily with an attention to sensuousness and form, possesses little substantive content of any kind" (410). Gabriel Roberts, "'Analysis Leaves off': The Use and Abuse of Philosophy in Walter Pater's 'Renaissance,'" *The Cambridge Quarterly* 37, no. 4 (2008): 407–25.

[32] David Carrier, "Walter Pater's 'Winckelmann,'" *Journal of Aesthetic Education* 35, no. 1 (2001): 99.

[33] Kate Hext, *Walter Pater: Individualism and Aesthetic Philosophy* (Edinburgh, UK: Edinburgh University Press, 2013), 165.

The poignant experience gives Marius the first theoretical propensity, as a "materialist," lying at the bottom of all his following reasoning and reception of ideas:

> It was to the sentiment of the body, and the affections it defined—the flesh, of whose force and color that wandering Platonic soul was but so frail a residue or abstract—he must cling. The various pathetic traits of the beloved, suffering, perished body of Flavian, so deeply pondered, had made him a materialist, but with something of the temper of a devotee. (Ch. 8, p.125)

Here the sentimental motivation is as important as the idea itself, for Marius's materialism is shaped by his devotion to Flavian's body, beautiful yet terribly fragile. After Flavian's death, Marius searches amongst ancient schools of thought that would explain the mystery of the transitory life, and synthesizes the thoughts of Heraclitus, Protagoras, and Cyrene, all of which abide by a skepticism that refuses knowledge of what lies beyond "the conditions of man's life" (Ch 8. p.133). The human temperament and past experience are what interpret for a metaphysical doctrine its ethical import, and thus directs the specific program of the aesthetic cultivation. Marius's reception of ideas is always colored by "the deep original materialism or earthliness of human nature itself, bound [sic] so intimately to the sensuous world" (Ch.8, p.146). By contrast, the Stoic emperor Marcus Aurelius whom Marius will soon meet, although likewise believing in the transience of life, translates the very same metaphysical doctrine into a completely different spiritual precept: "'the world and the thinker upon it, are consumed like a flame', said Aurelius, 'therefore will I turn away my eyes from vanity: renounce: withdraw myself alike from all affections'" (Ch. 27, p. 201). Responding to the same metaphysical idea that life is transient, Pater's unique genre argues forcefully that it is one's individual temperament, experience, and sentimental motivation that shape what the idea entails—how then should one leads one's life if one is to adhere to a certain idea.

Marius's meditation on the Cyrenaic philosophy articulates what might be considered the gist of Pater's aesthetic efforts, of "translating the abstract thoughts of the master into terms, first of all, of *sentiments*" (Ch. 8, p. 135, emphasis original). Pater believes that this sentiment is what reveals to a person the ethical significance of a metaphysical stance, and hence transforms the abstract idea to affective practices.

> It has been sometimes seen, in the history of the human mind, that when thus translated into terms of sentiment—of sentiment, as lying already half-way towards practice—the abstract ideas of metaphysics

for the first time reveal their true significance. The metaphysical principle, in itself, as it were, without hands or feet, becomes impressive, fascinating, of effect, when translated into a precept as to how it were best to feel and act; in other words, under its sentimental or ethical equivalent. (ibid.)

In setting philosophy into life, Marius mobilizes metaphysical ideas into a way to feel about things and to comport oneself—and thus includes the entirety of his life into the domain of ethical contemplation. Pater's imaginary portrait serves to delineate an intimate relation between idea and meaning, to translate an abstract metaphysical truth into affective practices, and to render life a work of art by drawing these connections between sentiments, aesthetic practices, spiritual beliefs, and metaphysical principles.

For Marius, to be an aesthete means that he lives an examined life. Marius's temperament and experience decide for him the reception of an idea and how the idea should prescribe to him a set of practices to live his life. Following it, he must live up to one's idea through aesthetic cultivation. The regime of aesthetic education is a "practical consequence" of a philosophical doctrine. In *Marius the Epicurean*, aesthetic education is defined as developing and refining our sensitivity.

> *Life as the end of life*, followed, as a practical consequence, the desirableness of refining all the instruments of inward and outward intuition, of developing all their capacities, of testing and exercising one's self in them, till one's whole nature become one complex medium of reception, towards the vision—the "beatific vision," if we really cared to make it such—of our actual experience in the world. (Ch. 8, p. 143)

For Marius, this very aesthetic education that elevates one's experience into a beatific vision is a means of redemption when one faces the empiricist predicament. The contemporary empiricist predicaments in the novel are tagged as Cyrenaic metaphysics, the dual-front limits that "all that is real in our experience but a series of fleeing impressions" but also "we are never to get beyond the walls of the closely shut cell of one's own personality" (Ch. 9, p. 146). Facing sensations anthropomorphic and fleeting, a world certain neither to intellect nor to sense, Marius firmly grounds the meaning in subjective transformation:

> With this view he would demand culture, *paideia*, as the Cyrenaics said, or, in other words, a wide, a complete, education—an education partly negative, as ascertaining the true limits of man's capacities, but

for the most part positive, and directed especially to the expansion and refinement of the power of reception; of those powers, above all, which are immediately relative to fleeting phenomena, the powers of emotion and sense. (Ch. 9, p. 147)

Marius transforms the metaphysical predicaments into an imperative on his aesthetic education: if sensations are fleeting and our attention is highly selective, then the only way to grasp the passing experience a little better is by expanding and refining our powers of reception. In another passage in *Plato and Platonism*, Pater articulates even more clearly the connection between aesthetics and ethics, that the purpose of art lies with this cultivation of the self. The regime of aesthetic education differs in the context of Pater's discussion, as in his lectures on Platonism, the aesthetic education composes not of training of one's receptive powers, but of, similar to Baudelaire's dandyism, rigorous control of one's manner and to bring an order to one's impassioned body:[34]

And Platonic aesthetics, remember! As such, are even in close connexion with Plato's ethics. It is life itself, action and character, he proposes to colour; to get something of that irrepressible conscience of art, into the general course of life, above all into its energetic or impassioned acts. (183)

In either case, Pater shows us how a metaphysical belief is translated into a regime of aesthetic education, based on the hero's temperament and personal experience. Pater's heroes seek to foster meaningful relationships with the world not by dint of what is given, but by what might be created and intentionally lived, even in the face of insurmountable metaphysical predicaments. Encouraging a synthesis of ethics, aesthetics, and epistemology, Pater's project would be of interest to the growing field of virtue epistemology in today's academia. Pater's project explores what Abrol Fairweather calls "epistemic motivation"—the affective conditions in which one accepts an idea and transforms it into a personal belief, and argues for

---

[34] Walter Pater, *Plato and Platonism: A Series of Lectures* (Adelaide: Cambridge Scholar Press, 2002).

what Lorraine Code calls "epistemic responsibility"—that one is held ethically responsible for one's intellectual belief.[35]

In the *Bildungsroman*, Marius the hero begins his aesthetic education with an Epicurean hunger for fine sensations, but gradually he develops *sympathy—the capacity to feel the reality for Others as for oneself*—as what one may "hold by" against the empiricist doctrine, "even in the dissolution of a world, or in that dissolution of self, which is, for everyone, no less than the dissolution of the world it represents for him" (Ch. 25, p.181). Marius's sympathy originates from his earthy bond to the sensuous world, which seems a stronger attachment than the metaphysical doubts of empiricism, convincing him that the world is real:

> Then, he, at least, in whom those fleeting impressions—faces, voices, material sunshine—were very real and imperious....Amid abstract metaphysical doubts, as to what might lie one step only beyond that experience, reinforcing the deep original materialism or earthliness of human nature itself, bound [sic] so intimately to the sensuous world, let him at least make the most of that was "here and now." (Ch. 9, p.146)

Even in the most recent criticisms, Marius bears an idealist reputation, as Romana Byrne writes that "in *Marius,* the barrier that subjectivity erects between the self, others, and an objective reality is detailed with a condescending tone in which subjective perception is cherished as a refinement of objective vulgarity."[36] But I argue that Marius's aesthetic education traces precisely how Marius outgrows his idealist tendency as he cultivates his aesthetic receptivity of material sensations and as later, this receptivity grows into a selfless love toward the world at large. Marius justifies his literary career as a vocation "to satisfy, with a kind of scrupulous equity, the claims of these concrete and actual objects on his sympathy, his intelligence, his senses," as well as to "become the interpreter of them to others" (Ch. 9, p.152). Out of sympathy, Marius eventually sacrifices himself for the love of his Christian friend, Cornelius. On his dying bed, Marius is blessed with mental peace by thinking of the people that he has loved, on

---

[35] Abrol Fairweather, "Epistemic Motivation," in *Virtue Epistemology: Essays on Epistemic Virtue and Responsibility*, ed. Linda Trinkaus Zagzebski and Abrol Fairweather (New York: Oxford University Press, 2000), 63–81; Lorraine Code, *Epistemic Responsibility* (Hanover, N.H: Published for Brown University Press by University Press of New England, 1987).

[36] Romana Byrne, "Sadistic Aestheticism: Walter Pater and Octave Mirbeau," *Criticism* 57, no. 3 (2016): 411.

how he has loved them rather than how he has been loved: "all the persons he had loved in life—[contemplating] on his love for them...rather than on theirs for him" (Ch. 28, p. 216-17). His love toward the world becomes the only salvage from the metaphysical predicament of subject-object divide: "In the bare sense of having loved he seemed to find, even amid this foundering of the ship, that on which his soul might 'assuredly rest and depend'" (Ch. 28, p.217). It is also this sympathy that grants him this sense of immortality, for he can "link himself to the generations to come in the world he was leaving": "Yes, through the survival of their children, happy parents are able to think calmly, and with a very practical affection, of a world in which they are to have no direct share" (Ch. 28, p. 216).

Of course, sympathy itself is not a metaphysical solution that warrants knowledge of certainty. Rather, this capacity to identify oneself with the Other is a concrete expression of *the structure of the perpetual quest*, the central quality of Marius's aesthetic education and a synonym to Marius's cultivated receptive powers to contemplate upon various theoretical stances. In the "Conclusion" to *Renaissance*, Pater calls for a perpetual curiosity not only of sense, but also of intellect: "what we have to do is to be forever curiously testing new opinions and courting new impressions, never acquiescing in a facile orthodoxy of Comte or of Hegel, or *of our own*" (120, emphasis added). Whereas for Hegel *Bildung* as a spirituality of the Enlightenment is an educational process of "self-alienation" that moves from one's particular disposition to the universal,[37] Pater removes the destination of the absolute and makes Marius's quest a perpetual flight toward the Other. Marius often terms this perpetual progression as, despite the novel's setting in ancient times, his modernity:

> He was ready to boast in the very fact that it was modern. If in a voluntary archaism, the polite world of that day went back to a choicer generation, as it fancied, for the purpose of fastidious self-correction, in matters of art, of literature, and even, as we have seen, of religion, at least it improved, by a shade or two of more scrupulous finish, on the old pattern; and the new era, like the *Neu-zeit* of the German enthusiasts at the beginning of our own century, might perhaps be discerned, awaiting one just a single step onward—the perfect new manner, in the consummation of time, alike as regards the things of imagination and the actual conduct of life. (Chapter IV, p. 48)

---

[37] G.W.F. Hegel, *Hegel's Phenomenology of Spirit*, trans. A.V. Miller (Oxford: Oxford University Press, 1977), 557.

Unlike Hegel's conception of *Bildung*, the novel does not end with Marius resting at a final, highest truth. Rather, as Buckler and Judith Ryan point out,[38] it promises an endless quest and continual transformation, "while the pursuit of an ideal like this demanded entire liberty of heart and brain" (*Marius*, 48).

By the end of the novel, Marius identifies himself as a modern spirit which constantly seeks to expand oneself by questing for the unknown. In the same way, Baudelaire in his poem "Le Voyage" recasts the meaning of Death as a quest for the unknown—"Ô Mort, vieux capitaine, il est temps! levons l'ancre!/.../ Au fond de l'Inconnu pour trouver du *nouveau*!"[39]—, Pater leaves blank the contents of Marius's cultivated receptivity:

> Throughout that elaborate and lifelong education of his receptive powers, he had ever maintained the purpose of a self-preparation towards possible further revelation, some day—an ampler vision... At this moment, his unclouded receptivity of soul, grown so steadily through all those years, from experience to experience, was at its height;...Surely, the aim of a true philosophy must lie...in the maintenance of a kind of ingenuous discontent, in the face of the very highest achievement; the unclouded and receptive soul quitting the world finally, with the same fresh wonder with which it had entered it still unimpaired, and going on its blind way at last with the consciousness of some profound enigma in things, as its pledge of something further to come. (Ch 28, p. 214-15)

The modern hero at his deathbed grounds the meaning of the quest not in a promised redemption, but in his continuous spiritual cultivation, in his professed curiosity and avowed recognition of the profound enigma in ideas, people, and things that he encounters. Just as Marius rejects any strong commitment to any metaphysical belief except for the only formal doctrine—to continue cultivating his receptive powers for new ideas, new impressions, Pater's imaginary portrait remains a literary mechanism to test how, for a life, what any idea feels and what it compels. Here, Pater replaces Kantian universal subjectivity with an aesthetics of the self: art differs from metaphysics in that it translates ideas into sentiments and practices, in that its ultimate meaning is not knowledge of certitude, but a perpetual quest which propels oneself to

---

[38] Buckler, *Walter Pater: The Critic as Artist of Ideas*, 266; Judith Ryan, *The Vanishing Subject: Early Psychology and Literary Modernism* (Chicago: University of Chicago Press, 1991), 37.

[39] Charles Baudelaire, *Les Fleurs du Mal* (Poulet-Malassis et de Broise, 1861), 312–13.

continually experiment with new theoretical stances. Sympathy, or this insatiable flight toward the Other, is Pater's answer to the metaphysical crisis that perception is anthropomorphic and sensation, fleeting.

IV. Proust's Irony

So straightforwardly simple is Pater's exhortation to cultivate one's receptive faculty that its value might be missed without a negative comparison, which I will supplement with an account of Proust. Proust's *Recherche* details the hero's conversion from empiricism to idealism: to an idealistic belief that, as Emmanuel Lévinas comments, "everything that encounters me exists as coming from me."[40] And yet, the psychological motivation that Proust depicts for such a conversion is that idealism is the only means through which one may possess completely the object of love, by granting it an existence only in one's imagination. Setting the philosophical idea in the laboratory of human life, depicting the psychological cause of idealism as one which cannot endure any mystery of material things, Proust's ironic (self-)criticism of idealism should not escape a discerning reader. The novel indeed delineates the most ironic auto-philosophical fiction of idealism, one that reveals idealism not as any innocent belief in the purity of imagination, but a sophisticated self-deception of a hero who, fascinated by the plenitude of the material world but unable to fulfill his doomed desire to hold captive his object of love, convinces himself that the only way to savor sensual pleasure without fear is by appropriating it in the edifice of his memory. The irony of *Recherche*, if read as a psychological account of idealism, is indeed a "narrative of its own destruction," to borrow a term from Paul de Man,[41] one that ironically reveals the pathetic solitude of idealism. Marcel's eventual conversion is only an intellectual conviction and not a spiritual cultivation; a forced disbelief in the reality of the sensuous object, rather than a courage to forever anticipate, as Pater writes, "some profound enigma in things." The present section discusses Proust's incisive psychoanalysis of idealism, and to again accentuate the value of spiritual cultivation with an example of its negative counterpart, that of intellectual conviction.

---

[40] Emmanuel Lévinas, "The Other in Proust," in *The Levinas Reader*, ed. Seán Hand (New York, NY: B. Blackwell, 1989), 164.
[41] Paul de Man, *Allegories of Reading: Figural Language in Rousseau, Nietzsche, Rilke, and Proust* (New Haven: Yale University Press, 1979), 77.

À la recherche du temps perdu[42] begins with the central problem of empiricist psychology, that our intellect cannot grasp sensations that are constantly fleeting. Marcel regrets that his intellect cannot remember much of the sensuous surroundings of his childhood, except for the passage that his mom will walk through to kiss him at seven o'clock: "comme si Combray n'avait consisté qu'en deux étages reliés par un mince escalier et comme s'il n'y avait jamais été que sept heures du soir." (V1, p. 64). And yet, unlike Pater and Woolf, who are dedicated to train their receptive faculty so as to open themselves up to the fleeting present of "throwing himself into the stream,"[43] Marcel troubles himself with the problem of *possession*, of retaining in his mind, in the form of memory, the time that is irrevocably lost.

For Marcel, there is no certainty in knowledge if all is constantly changing, and as a result, only his memory that stands above time, subjective and solitary as it is, might offset this metaphysical crisis. And yet, for Marcel, his solipsism is not a predetermined philosophical stance, not an intellectual belief simply because it is true. It is rather an acquired attitude, in fact, a coping strategy, after a series of heart-rending failures in his love affairs. Marcel begins his *Recherche* by believing in the objectivity of love, that his pleasure originates from and resides in the object of his love. But then Marcel realizes that he can never take full possession of his object of love, whose inwardness consists of the flowing stream of thoughts that he can never get hold of. For Marcel, the empiricist uncertainty mainly manifests in the aspect that he does not know the ever-changing thoughts of other people, especially since empiricist psychology refuses to reduce a person to a fixed identity, but rather conceptualizes the self as the swift, everchanging passage of our stream of thoughts. Utterly failed to completely possess his beloved by grasping comprehensively all her inward activities, Marcel eventually turns back upon himself to recognize that his feelings of love originate from within himself, and that he at least has access to his own feelings. Deleuze documents how this solipsism eventually develops into idealist art, and calls Marcel's pathological journey his "apprenticeship" to art.[44] But I argue that it is precisely by setting idealism in the context of Marcel's amorous pursuit, in

---

[42] Marcel Proust, *À la Recherche du temps perdu*, 15 vols. (Gallimard, 1946).
The Gallimard edition is divided in 7 books but published in 15 volumes: I. *Du côté de chez Swann* (V1-V2). II. *À l'ombre des jeunes filles en fleurs* (V3-V5). III. *Le Côté de Guermantes* (V6-8). IV. *Sodome et Gomorrhe* (V9-V10). V. *La Prisonnière* (V11-V12). VI. *Albertine disparue* (titre original : *La Fugitive*) (V13). VII. *Le Temps retrouvé* (V14-V15).
[43] Walter Pater, *Marius the Epicurean: His Sensations and Ideas* (Macmillan, 1913), Chp. 8, p. 139.
[44] Deleuze, *Proust and Signs*, 26–38.

the genre of auto-philosophical fiction, that Proust reveals the piteous limit of idealism—that the disciple of idealism in the castle of memory can never rejoice in intimacy with the beloved, which is, however Marcel denies it, his true desire. Although in the *Recherche* Marcel likewise offers his personal experience—his discovery of the involuntary memory that transcends fleeting time in this case—to counteract this metaphysical conundrum, what Marcel does is merely "subjective compensation" that involves only an intellectual conversion and no true spiritual transformation. Marcel by the end of the novel confesses that his so-called "deficit" has never been improved—that he cannot savor the present moment unless it is transported to his mind.

Three lines of development run through the epical *Recherche*: Marcel's pursuits of his sensuous memory, of love, and of art. Marcel's quest for his sensuous memory is the most famous among the three lines but, as I will later discuss, what really determines Marcel's final idealist stance is his experience in love. At the outset of the novel, the hero aims at retrieving the sensuous memory *stored in the object*. *Recherche* begins by announcing the purpose of the hero's quest with the famous madeleine episode, where Marcel, by taking a morsel of the shell-shaped cake soaked in the tea, experiences a flush of involuntary memory that brings back vividly all his childhood impressions of Combray. Here Marcel believes in the *objectivity* of his memory since the sensation is given by the object. He even suggests that the memory, residing in the object, will persist longer than his own existence.

> Je trouve très raisonnable la croyance celtique que les âmes de ceux que nous avons perdus sont captives dans quelque être inférieur, dans une bête, un végétal, une chose inanimée, perdues en effet pour nous jusqu'au jour, qui pour beaucoup ne vient jamais, où nous nous trouvons passer près de l'arbre, entrer en possession de l'objet qui est leur prison. Alors elles tressaillent, nous appellent, et sitôt que nous les avons reconnues, l'enchantement est brisé. Délivrées par nous, elles ont vaincu la mort et reviennent vivre avec nous.
>
> Il en est ainsi de notre passé. C'est peine perdue que nous cherchions à l'évoquer, tous les efforts de notre intelligence sont inutiles. Il est caché hors de son domaine et de sa portée, en quelque objet matériel (en la sensation que nous donnerait cet objet matériel) que nous ne soupçonnons pas. Cet objet, il dépend du hasard que nous le rencontrions avant de mourir, ou que nous ne le rencontrions pas. (V1, p. 64-65)

Against the empiricist background that our intellect is barely aware of our sensuous experience, the leitmotif of involuntary memory here suggests a structure of a yearning openness, a desire of restoration, in which the material object external to and other than the self should by chance and grace restore the lost past.

Toward the end of the novel, however, Marcel revises his initial theory of involuntary memory, and argues with a scientific tone that, of course, material things cannot retain for us our affections and thoughts. Refuting the Celtic myth, Marcel by the end of *Recherche* proclaims that his initial theory would be true only if he firmly understands that the reality of his memory exists in himself;[45] that physical things might bring back our past memory not by virtue of their sensuous power, but because their current existence serves as signposts to recall our past memory:

> Certains esprits qui aiment le mystère veulent croire que les objets conservent quelque chose des yeux qui les regardèrent, que les monuments et les tableaux ne nous apparaissent que sous le voile sensible que leur ont tissé l'amour et la contemplation de tant d'adorateurs pendant des siècles. Cette chimère deviendrait vraie s'ils la transposaient dans le domaine de la seule réalité pour chacun, dans le domaine de sa propre sensibilité.
>
> Oui, en ce sens-là, en ce sens-là seulement ; mais il est bien plus grand, une chose que nous avons regardée autrefois, si nous la revoyons, nous rapporte, avec le regard que nous y avons posé, toutes les images qui le remplissaient alors. *C'est que les choses — un livre sous sa couverture rouge comme les autres — sitôt qu'elles sont perçues par nous, deviennent en nous quelque chose d'immatériel, de même nature que toutes nos préoccupations ou nos sensations de ce temps-là, et se mêlent indissolublement à elles.* (V15, p. 29-30, emphasis mine)

An involuntary memory flushes over Marcel when he, waiting to meet the Prince de Guermantes at his library, sees the red book titled *François le Champi*, which was the book Marcel's mother read to him (while leaving out all incestuous scenes) at the night when the child finally musters all his strength to seek his mother's attention. The physical book for Marcel is a sign

---

[45] For Proust's philosophical perspectivism, see Duncan Large, "Epistemoptics: Proust's Perspectivism," in *Nietzsche and Proust: A Comparative Study* (Oxford University Press, 2001), 111–61.

that recalls the sensorium it was metonymically situated at: the sensitive child's bedroom, his temperament that was prone to daydreaming, his anguish about his mother's bedtime kisses. By the end of the novel, Marcel concludes his quest by revising the structure of involuntary memory from an openness that seeks the lost self in material objects, to that of an idealist appropriation: as far as things are perceived, Marcel proclaims, they are transferred into the immaterial realm of our sensibility. Marcel's ecstasy at the reflux of his memory is not due to the fact that he has lived it, but more because he can now elevate his past life into an immaterial terrain: the memory is now, "débarrassé de ce qu'il y a d'imparfait dans la perception extérieure, pur et désincarné" (V15, p. 10-11).

As Deleuze argues in *Proust and Signs*, Marcel's discovery of the mechanism of involuntary memory inspires him onto the path of idealist art. This bliss that elevates Marcel above the passing time prepares Marcel to embark on his career of writing, as Deleuze comments: "In art, substances are spiritualized [that is, idealized], media dematerialized. The work of art is therefore a world of signs, but they are immaterial and no longer have anything opaque about them, at least to the artist's eye, the artist's ear."[46] The mechanism of involuntary memory connects a present sensation with past memories and therefore gives the past memories their concrete reality, and grants these memories special existences that are "réels sans être actuels, idéaux sans être abstraits" (V15, p. 15). But the connection again *substitutes* the present reality with the perceiver's memory, and Marcel comments that this substitution leads him onto the path of art:

> La nature elle-même, à ce point de vue, ne m'avait-elle pas mis sur la voie de l'art, n'était-elle pas commencement d'art, elle qui souvent ne m'avait permis de connaître la beauté d'une chose que longtemps après, dans une autre, midi à Combray que dans le bruit de ses cloches, les matinées de Doncières que dans les hoquets de notre calorifère à eau? Le rapport peut être peu intéressant, les objets médiocres, le style mauvais, mais tant qu'il n'y a pas eu cela il n'y a rien eu. (V15, p. 37)

From the mechanism of involuntary memory, Marcel infers the law of literature, whose aim is to find the metaphor that connects two different sensations, and this connection will reveal the essence of things:

---

[46] Deleuze, *Proust and Signs*, 50.

> On peut faire se succéder indéfiniment dans une description les objets qui figuraient dans le lieu décrit, la vérité ne commencera qu'au moment où l'écrivain prendra deux objets différents, posera leur rapport, analogue dans le monde de l'art à celui qu'est le rapport unique de la loi causale dans le monde de la science, et les enfermera dans les anneaux nécessaires d'un beau style, ou même, ainsi que la vie, quand, en rapprochant une qualité commune à deux sensations, il dégagera leur essence en les réunissant l'une et l'autre, pour les soustraire aux contingences du temps, dans une métaphore, et les enchaînera par le lien indescriptible d'une alliance de mots. (V15, p. 37)

Metaphor that cuts across time and substitutes the real for the ideal serves to prove the narrator's artistic agency, if it can successfully summarize in totality the metonymic association that was only given by chance. More simply put, Proust's metaphor does not depart much from the romantic tradition: it is an anthropomorphic appropriation of a sensuous object, now reduced to a signpost to a past memory, as it enters the writer's poetic vision.

However, doubts occur as to whether this idealist appropriation can truly cut itself from the material origin. As de Man rightly suspects, the metaphor that is produced by involuntary memory remains metonymic, contingent upon the coincidence given by his chance encounter and his past experience, even as it pretends to exist in the immaterial realm of art. Marcel's metaphor is appropriated from real life but cannot cut itself from it, and seems "oddly unable to remain sheltered within this intra-textual closure" (70). Similarly, Deleuze[47] comments that "reminiscences are inferior metaphors…memory unites two objects that still depend on an opaque substance and whose relation depends upon an association."[48] Deleuze seeks to resolve the contradiction by asserting that there is for Marcel yet another realm of art solely composed by his imagination, detached from his sensuous memory: "We must regard involuntary memory as a stage, which is not even the most important stage, in the apprenticeship to art" (ibid., 65). In either case, insofar as the occasion of Marcel's involuntary memory is accidental, Marcel's idealism, one that seeks to persuade himself that the sensuous plentitude exists only in his own mind in the form of memory, is hardly convincing.

Marcel's aesthetic manifesto feels dubious, and the circumstances that produce this idealism are even more problematic. In his *Proust and Signs*, Deleuze analyzes how Marcel's artistic manifesto is derived from his life

---

[47] Gilles Deleuze, *Proust and Signs* (New York: G. Braziller, 1972), 26–38.
[48] Deleuze, *Proust and Signs*, 64.

experience: that is, we might read *Recherche* as an auto-philosophical fiction. Proust sets in parallel Marcel's hope to restore his sensuous memory with his relentless desire to completely possess his object of love, and, by confusing Marcel's two pursuits, interweaves in the auto-philosophical fiction ideas and life, and therefore underwrites Marcel's aesthetic idealism with a psychological motivation. Unbeknownst to Marcel himself but ironically clear to his reader is the foible that causes Marcel's tragic experience: his uncompromising need to completely possess his object of desire and to strip it off its mysterious Otherness. Such a desire is in part triggered, in part made impossible to fulfill, by the empiricist view that recognizes a person (or a thing) cannot be encased in an identity.

> Par instants, dans les yeux d'Albertine, dans la brusque inflammation de son teint, je sentais comme un éclair de chaleur passer furtivement dans des régions plus inaccessibles pour moi que le ciel, et où évoluaient les souvenirs, à moi inconnus, d'Albertine. Alors cette beauté qu'en pensant aux années successives où j'avais connu Albertine, soit sur la plage de Balbec, soit à Paris, je lui avais trouvée depuis peu, et qui consistait en ce que mon amie se développait sur tant de plans et contenait tant de jours écoulés, cette beauté prenait pour moi quelque chose de déchirant. Alors sous ce visage rosissant je sentais se creuser, comme un gouffre, l'inexhaustible espace des soirs où je n'avais pas connu Albertine. Je pouvais bien prendre Albertine sur mes genoux, tenir sa tête dans mes mains ; je pouvais la caresser, passer longuement mes mains sur elle, mais, comme si j'eusse manié une pierre qui enferme la salure des océans immémoriaux ou le rayon d'une étoile, je sentais que je touchais seulement l'enveloppe close d'un être qui, par l'intérieur, accédait à l'infini. (V12, p. 229-230)

At this point, Marcel hides Albertine in his house as his mistress, whose presence is completely unknown to any friends who come visiting. Marcel holds Albertine's body captive as if he has "enfermée dans une bouteille la Princesse de la Chine", but at the same time with her infinite inwardness "elle était plutôt comme une grande déesse du Temps" (*ibid*) that he can never get hold of since Time grants any person or thing a rich history with all that it has experienced. Despite Marcel's fear, he depicts so beautifully the rich inwardness of any person or object, which is an eternal mystery forever withdrawn from his inquiry. Not only that a person has in herself all her passing memories and thoughts, an object, such as a mute, plain stone, could have enclosed within it salts deposited from ancient oceans or distant stars. But it is also precisely this empiricist view that provokes in Marcel insatiate jealousy—he can never get hold of his beloved if she cannot be encased in an identity. Unable to fathom the inwardness of his object of love, Marcel's final resort is to perform the Copernican turn: he learns the lesson that he can only get hold of what exists in his own mind, but not in an Other.

In Marcel's pursuit of sensuous memory, Marcel clearly understands that his intellect is powerless and should better remain receptive. In his amorous pursuit, however, Marcel obviously errs on the side of over-exerting his intellect and therefore significantly weakens his receptive faculty. Like a detective, Marcel reads and follows closely all signs that Albertine emits in his tenacious desire to divest Albertine of all mysteries about her, but his frenetic undertakings never reveal to him the essence of love. By contrast, precisely because his intellect is so caught up in all these perplexing signs, his receptivity is debilitated to the point that he no longer feels any joy of love inspired by Albertine.

> Sans me sentir le moins du monde amoureux d'Albertine, sans faire figurer au nombre des plaisirs les moments que nous passions ensemble, j'étais resté préoccupé de l'emploi de son temps ; certes, j'avais fui Balbec pour être certain qu'elle ne pourrait plus voir telle ou telle personne avec laquelle j'avais tellement peur qu'elle ne fît le mal en riant, peut-être en riant de moi, que j'avais adroitement tenté de rompre d'un seul coup, par mon départ, toutes ses mauvaises relations. (V11, p. 25)

In effect, however, the more Marcel is obsessed with his object of desire, the further he will be trapped in his own jealousy and suspicions—and hence the more elusive he finds Albertine to be: "plus le désir avance, plus la possession véritable s'éloigne" (V13, p.45). Utterly failing to get hold of his object of desire, Marcel is only dimly aware that it is his intellect—and not Albertine who is all too submissive to his desire of possession—who is the author of his own suspicion and inflicts on himself all these pains.

After a long, exhausting, and futile quest in which Marcel finds he can never get hold of his object of the beloved, Marcel revises his philosophy of involuntary memory. At the outset of the novel, we remember, Marcel suggests an aesthetic quest whose holy grail is his sensuous memory, which is more enduring, more objective, and like souls, more essential to the selfhood than thoughts:

> Mais, quand d'un passé ancien rien ne subsiste, après la mort des êtres, après la destruction des choses, seules, plus frêles mais plus vivaces, plus immatérielles, *plus persistantes*, plus fidèles, l'odeur et la saveur restent encore longtemps, comme des âmes, à se rappeler, à attendre, à espérer, sur la ruine de tout le reste, à porter sans fléchir, sur

leur gouttelette presque impalpable, l'édifice immense du souvenir. (V1, p. 70; emphasis mine)

At the end of the novel, Marcel's involuntary memory no longer teaches him to cherish the sensuous plenitude of the material world. Rather, the mechanism that transports the elusive reality to his memory serves to teach him the joy of idealist appropriation. To our surprise, further, Marcel now does not attempt to write about the idealized sensuous memory. Rather, he insists on performing an analysis of his jealous intellect. William James recognizes that our intellect or the "Knower I" is not an abiding entity prior to our experience as Kant conceives of, but rather the most memorable part of ourselves that follows us and evolves along with time: "It is a *thought*, at each moment different from that of the last moment, but *appropriative* of the latter, together with all that the latter called its own."[49] What Marcel pronounces here bears a surprising similitude with James's empirical psychology. By the end of the novel, mostly pathetically, instead of sensuous memory Marcel pronounces that it is rather his jealousy, the product of his mind, that is the most enduring part of himself underlying all his love directed toward different objects. This jealousy is what he calls the general rule of humanity, the purpose of his work of art.

> *Il est une portion de notre âme plus durable* que les moi divers qui meurent successivement en nous et qui voudraient égoïstement le retenir, portion de notre âme qui doit, quelque mal, d'ailleurs utile, que cela nous fasse, se détacher des êtres pour que nous en comprenions, et pour en restituer la généralité et donner cet amour, la compréhension de cet amour, à tous, à l'esprit universel et non à telle puis à telle, en lesquelles tel puis tel de ceux que nous avons été successivement voudraient se fondre. (V15, p. 46)

Marcel's aesthetic theory in *Time Regained* contradicts starkly with what he proposes at the outset of the novel. It is now his conscious jealousy, rather than his joyous sensuous memory, now persists beyond his mortal life, transcends Time and constitutes his work of art.

The novel itself, as a literary form, regulates the reader's reading experience in linear time. With an expectation that Marcel is on a quest to retrieve sensuous memory, we read first Marcel's hope to find it in a material object, but then this hope gradually, surreptitiously morphs toward a pathological

---

[49] James, *Psychology: The Briefer Course*, 82.

idealism. Marcel's idealism that he announces by the end of the autophilosophical novel is not a disinterested stance: it bears Marcel's journey of disillusion, and reinterprets idealism not as a glorification of the mind, but as a weary resignation—a deep sigh that the object of love is forever withdrawn. Setting Marcel's idealism in the context of his romantic fiasco, Proust might have, I venture to argue, jeered at idealism as a possessive mania. I do not mean to argue that Proust completely rejects idealism, but rather wish to remind my reader that this heightened self-reflexivity and harsh irony of one's own aesthetic belief is characteristic of modernist literature.

This book argues that fin-de-siècle is an age where the artists can no longer sustain the naïve idealist pride that immaterial art is more superior to opaque matter. Rather, the artists begin to feel a yearning toward the material world, as Baudelaire loves the enigmatic stone, or as Richard Wagner comments on idealism as a doomed tragedy: "the objectless and self-devouring fervor of the soul, all ignorant of its source, is nothing but itself, nothing but yearning, tossing, pining—and *dying out, i.e.* dying without having assuaged itself in any 'object'."[50] In a similar fashion, in Mallarmé's poem "L'Azur" (1864),[51] the cloudless, blue sky, the symbol of the absolute mind that contains nothingness, while serene and beautiful, becomes for him an oppressive irony: "De l'eternel Azur la sereine ironie / Accable, belle indolemment comme les fleurs." The impotent poet ("Le poëte impuissant") is desperate to flee from his own void soul ("mon âme vide"), his own consciousness that traps him and isolates him from the objective world. The poet desperately summons up anything material to cover up the void sky, fog or chimney smoke, and exclaims out loud that he wishes to flee toward matter while forgetting the cruel ideal of emptiness: "Vers toi, j'accours ! Donne, ô Matière, / L'oubli de l'Idéal cruel." But how can the poet flee from his own consciousness? The poem famously ends with the poet's horrified cry that he is haunting by his consciousness that contains only nothingness:

> Où fuir, dans la révolte inutile et perverse ?
> *Je suis hanté.* L'Azur ! l'Azur ! l'Azur ! l'Azur !

For Mallarmé, as articulated by his poem "L'Azur" (1864), the Kantian finitude is absolute, just as the nothingness of our language is as beautiful, oppressive,

---

[50] Richard Wagner, "The Art-Work of the Future," in *Richard Wagner's Prose Works*, vol. 1 (London: Kegan Paul, 1892), 116.
[51] Judith Ryan, *The Vanishing Subject: Early Psychology and Literary Modernism* (Chicago: University of Chicago Press, 1991), 28.

and inescapably haunting. The poet's incapacity to include in his poem anything material is for him an impotence of the idealist age.

But empiricist psychology opens up a possibility for the artists to cultivate and expand their powers of reception so as to see beyond the limits of the transcendental ego, which is now reconceptualized as a negotiable psychological tendency, rather than an *a priori* structure that we can never escape. Against the intellectual background of empiricist psychology, which Proust certainly is well versed in,[52] Marcel's impotence (compared to that of Mallarmé who openly recognizes his failure) is not heroic but self-indulgent, for what motivates him toward the final idealist stance has never been a *beau idéal* that he actively aims to achieve, but rather, as Deleuze comments, a "mechanism of objective disappointment and of subjective compensation."[53] Proust's *Recherche* lays bare the psychological motivation of idealism, and serves to tell us *how, in literature, what seems like a metaphysical belief can be a result of a personal choice and bears ethical significance*. To conclude my discussion on the *Recherche*, I compare Marcel's idealist tendency, whose tone is of the signature irony of the fin-de-siècle, with Pater's exhortation to cultivate one's receptive faculty.

Marcel's tragedy in love can be ascribed to the fact that his sensibility is not trained to enjoy the sensuous plenitude. Evoking the fashionable fin-de-siècle metaphor for the artist—an indoor, imaginative invalid—Marcel likes to stay in bed and imagine the air and atmosphere of the morning that he has refused his senses to savor: "Cette matinée idéale comblait mon esprit de réalité permanente, identique à toutes les matinées semblables, et me communiquait une allégresse que mon état de débilité ne diminuait pas" (V11, p. 31). Towards the end of the novel, Marcel tells us his amorous tragedy originates from the fact that he can only savor in imagination what is absent, and cannot feel any joy of love when Albertine is present:

> Tant de fois, au cours de ma vie, la réalité m'avait déçu parce que, au moment où je la percevais, mon imagination, qui était mon seul organe pour jouir de la beauté, ne pouvait s'appliquer à elle, en vertu de la loi inévitable qui veut qu'on ne puisse imaginer que ce qui est absent. (V15, p. 14)

---

[52] For an intertextual reading between *Recherche* and empiricist psychology, see Marilyn M. Sachs, *Marcel Proust in the Light of William James: In Search of a Lost Source* (Lanham, Maryland: Lexington Books, 2014).
[53] Deleuze, *Proust and Signs*, 35.

Now, discovering involuntary memory, Marcel finds the most powerful mechanism that supplements the barrenness of his faculty. The present sensation does not exist in its own right, but rather serves to recall the past and at the same time add a sense of concrete reality to his memory, which in turn gives Marcel inexplicable joy. Again, Marcel's peculiar theory deserves to be quoted in length:

> Il languit dans l'observation du présent où les sens ne peuvent la lui apporter, dans la considération d'un passé que l'intelligence lui dessèche, dans l'attente d'un avenir que la volonté construit avec des fragments du présent et du passé auxquels elle retire encore de leur réalité, ne conservant d'eux que ce qui convient à la fin utilitaire, étroitement humaine, qu'elle leur assigne. Mais qu'un bruit déjà entendu, qu'une odeur respirée jadis, le soient de nouveau, à la fois dans le présent et dans le passé, réels sans être actuels, idéaux sans être abstraits, aussitôt l'essence permanente et habituellement cachée des choses se trouve libérée et notre vrai moi qui, parfois depuis longtemps, semblait mort, mais ne l'était pas autrement, s'éveille, s'anime en recevant la céleste nourriture qui lui est apportée. (V15, p. 15)

Marcel is aware of the fact that his memory, as retained by the intellect, is only intended for utilitarian purpose, such as that we remember our address or phone number. With the mechanism of involuntary memory, he is now finally capable of savoring a sensuous plenitude. Curiously, however, the sensuous plenitude he seeks to retrieve must exist only in his memory in order that he may relish it—Marcel never seeks to enjoy the sensuous plenitude in the present. Marcel's eventual idealism is only a strategy of subjective compensation: one that re-present, in the domain of immaterial art, all that he has missed, the shadow of sensuous plenitude.

The tension of the *Recherche* is indeed sustained by *the absence of the Object and its redemption in the mind,* as Stephen Brown comments that it is "an ongoing dialectic…between the illusory nature of desire, the disillusionment of experience, and the recuperative power of remembrance,"[54] while a joyous harmony with the Other at the present has never happened. Marcel's "idealizing imagination is like an arrow that overshoots its target: reality."[55] Benjamin is also clear to note that Marcel's involuntary memory never fulfills his fundamental

---

[54] Stephen Gilbert Brown, *The Gardens of Desire: Marcel Proust and the Fugitive Sublime* (SUNY Press, 2012), 146.
[55] Brown, *The Gardens of Desire*, 147.

desire of being in connection with an Other: "Proust's [*Recherche*], too, has as its center a loneliness which pulls the world down into its vortex with the force of a maelstrom."[56] Benjamin quotes Jacques Rivière to identify Marcel's weakness as that his idealist transportation places the salvation in art, and not in life: "He died of ignorance of the world and because he did not know how to change the conditions of his life which had begun to crush him. He died because he did not know how to make a fire or open a window".[57] Despite that Marcel is ecstatic that he can recuperate the past in his memory, in the final analysis the adult Marcel is still entirely powerless, as powerless as the child desires his mother's bedtime kisses, for the occasion of involuntary memory is entirely "a matter of chance," bearing "the marks of the situation which gave rise to it."[58] But then, isn't it possible, readers who hope for Marcel's wellbeing might think, that he could cultivate his receptive faculty so that he may apply his senses to relish the present, "gathering all we are into one desperate effort to see and touch," as Pater exhorts?

Marcel does utilize his mental efforts to retain precious sensation, only that, in the auto-philosophical fiction, Marcel's intellect is employed in very specific contexts. On nights when there were guests at the house, his mother would kiss him just briefly at the dining table, rather than, as on other nights, she would kiss him in his bedroom several times. For Marcel, the fact that his bedtime ritual must be thus curtailed incurs intense pain, and he would need to prepare himself to concentrate on the moment of his mother's furtive kiss in order to compensate for its brevity.

> Aussi je me promettais, dans la salle à manger, pendant qu'on commencerait à dîner et que je sentirais approcher l'heure, de faire d'avance de ce baiser qui serait si court et furtif, tout ce que j'en pouvais faire seul, de choisir avec mon regard la place de la joue que j'embrasserais, de préparer ma pensée pour pouvoir grâce à ce commencement mental de baiser consacrer toute la minute que m'accorderait maman à sentir sa joue contre mes lèvres, comme un peintre qui ne peut obtenir que de courtes séances de pose, prépare sa palette, et a fait d'avance de souvenir, d'après ses notes, tout ce pour quoi il pouvait à la rigueur se passer de la présence du modèle. (VI, p42-43)

---

[56] Walter Benjamin, "The Image of Proust," in *Illuminations*, ed. Hannah Arendt, trans. Harry Zohn (New York: Schocken Books, 1985), 212.
[57] Benjamin, "The Image of Proust," 213.
[58] Walter Benjamin, "On Some Motifs in Baudelaire," in *Illuminations: Essays and Reflections*, ed. Hannah Arendt, trans. Harry Zohn (New York: Schocken Books, 1985), 158.

Here, even as Marcel promises himself that he will consecrate with his mental acuity the entire brief moment that his mother kisses him, the precious sensation does not simply exist in its own right—it must be retained to accompany and to comfort Marcel for the horribly lonely night where he must go to the bedroom by himself, tucking himself into bed, and then endure hours of solitude in darkness. Marcel here compares his mental efforts to what a painter must incur if his model offers only a brief sitting, and this comparison seems to allude to Baudelaire's painter of modern life, but the meaning of it is completely changed—*for his intellect here does not serve to open himself to the shock of the intense sensation per se, but rather to protect himself from suffering yet another greater one to come.* In Benjamin's analysis, Marcel knows all too early and well that the only way to protect oneself from a traumatic experience is by being conscious of it, and even by preparing for it in advance: "the more readily consciousness registers these shocks, the less likely are they to have a traumatic effect."[59] That is to say, for Marcel, consciousness functions to bar and to deplete the impact of the shock rather than to experience it. In Proust's auto-philosophical fiction, he explains lucidly how his intellect functions: it is an armor against the feeling and vulnerable heart. And any intellectual memory thus captured must necessarily be sterilized so as not to hurt the heart. Marcel lives under the dutiful protection of his brain to the point that all that he remembers is tasteless, to the point that he must search for what has not passed the guard of his dutiful brain through his gimmick of involuntary memory, as Benjamin notes: "this means that only what has not been experienced explicitly and consciously, what has not happened to the subject as an experience, can become a component of the *mémoire involontaire.*"[60]

Here, we find that the issues discussed in auto-philosophical fiction are indeed complicated. Whereas for Baudelaire and Pater, it is still easy and straightforward to exhort the artist to willfully open themselves to experience fleeting sensations, half a century later for Proust and Woolf, the role of consciousness is qualitatively changed, into a stubborn protective mechanism that would not yield to the artist's will. We may attribute it to the development of Freudian psychology in the twentieth century: Proust asserts that he has never read Freud[61] but it was easy for Benjamin to read Freud in Proust,[62]

---

[59] Benjamin, "On Some Motifs in Baudelaire," 161.
[60] Benjamin, "On Some Motifs in Baudelaire," 160-161.
[61] Céline Surprenant, "Freud and Psychoanalysis," in *Marcel Proust in Context* (Cambridge: Cambridge University Press, 2013), 107.
[62] Benjamin, "On Some Motifs in Baudelaire," 160.

whereas Woolf has published an English translation of Freud's work.[63] But then the theoretical conundrum can be further explored only if the writer sets it in the experiment of one's life in an auto-philosophical fiction. In it, Marcel seeks to recuperate the unconscious with involuntary memory, but he can only do it retroactively, while missing the entire reality in the present moment. In the next section, I will discuss how consciousness is likewise a problem for Woolf: she finds an exit to escape individual consciousness by consigning herself to the hypnotic rhythm of universal sensation, but then she finds that once she wants to write down such experience, she would again need to employ her consciousness that threatens to evaporate the essence of her experience. Auto-philosophical fiction serves to set ideas in the laboratory of life, and to point out the arenas necessary for cultivation. It is a genre in which one finds the conflicts between ideas and practices, and reminds us that an idea needs not only be intellectually convincing, but one that, when implemented in life, constantly raises questions as to whether the original goal has been achieved.

V. Woolf's Universal Sensation, and Her Problems with Writing

Against a general empiricist milieu, each writer begins with a different premise or emphatic concern, on which the aesthetic project is built. An idea that is absent in Proust, but motivates Pater's and Woolf's aesthetic education is that we are fundamentally *part of* what Pater calls "concurrence" or "perpetual motion,"[64] or what Woolf calls "waves of that divine vitality,"[65] a summative term for all material elements and sensuous forces that constitutes us, but extends much beyond ourselves. In Pater's famous conclusion to *the Renaissance*:

> But these elements, phosphorus and lime and delicate fibres, are present not in the human body alone: we detect them in places most remote from it. Our physical life is a perpetual motion of them—the passage of the blood, the wasting and repairing of the lenses of the eye, the modification of the tissues of the brain by every ray of light and sound—processes which science reduces to simpler and more elementary forces. Like the elements of which we are composed, the

---

[63] Sigmund Freud, *Civilization and Its Discontents*, trans. Joan Riviere (London: Hogarth Press, 1930)
[64] Pater, *The Renaissance: Studies in Art and Poetry*, 247, 246.
[65] Woolf, *Mrs. Dalloway*, 9.

action of these forces extends beyond us; it rusts iron and ripens corn.[66] ("Conclusion," 246-47)

For Kate Hext, this passage in "Conclusion" immediately reminds us of David Hume's thesis that challenges the notion of a stable and coherent identity. Minute changes constantly happen to our physical life, cells die and are replaced. Our inner life changes more drastically, which consists of, for Hume, "nothing but a bundle or collection of different perceptions, which succeed each other with an inconceivable rapidity, and are in a perpetual flux and movement," and for Pater, similarly, of "impressions unstable, flickering, inconsistent."[67] This observation for Hext raises epistemological crises both of knowledge and of our selfhood. Empiricism (or New Materialism, as it is called in contemporary academia) challenges the stability for knowledge, for "there is no order, only the disorder of fluctuating reality." [68] And Hext argues that "the most vexing question that Pater has inherited from Hume is: if I cannot depend on continuous consciousness to give coherence to my empirical impressions then 'what am *I*?'" (ibid.). But this epistemological despair, I argue, is not what Pater here is driving at. Rather, if we read the above-quoted passage more carefully, Pater indeed distances himself from "the tendency of modern thought" that tends to merely "regard all things and principles of things as inconstant modes or fashions" ("Conclusion," 246). Pater recasts the Humean stance by arguing that although our physical lives are in constant changes, we are *part of* the material and sensuous forces that *extend much beyond us*, which rust iron, ripen corn, and produce impressions that occupy our minds. The difference between Hume's and Pater's own stance can be easily missed because Pater's transitional word here is one single "but": "*But* these elements, phosphorus and lime and delicate fibres, are present not in the human body alone: we detect them in places most remote from it" (ibid., 246; emphasis mine). Whereas our selfhood might seem incoherent and fragmentary, we will gain a sense of the order if we look beyond our illusory identity and at the universal motion of these forces. The confluence of the sensuous and material forces still weaves a "web," which is Pater's metaphor of a sense order—only that the web does not end at our individual self, in the same way our nerves receive and transmit information

---

[66] Pater, *The Renaissance*, 246-247.
[67] David Hume, *A Treatise of Human Nature*, ed. Norton David Fate and Norton Mary J., The Clarendon Edition, vol. 1 (Oxford: Oxford University Press, 2007), 165; Pater, *The Renaissance: Studies in Art and Poetry*, 248.
[68] Kate Hext, *Walter Pater: Individualism and Aesthetic Philosophy* (Edinburgh, UK: Edinburgh University Press, 2013), 29.

much beyond our body. Our image of a delimited self is illusory, but Pater does not end at debunking the illusion as Hume does—the positive meaning lies with seeing the web that extends beyond us: "That clear, perpetual outline of face and limb is but an image of ours, under which we group them—a design in a web, the actual threads of which pass out beyond it" (ibid., 247). Whereas for Lacan, an infant recognizes the unity of the self in the mirror image,[69] Pater gracefully remarks that this mirror image is illusory, with his posthumanist insight that the body is constituted by material forces that extend much beyond the delimited selfhood. The strongest sense of order in Pater's monism is articulated through his hero in *Marius the Epicurean*, borrowing vocabulary from ancient philosophy: "the movement of the universal life, in which things, and men's impressions of them, were ever 'coming to be': "the sleepless, ever-sustained, inexhaustible energy of the divine reason itself, proceeding always by its own rhythmical logic, and lending to all mind and matter, in turn, what life they had" (Ch.8, p.130-31). Here, all matter and mind are part of the universal energy, which lends us our psychical and physical life and extends much beyond ourselves.

Whereas Pater's vision of our place in the universe might indeed feel decentering and disorienting as we are but an accidental combination of a motion perpetually moving beyond us, Woolf pictures this universal motion as a rhythmic continuity that supports us. Woolf's image of the universal motion is the cadence of the waves, hypotonic and would induce an individual to relinquish its burden *qua* individual. In the first few pages of Woolf's autobiographical essay, "A Sketch of the Past," she describes a "first memory" that her life stands upon: as a child lying at the nursery of St Ives, half-consciously, Woolf listens to the waves lapping, repetitive and continuous.

> It is of lying half asleep, half awake, in bed in the nursery at St Ives. It is of hearing the waves breaking, one, two, one, two, and sending a splash of water over the beach; and then breaking, one, two, one, two, behind the yellow blind. It is of hearing the blind draw its little acorn across the floor as the wind blew the blind out. It is of lying and hearing this splash and seeing this light, and feeling, it is almost impossible that I should be here; of feeling the purest ecstasy I can conceive. (64-5)

---

[69] Jacques Lacan, "The Mirror Stage as Formative of the I Function as Revealed in Psychoanalytic Experience," in *Écrits: The First Complete Edition in English*, trans. Bruce Fink (New York: W. W. Norton & Company, 2005), 76.

Her language mimicking the breaking of the waves, Woolf explains why the memory is so strong: it was because "I am hardly aware of myself, but only of the sensation. I am only the container of the feeling of ecstasy, of the feeling of rapture" (67). Here Woolf tells us her peculiar constitution: the moment of pure rhythmic sensation that envelops her and envelops all, continuous and hypotonic, without the intervention of isolated consciousness, brings her memorable ecstasy.

Reading through Woolf's oeuvre, we might gather why this trance grants Woolf inexplicable rapture: the ebb and flow of the waves is a symbol of Pater's "concurrence," which promises her a continuity much larger than the individual consciousness, and proves to her that she is part of the whole, one with the oceanic sensation. Later on in the "Sketch" essay, Woolf invokes an imagery similar to that of Pater, that many nonhuman forces traverse us in every moment.

> The lemon-coloured leaves on the elm tree; the apples in the orchard; the murmur and rustle of the leaves make me pause here, and think how many other than human forces are always at work on us. While I write this the light glows; an apple becomes a vivid green; I respond all through me; but how? Then a little owl [chatters] under my window. Again, I respond. Figuratively I could snapshot what I mean by some image; I am a porous vessel afloat on sensation; a sensitive plate exposed to invisible rays; and so on. (133)

Facing the changes moment to moment, Woolf's emotional tone is characteristically different from that of Pater. For Pater, it is decentering as we recognize that the forces move on beyond us and continue to rust iron and ripen corn. But Woolf describes the scene at St. Ives as "pure delight," and her language departs a serenity and gratitude to the sensuousness of the earth, for she finds herself capable of receiving and responding to the nonhuman forces; she is part of the whole. A main difference between Pater and Woolf may be ascribed to that here Woolf detracts her individual consciousness from the scene—she is like a camera exposed to invisible rays and registers all rich colors;[70] she is a porous vessel that allows the nonhuman forces to freely go through her without any attempts of resistance or retention. There would be no giddy sense of decentering if Woolf does not pose her consciousness as a center.

---

[70] For a discussion of how Woolf compares her sensibility to a camera without a consciousness, see Timothy Mackin, "Private Worlds, Public Minds: Woolf, Russell, and Photographic Vision," *Journal of Modern Literature* 33, no. 3 (2010): 112–30.

But to say that Woolf's consciousness is not the center does not mean that it is not present—rather, we realize that in fact Woolf makes this observation from her subjective voice, whereas Pater makes the statement about the concurrence as an objective truth. It would be more accurate to say, then, that Woolf's concurrence differs from that of Pater because she participates in the concurrence not only on the level of physical forces, but with all her thoughts and emotions. Woolf's monism is so radical that, as Erich Auerbach analyzes, she would interweave voices from different consciousnesses into a single stream of thought.[71] Woolf's aesthetic cultivation, against the empiricist predicament that conceives individual consciousness to be incoherent and illusory, involves relaxing the boundary of the selfhood so as to immerse oneself in the universal stream. Whereas Pater's self-cultivation involves an intense focus to register transitory sensations, for Woolf it is by relaxing the boundary of individual consciousness that she would become a porous translucent receptacle of the confluence larger than herself.

James Naremore writes a monograph, *The World without a Self*, on Woolf's oceanic feeling and her peculiar propensity for self-dissolution, which deserves to be quoted in length.

> Her attraction to a watery element gives her writing another of its unusual attributes. Reading her, one sometimes has the impression of being immersed in a constantly moving liquid, immersed so deeply that the people and things in her books become muffled and indistinct, like blurred and ghostly shadows. ...Such a characteristic of her mature fiction is precisely described in a later passage from *A Room of One's Own*, where, looking out her window, she detects "a signal pointing to a force in things which one had overlooked. It seemed to point to a river, which flowed past, invisibly, round the corner, down the street, and took people and eddied them along" (p. 144).[72] At its extreme, this invisible river combines with the sleepy, hypnotic moods and the moments of exhilaration and fear to reproduce the strangest feeling of all: both the author and her

---

[71] Erich Auerbach, *Mimesis: The Representation of Reality in Western Literature* (Princeton University Press, 2003), 536.
[72] Virginia Woolf, *A Room of One's Own* (London: Hogarth Press, 1935).

characters appear on the verge of dissolving, or sinking forever into what Mrs. Ramsay famously calls a "wedge-shaped core of darkness."[73]

Naremore associates Woolf's self-dissolution with her "fascination with death" (3). But I argue that there is a strong positive meaning that Naremore does not notice: for Woolf to let go one's personality means to join the universal sensation much larger, and more continuous, than the fragile individual consciousness. This oceanic sensation does not lead to death, but is rather a protective power that might help her to affirm the continuity of our everyday life against unprecedented trauma and death. Woolf in her writing more often associates the oceanic sensation with the continuity of a universal concurrence, with an invisible river round the corner and down to the bustle of the London streets, with the rhythm of her everyday life. As Michele Pridmore-Brown accurately notes, Woolf's depiction of her oceanic sensation "follows from Woolf's vision of the world as a pulsating field of mind and matter in which everything is interconnected."[74]

A central passage in Woolf's novel *Mrs. Dalloway* reveals Woolf's valorization about individual consciousness as against the universal, oceanic sensation. The heroine of the novel, Clarissa Dalloway, is frustrated by the fact that she is not invited to a luncheon, and upon the social stress, she withdraws into her room to look into the mirror and contemplate about her individuality, as if her individuality is the original cause that she should suffer social exclusion:

> How many million times she had seen her face, and always with the same imperceptible contraction![75] She pursed her lips when she looked into the glass. It was to give her face point. That was her self—pointed; dartlike; definite. That was the self when some effort, some call on her to be her self, drew the parts together, she alone knew how different, how incompatible and composed so for the world only into one center, one diamond, one woman who sat in her drawing-room

---

[73] James Naremore, *The World without a Self: Virginia Woolf and the Novel* (New Heaven: Yale University Press, 1973), 2.

[74] Michele Pridmore-Brown, "1939-40: Of Virginia Woolf, Gramophones, and Fascism," *PMLA* 113, no. 3 (1998): 411. For an excellent discussion on Woolf's writing on the non-human, see Louise Westling, "Virginia Woolf and the Flesh of the World," *New Literary History* 30, no. 4 (1999): 855–75.

[75] In "Sketch" Woolf confesses that she has a "looking-glass shame" that follows her throughout her life. Virginia Woolf, "A Sketch of the Past," in *Moments of Being: A Collection of Autobiographical Writing*, ed. Jeanne Schulkind, 2nd ed. (San Diego: Harcourt, 1985), 68.

and made a meeting-point, a radiancy no doubt in some dull lives, a
refuge for the lonely to come to, perhaps; she had helped young
people, who were grateful to her; had tried to be the same always,
never showing a sign of all the other sides of her—faults, jealousies,
vanities, suspicions, like this of Lady Burton not asking her to lunch;
which, she thought (combing her hair finally), is utterly base! Now,
where was her dress? (42)

The passage is a remarkable meta-discourse on individuality. An individual is not an autonomous entity by virtue of its unique personality, but only a social construction[76] that requires subordination of incompatible parts of the self. Clarissa is aware that she is compliant with the shaping force of society, and aware of how much effort it requires to draw herself together into a coherent, recognizable individuality.

But then, Clarissa escapes the social pressure related to individuality by resorting back to the oceanic feeling deeply ingrained in her bodily memory. Individuality is the locus where one suffers sudden shock and feels isolated by the pain, while to resume tranquility, one may fall back into the universal sensation that carries the self, like the waves that carry the shell. For Woolf, universal sensation is not a given bliss pure and simple, it rather is the opposite side of shock and trauma, which are symptoms of modernism that I will go on to discuss. It is only as the shock is too much for one to bear that one must seek to escape individual consciousness. And Woolf identifies her aesthetic achievement with finding a way to assuage the heightened consciousness, which is remarkable indeed. Here, Clarissa finds that the dress that she is to wear at the party tonight is torn, and she will mend it. The act of mending the dress is a metaphor for Woolf's mission as a writer, to "put the severed parts together" and "make it whole" again ("Sketch" 72) after her sense of order has been disrupted. Mending her dress, Clarissa regains her tranquility as she associates her repetitive movements of sewing with the repetitive movements of waves flapping.

> Quiet descended on her, calm, content, as her needle, drawing the silk
> smoothly to its gentle pause, collected the green folds together and
> attached them, very lightly, to the belt. So on a summer's day waves
> collect, overbalance, and fall; collect and fall; and the whole world

---

[76] For an essay on Woolf's criticism of the social construction of identity, see Ban Wang, "'I' on the Run: Crisis of Identity in Mrs. Dalloway," *Modern Fiction Studies* 38, no. 1 (1992): 177–91.

> seems to be saying "that is all" more and more ponderously, until even the heart in the body which lies in the sun on the beach says too, That is all. Fear no more, says the heart. Fear no more, says the heart, committing its burden to some sea, which sighs collectively for all sorrows, and renews, begins, collects, lets fall. (44-5)

Clarissa here inherits Woolf's comforting oceanic rhythm that she has internalized as a child, which would surface up along with her own rhythmic bodily movement. At this moment of Clarissa's frustration, the waves with their mesmerizing cadence begin by persuading the whole world to chant together "that is all," more and more ponderously, so that eventually the heart in the body, most stubborn of all, relinquishes its individuality to say "that is all." One can relinquish its individual burden to some sea. Unlike an individual that shoulders its own success and downfall, here living in the concurrence, like a shell or a starfish floating along with the waves, one should not be worried if oneself rises and falls—it is the waves that are doing it. The somatic cadence that resides in our body, such as our breathing, always assures us we are part of the whole. The flapping of the waves become, in each of her books, a metaphor for comfort, collectivity and continuity, a hypnotizing rhythm that can induce one to resign her bounded selfhood along with any burden as an individual. To be part of the whole for Woolf means to relax her self-consciousness and to immerse oneself in universal sensation.

This dynamic between individual consciousness and the confluence larger than oneself is repeated again in *To the Lighthouse*.[77] Mrs. Ramsay is doing her needlework deep at night, alone. Here she contemplates to herself, as Clarissa does, that her personality is only a superficial social construction. Listening to the oceanic rhythm of her bodily movement, that of herself knitting, she feels her essence is rather part of the deep sea in darkness, while we recognize one another as you see a whale occasionally rising to the surface of the water: "Beneath it is all dark, it is all spreading, it is unfathomably deep; but now and again we rise to the surface and that is what you see us by" (73). Hypnotized, Mrs. Ramsay has a propensity to lose herself to things that she looks at, such as the steady strokes of the lighthouse, which resonates with the rhythm of herself knitting. At the quiet moment of the night, the stokes with the lighthouse and the strokes of her knitting fuse into one, inseparable.

> Losing personality, one lost the fret, the hurry, the stir; and there rose to her lips always some exclamation of triumph over life when things

---

[77] Virginia Woolf, *To the Lighthouse* (London: Hogarth Press, 1927).

> came together in this peace, this rest, this eternity; and pausing there she looked out to meet that stroke of the Lighthouse, the long steady stroke, the last of the three, which was her stroke, for watching them in this mood always at this hour one could not help attaching oneself to one thing especially of the things one saw; and this thing, the long steady stroke, was her stroke. Often she found herself sitting and looking, sitting and looking, with her work in her hands until she became the thing she looked at—the light for example. (73)

And here, Mrs. Ramsay gives the most direct expression of Woolf's essential sense of herself: that she is one with things.

> It was odd, she thought, how if one was alone, one leant to inanimate things; trees, streams, flowers; felt they expressed one; felt they become one; felt they knew one, in a sense were one; felt an irrational tenderness thus (she looked at that long steady light) as for oneself. (74)

Throughout her oeuvre, Woolf cannot refrain from imbuing this of her vision in her characters: that the world is one, that one should let go of her restrictive individual consciousness in order to be part of the whole, that one could do so by listening to her bodily rhythm which resonates with the cadence of the universal sensation.

Besides the cadence of the waves, another of Woolf's favorite symbols for the concurrence is the bustle of the London streets. In *Mrs. Dalloway*, the heroine Clarissa articulates Woolf's conception that the bustle of London streets is itself the concurrence which proves to her that she is part of the whole, of people she never meets and inanimate things, of ugly houses and bare trees:

> But that somehow in the streets of London, on the ebb and flow of things, here, there, she survived, Peter survived, lived in each other, she being part, she was positive, of the trees at home, of the house there, ugly, rambling all to bits and pieces as it was; part of people she had never met; being laid out like a mist between the people she knew best, who lifted her on their branches as she had seen the trees life the mist, but it spread ever so far, her life, her self. (11-12)

As Cristina Delgado Garcia rightly notes, this passage "illustrates how Clarissa views her selfhood not as a non-transferable, inherent essence, but as a ubiquitous relation between her and immediate places, objects and animate beings that are 'here, now, in front of her'."[78] The bustle of London streets is a shared sensation that envelops all people and things, which Clarissa feels she is being part of. Along with Clarissa's everyday life—ebb and flow of things—the traffic of the street is associated with the continuous cadence of the waves, and, just as the pulsations of the waves allow Woolf to relax her self-consciousness, Clarissa walking on the London streets experiences a kind of self-dissolution—she feels like "being laid out like a mist" which "spread ever so far." To relax the boundary of the selfhood for Woolf is in turn associated with her intuition that she is being supported, like trees lifting the mist. Walking on the streets, Clarissa is absorbed in the commotions of the streets, and yet she is part of what she sees or thinks of, undifferentiated from the whole: "and yet to her it was absolutely absorbing; all this; the cabs passing; and she would not say of herself, I am this, I am that" (11). Like Mrs. Ramsay, Clarissa has a tendency to attach herself to things she looks at. This attachment allows her to join the larger whole: "What she loved was this, here, now, in front of her; the fat lady in the cab" (11).

At these moments when Woolf's characters experience a oneness with the world, we see also some repeated details that seem to have an autobiographical significance. We read in *Mrs. Dalloway,* "Arlington Street and Piccadilly seemed to chafe the very air in the park and lift its leaves hotly, brilliantly, on waves of that divine vitality which Clarissa loved. To dance, to ride, she adored all that" (9). In *A Room of One's Own*, where Woolf speaks from her own authorial voice, we read again the passage that Naremore quotes, and find that Naremore omits the most important contextual information that belies Woolf's original inspiration. When the street is quiet, she had seemed a leaf signals to her a rhythmical order, like an invisible river that flows on the street, and envelops all people and carry them along.

> A single leaf detached itself from the plane tree at the end of the street, and in that pause and suspension fell. Somehow it was like a signal falling, a signal pointing to a force in things which one had overlooked. It seemed to point to a river, which flowed past, invisibly, round the corner, down the street, and took people and eddied them along...the sight was ordinary enough; what was strange was the rhythmical order with which my imagination had invested it. (144-45)

---

[78] Cristina Delgado García, "Decentring Discourse, Self-Centred Politics: Radicalism and the Self in Virginia Woolf's 'Mrs Dalloway,'" *Atlantis* 32, no. 1 (2010): 18.

Reading through Woolf's entire oeuvre, we find that often the heroines in the novel share a part of Woolf's sense of the self, and would articulate her vision of oneness here and there. In a sense, all of Woolf's novels are auto-philosophical fictions, vehicles through which she explores her mystic vision.

Woolf's conception of the crowd is unique among the modernist writers. Woolf here associates the modernist crowd with oceanic sensation and with interconnectivity, whereas—as theorized by Benjamin—for Edgar Poe and Baudelaire, the crowd is seen more as an expression of alienation. For Benjamin, one important leitmotif of modern experience is the shock produced by technology, which has greatly altered our sensorium environment.[79] The crowd in the metropolis is one of the important sites in which modern writers experience shock, though they might at the same time be enchanted by it. Benjamin senses that there is something mechanical and inhuman in Poe's presentation of the crowd, who wear "an absent and overdone smile upon the lips," and "if jostled, they bowed profusely to the jostlers."[80] Although Poe's crowd are composed of successful businessmen, for Benjamin, their absent-minded docility makes them somewhat similar to the workers in the factory, who lose their agency and become part of the great machine on an assembly line:

> Independently of the worker's volition, the article being worked on comes with his range of action and moves away from him just as arbitrarily. "It is a common characteristic of all capitalist production…," wrote Marx, "that the worker does not make use of the working conditions. The working conditions make use of the worker; but it takes machinery to give this reversal a technically concrete form." In working with machines, workers learn to co-ordinate "their own movements with the uniformly constant movements of an automaton." These words shed a peculiar light on the absurd kind of uniformity with which Poe wants to saddle the crowd—uniformities of attire and behavior, but also uniformity of facial expression. Those smiles provide food for thought. They are probably the familiar kind, as expressed in the phrase "keep smiling."[81]

---

[79] Benjamin, "On Some Motifs in Baudelaire," 175.
[80] Benjamin, "On Some Motifs in Baudelaire," 171.
[81] Benjamin, "On Some Motifs in Baudelaire," 175. Benjamin here did not cite the source of the quotations from Marx.

Benjamin intuits that the physiognomy of the modernist crowd somehow expresses the shock the workers suffer in the factory, because the urban environment is likewise technologically mediated—even as the modernist writers themselves might not be interested in the capitalist production. For Benjamin, the mechanical features of the crowd fascinate Poe as well as Baudelaire for this very reason:

> The shock experience which the passer-by has in the crowd corresponds to what the worker "experiences" his machine. This does not entitle us to the assumption that Poe knew anything about industrial work processes. Baudelaire, at any rate, did not have the faintest notion of them. He was, however, captivated by a process whereby the reflecting mechanism which the machine sets off in the workman can be studied closely, as in a mirror, in the idler.[82]

As Benjamin theorizes it, the crowd is a mirror of modernity. It is straightforward to associate the crowd with its other salient feature, that of mechanization.

Interestingly, however, Woolf finds in the crowd a salvation of what the machine destroys. That people casually walking on the streets, going about their everyday errands such as buying flowers, is seen as a site of shared experience and a symbol of interconnectivity for Woolf, as she has experienced the destruction of the war. In the quotation above—"but that somehow in the streets of London, on the ebb and flow of things, here, there, she survived, Peter survived, lived in each other"—the fact that she and her old lover survive to enjoy yet another ordinary day, freely roaming about the streets, is deeply appreciated when she sets it in contrast with the devastating war where all such enjoyment is suspended. But Clarissa feels fortunate not simply because she has survived the war, but more importantly because the death of her individual life does not matter that much, if she focuses not on her individual self, but rather identifies herself with the crowd: "Did it matter then, she asked herself, walking toward Bond Street, did it matter that she must inevitably cease completely; all this must go on without her" (11). Different from how Benjamin reads Poe and Baudelaire, here Woolf associates the crowd with collectivity and continuity, as well as her aesthetics of universal sensation, against the backdrop of the war.

Benjamin encapsulates modernity with his keyword "shock," by which he means, as Anna Jones Abramson summarizes it, "the subject is bombarded

---

[82] Benjamin, "On Some Motifs in Baudelaire," 176–77.

with novel sensory stimuli," "in a fast-paced, technologically mediated, and constantly changing urban milieu."[83] The subject must employ its consciousness to protect itself from excessive stimuli by shutting up the synesthetic system, as Benjamin discerns in Baudelaire's poetry "the image of the fencer": "the blows he deals are designed to open a path through the crowd for him."[84] In Benjamin's paradigm, "the individual is at odds with the city, clashing with its many disruptive and jarring technologies."[85] But for Woolf, the shock provokes not self-defense but rather a collective reaction that serves a unit of the crowd. In *Mrs. Dalloway*, Woolf writes about the crowd hearing a pistol shot coming from a motor car (16), while people begin to guess who the important person sitting in the motor car is. This shared concern immediately unites the crowd, which was disorderly a moment ago.

> Yet rumours were at once in circulation from the middle of Bond Street to Oxford Street on one side, to Atkinson's scent shop on the other, passing invisibly, inaudibly, like a cloud, swift, veil-like upon hills, falling indeed with something of a cloud's sudden sobriety and stillness upon faces which a second before had been utterly disorderly. (17)

The cloud image here metaphorically buffers and absorbs the shock, for the very reason that it is a collective experience. As Abramson observes, here it is "the urban atmosphere itself," rather than the overwrought and defensive psyche, that "functions as shock absorber."[86] Here Woolf incorporates modern shock and crowd into her aesthetics of universal sensation: after the shock, the author or her characters would turn their attention to the collective for a sense of comfort and tranquility.

In addition to the crowd, the everyday life for Woolf is another site to feel the pulsation of the universal sensation shared by all. Whereas for Pater the universal sensation passes by relentlessly, like Heraclitus's stream, Woolf finds a way to participate in, and in fact organize, the universal sensation. This somatic rhythm that punctuates the universal sensation can be found, Woolf

---

[83] Anna Jones Abramson, "Beyond Modernist Shock: Virginia Woolf's Absorbing Atmosphere," *Journal of Modern Literature* 38, no. 4 (2015): 41.
[84] Benjamin, "On Some Motifs in Baudelaire," 165.
[85] Abramson, "Beyond Modernist Shock," 41.
[86] Abramson, "Beyond Modernist Shock," 41.

proposes, on the site of our habitual everyday life.[87] The everyday is where we can relax our individual consciousness to follow the bidding of our biological pattern, pattern that is shared universally by all organic lives, pattern that is responsive to the cyclical structure of the earth, such as day and night. Woolf calls the rhythm of our everyday life "a kind of nondescript cotton wool" that insulates and protects us from moments of heightened consciousness.[88] Despite the fact that our everyday life is not consciously lived, this relaxation of our consciousness in order to join the universal pattern for Woolf is already an inner strength of ours that is capable of punctuating the flux of universal sensation with a habitable rhythm. For Woolf who has suffered the traumas of the wars and her own mental illness, days as ordinarily lived, without much effort to maintain it, is even more precious. In *Mrs. Dalloway*, where Septimus, who suffers from shell shock, is troubled by his hallucinations, he feels grounded by looking at how his wife runs about her everyday life, which builds a comforting order for the household. Rezia is in the habit of treating the newspaper girl with some candies:

> What always happened, then happened—what happened every night of their lives. The small girl sucked her thumb at the door; Rezia went down on her knees; Rezia cooed and kissed; Rezia got a bag of sweets out of the table drawer. For so it always happened. First one thing, then another. So she built it up, first one thing and then another. (159)

The everyday life follows a cyclical pattern, repetitive, familiar. The everyday life provides a comforting cadence like that of the waves, which by contrast allows human participation and organization of the universal sensation that passes relentlessly. Here Rezia and Septimus are enjoying their happiest moment, as Septimus directs Rezia sewing an odd combination of ribbons, beads, tassels, and artificial flowers onto one hat: "She built it up; first one thing, then another, she built it up, sewing" (160). First one thing, then another: through the familiar everyday rituals Rezia builds an order. The hat is a gift to Mrs. Peters. For Septimus, the order of the everyday helps to ground his heightened consciousness of hallucination: "It was so real, it was so substantial, Mrs. Peters' hat" (159). In Rezia's as well as Clarissa's sewing, the

---

[87] For scholarship on Woolf's conceptions about everyday life, see Liesl M. Olson, "Virginia Woolf's 'Cotton Wool of Daily Life,'" *Journal of Modern Literature* 26, no. 2 (2003): 42–65; J. Hillis Miller, "Mrs. Dalloway: Repetition as the Raising of the Dead," in *Fiction and Repetition: Seven English Novels* (Harvard University Press, 1982), 176–202.
[88] Virginia Woolf, "A Sketch of the Past," in *Moments of Being: A Collection of Autobiographical Writing*, ed. Jeanne Schulkind, 2nd ed. (San Diego: Harcourt, 1985), 70.

everyday rhythm is cherished in the sense that it is not merely a given; it is an effort to relax again the startled, overwrought individual consciousness—a symbol of recovery, an inner strength to participate in the universal sensation.

Both Rezia sewing ribbons and beads onto a hat to make a gift, and Clarissa mending the torn dress for the party, are symbols of Woolf's writing, of her mission "to put the severed parts together."[89] Writing for Woolf is the bridge between the heightened individual consciousness and the rhythmic universal sensation, as the painter Lily Briscoe in *To the Lighthouse* remarks: "It was a question, she remembered, how to connect this mass on the right hand with that on the left."[90] In her memoir essay "A Sketch of the Past," Woolf confesses that writing for her is never merely a naïve reproduction of her childhood memory of the waves, but rather a *willed return* to her oceanic sensation. In the memoir essay, Woolf describes *violent shocks* that would suddenly startle her so that she can no longer comfortably stay in the rhythmic order of her everyday life, "this cotton wool, this non-being" (71). The shock might be negative as it shatters her sense of unity: for example as a child she heard a person committed suicide and felt her own body was "paralysed," herself in "a trance of horror" (71)—which we know is the original experience based on which Woolf constructs the scene in *Mrs. Dalloway*, that Clarissa hears Septimus throwing himself out the window. The shock might also be an epiphanic revelation of the order behind the appearance, for example, when young Virginia was looking at the flowerbed in the garden at St. Ives, she realizes that "the flower itself was a part of the earth" (71). Woolf analyzes the difference between the positive and negative shocks. Whereas the negative shocks held the child Virginia powerless, the positive one contains within it an order, and this order will help her, in time, to recuperate from the violent shock: "in the case of the flower I found a reason; and was thus able to deal with the sensation. I was not powerless. I was conscious—if only at a distance—that I should in time explain it" (72). Woolf supposes "that this shock-receiving capacity is what makes me a writer" (72). And from the positive experience of the flower, Woolf learns that writing for her essentially means a cerebral activity that *provides a reason* to her original shocks.

> I feel that I have had a blow; but it is not, as I thought as a child, simply a blow from an enemy hidden behind the cotton wool of daily life; it is or will become a revelation of some order; it is a token of some real thing behind appearances; and I make it real by putting it into words. It

---

[89] Woolf, "A Sketch of the Past," 72.
[90] Woolf, *To the Lighthouse*, 62.

is only by putting it into words that I make it whole; this wholeness means that it has lost its power to hurt me; it gives me, perhaps because by doing so I take away the pain, a great delight to *put the severed parts together* (72, emphasis mine).

Whereas Woolf feels connected when she can relax her self-consciousness, writing becomes a cathartic remedy after receiving a shock. Writing for Woolf is like Clarissa throwing a party, which she offers to assemble people after they have been separated for years: "And it was an offering," Clarissa musing to herself her purpose of being a hostess, "to combine, to create" (135). It aims to resume the order, after a certain shock that has intensified the individual consciousness. Here, we find Woolf's aesthetics centers around the dialectic between shock that shatters the world, and strength to put things back together. The most intense shocks that Woolf suffer in her lifetime, of course, are the two World Wars, while the loci where Woolf feels oceanic sensation—in shared experience such as in the crowd and in everyday life—are also characteristic of interwar modernity, as it becomes precious only after the war for people to walk casually on the streets, going about their everyday errands such as buying flowers. One question that troubles Woolf however, which she must explore through her auto-philosophical fiction *The Waves*, is whether reason provided by writing can replace relaxation bestowed by oceanic sensation, a question that I will further discuss in detail.

***

Two deep ironies are however always present in Woolf's reflection on her practice of writing. The first is that the order she finds in rhythmic sensation is only a remedy after trauma, an attempt to comfort herself after the shock. Woolf is capable of the most brutal irony of herself, indeed, as she would publish with her husband, at the Hogarth Press, an English translation of Freud's *Civilization and Discontent* (1930). In the book, Freud studies Woolfian "oceanic feeling"—"a feeling which embraced the universe and expressed an inseparable connection of the ego with the external world," but he deconstructs this beatified sense of oneness and gives it an apathetic scientific explanation: as a "primary ego-feeling" of an infant which does not know that it is separated from the world, and as it is retained in adults it becomes the source of religious feelings.[91] In this book, Freud uses the most

---

[91] Sigmund Freud, *Civilization and Its Discontents*, trans. Joan Riviere (London: Hogarth Press, 1930), 13.

unsympathetic terms to describe the infant's oceanic feeling as "limitless narcissism" (21), and to charge our religious sentiment in general as "palliative remedies" (25) to the hardship of life. Freud's criticism, as I will go on to argue, however, is neither entirely unfair nor entirely unrelated to Woolf's own assessment to her vocation as a writer.

The irony about Woolf's oceanic feeling is self-consciously present in *Mrs. Dalloway* when we realize that often Woolf's characters are extremely naïve, and the consolation offered by universal sensation is often subjectively sentimental, which does not deal with the traumatic experience itself. Clarissa who does not know Septimus in person mulls over the veteran's death for a moment and gets over it, while Rezia's sorrow is not mentioned at all in the novel. That is, the affirmation offered in the novel is in reality as superficial as an outsider looking at things happen. The figure of the artist, Lily Briscoe in *To the Lighthouse* therefore comments: "so much depends, she thought, upon distance: whether people are near us or far from us" (217). Surely, Woolf has firsthand experience of mental illness and she certainly sees a part of herself in Septimus, and critics have been reading Clarissa and Septimus as a double that presents different parts of one's psychology. But the question here is certainly not what Woolf has personally experienced, but rather the dramatic irony that Woolf employs to comment on the disparity between her vocation of writing, and her own aesthetic ideal of oceanic sensation.

Woolf often questions harshly if this writerly power of gaining a panoramic order, at the time when reason is capable of *detaching* from the shock of the original experience and look at it from the perspective of a disinterested observer, is congruous with her aesthetic ideal of *immersing* in the oceanic sensation. In a notable passage in *Mrs. Dalloway*, Clarissa's daughter Elizabeth *sits on top of the omnibus*, looking down to the uproar of the London street, and muses to herself that the military music might be consolatory to the witnesses of the dead, for no other reason but that this collective sensation, much larger than any fragile individual, will continue onward and carry us forward, unconscious and indifferent as it is. The remarkable passage deserves to be quoted in full:

> She liked the geniality, sisterhood, motherhood, brotherhood of this uproar. It seemed to her good. The noise was tremendous; and suddenly there were trumpets (the unemployed) blaring, rattling about in the uproar; military music; as if people were marching; yet had they been dying—had some woman breathed her last, and whoever was watching, opening the window of the room where she had just brought off that act of supreme dignity, looked down on Fleet Street, that

uproar, that military music would have come triumphing up to him, consolatory, indifferent.

> It was not conscious. There was no recognition in it of one's fortune, or fate, and for that very reason even to those dazed with watching for the last shivers of consciousness of the faces of the dying, consoling.

Elizabeth's contemplation here is strangely heartless. The universal sensation might be consolatory for Elizabeth as for her the dead is a stranger, but surely not if the dead is my own mother. But such is Woolf's ironic interrogation upon herself as a writer: can the sorrow be explained away by a writer sitting on top of the omnibus, who can thus see that we are part of the universal sensation by virtue of her privileged perspective?

Whereas Clarissa has a natural disposition to immerse herself in universal sensation, here Elizabeth observes the phantasmagoric motion of it from a distance, on top of an omnibus. In Susan Buck-Morss's article, "Aesthetics and Anaesthetics," She discusses the anesthetic effect of phantasmagoria. While "shock is the very essence of modern experience,"[92] phantasmagoria, or a total view of the reality only as surface appearance, as technology has altered our environment to the point that we are constantly overwhelmed by sensory stimuli, "has the effect of anaesthetizing the organism"[93] from suffering shock. Although phantasmagoria is a shared reality for the moderns, for an experienced flaneur, who knows too well how to roam about the city, this phantasmagoric effect is willed:

> Benjamin describes the flaneur as self-trained in this capacity of distancing oneself by turning reality into a phantasmagoria: rather than being caught up in the crowd, he slows his pace and observes it, making a pattern out of its surface. He sees the crowd as a reflection of his dream mood, an "intoxication" for his senses.[94]

Here, the flâneur is marked by the capacity to detach oneself from reality, and to turn reality into surface representation. This is also the process where he can supplement reality with reason and order, "making a pattern out of its surface," and thereby shield the heart from suffering shock. But Woolf has qualms and guilt in the process of relieving herself from the original

---

[92] Buck-Morss, "Aesthetics and Anaesthetics," 16.
[93] Buck-Morss, "Aesthetics and Anaesthetics," 22.
[94] Buck-Morss, "Aesthetics and Anaesthetics," 24.

experience. Whereas Woolf has written that "this shock-receiving capacity is what makes me a writer," and explained that the purpose of writing is to free her from the original shock, she is troubled by the fact that the process of writing necessarily detaches her from the experience, in the same way Elizabeth offers her sympathy as an onlooker sitting on top of the omnibus. In a metaphysical sense, the act of writing also forces Woolf to maintain the position of a conscious observer, to extracts herself from the universal sensation she would like to immerse herself in, such as the bustles of the London crowds and streets, and to turn it into surface phantasmagoria. Such are the ironies innate in Woolf's vocation of writing and her ideal of universal sensation, which she explores in her auto-philosophical fictions.

The questions that Woolf here ask are, first: what is the power of her writing, and what is the power of her reason, which attempts to seal the wound and to put the severed parts together? Might it be that the affirmation offered by her writing is merely theoretical, and not experiential, as, in fact, *unrelated* as Clarissa and Septimus, as the onlooker and the one who suffers? Might it be that writing is a kind of technology that works like anesthetic, which serves to cut the neurological connection between the brain and the body, and allows the surgeon a privileged position to calmly dissect the body, without suffering the emotional burden of the patient's pain?[95] Ideally, the one who suffers intensively and finds herself isolated should find comfort if she can relax her frightened consciousness a little and seek connection with the oceanic rhythm that promises to carry and support her. But in Woolf's design, Septimus who suffers cannot be saved by it, while the figures of the artist, the figures who provide reason in Woolf's novels—Clarissa Dalloway and Lily Briscoe have never been playing a role more significantly than *an onlooker*. The trauma and the reason in Woolf's writing has never been integrated.

The second question, or Woolf's harsh self-critique, is that the order composed of words cannot, ontologically, replace the oceanic sensation on the street. Discussing Woolf's philosophy of writing in "A Sketch of the Past," Benjamin D. Hagen notes uncritically that Woolf's sense of order is essentially composed of words, and that she in fact transports her oceanic wholeness into a verbal composition: "To find the reason for a shock and to put it into words are, for Woolf, differential, creative activities that translate the world's fundamental operation into a verbal composition that acquires a sensuousness and *a truth of its own.*"[96] But I argue that for Woolf this composition of the artistic world is not

---

[95] Buck-Morss, "Aesthetics and Anaesthetics," 18.
[96] Benjamin D. Hagen, "Feeling Shadows: Virginia Woolf's Sensuous Pedagogy," *PMLA* 132, no. 2 (March 1, 2017): 132 (emphasis mine).

any artistic glory, but rather as ironic as Mallarmé's swan trapped in the nothingness of language. The reconciliations offered in the novel have always been merely *symbolic*, whose literary value does not extend beyond the world of fiction. In *Mrs. Dalloway*, the order composed by reason is symbolized by Clarissa's party, which assembles people only on a superficial level, while Septimus throws his life away. Likewise, in *To the Lighthouse*, the family's reconciliation, after war and death and the son's hatred toward his father throughout his adolescence, is brought about by the symbolic act of the family sailing together across the sea to the lighthouse. The reconciliation resides only in transitory, subjective, uncommunicated moods. And Woolf makes it clear that this order is brought about by her artistic authority: the figure of the artist, Lily Briscoe, finishes her painting at the same time and in parallel with the family landing at the lighthouse.

For Woolf, auto-philosophical fiction is the genre to examine the irony between representation and oceanic sensation, to unfold the distance between practice and ideal, to examine whether an idea is viable, and to, in a way, recognize the values of both her aesthetic ideal and her heroic attempts. Woolf's meditation on writing is symptomatic of the modernist writers: it is an extreme rigor of self-reflection, often leading to the point of self-defeating irony. In her auto-philosophical novel, *The Waves*,[97] Woolf painfully looks at this distance between theory and experience, between writing that provides a reason and the experience of those who suffer the shock, between representation that is the vision of an individual consciousness and oceanic sensation that asks one to join the whole.

The Waves is Woolf's most experimental novel, composed of sustained soliloquies of six closely tied characters that, stylishly harmonized, are obviously spoken by a single consciousness. As Woolf comments in her diary, "the thing is to keep them [soliloquies] running homogeneously in and out, in the rhythm of the waves" (*Diary*, Aug 20, 1930).[98] Among the six personas, Bernard is the writer who stands for Woolf's external self-expression, who possesses intellectual power and articulates Woolf's ideal of the primal union. With the character Bernard, Woolf comments on her vocation—in fact some kind of compulsion—to constantly draw with writing a dreamland in which the individual selves can dissolve. The novel begins with Jinny kissing Louis, Susan feeling alienated seeing them two kissing, and Bernard the writer attempting to redraw the union *with words*. Bernard's naïve and unreflective

---

[97] Virginia Woolf, *The Waves* (London: The Hogarth Press, 1931).
[98] Virginia Woolf, *A Writer's Diary*, ed. Woolf Leonard (San Diego: Harcourt, 1981), 156 (Aug 20, 1930).

confidence in the power of words, very ironically however, reads like a frank metafictional commentary on Woolf's writing career. But Bernard is very sincere when he considers writing to be the only means to put things back whole when the primal oneness is disrupted.

> 'But when we sit together, close,' said Bernard, 'we melt into each other with phrases. …We make an *unsubstantial territory'* (11, emphasis mine).

Bernard is the figure of the writer in *The Waves* who has the power to draw a dreamland of the primal union; in the novel, this land is underneath some rainforest where tree roots entangle, sensations muffled, and selves obscured, "the sunless territory of non-identity" (83). Bernard's "unsubstantial territory" is supposed to mimic the earth underneath the tree, which Louis feels himself to be connected to, but Susan expresses her mistrust: "But you wander off; you slip away; you rise up higher, with words and words in phrases" (11). To Susan, Bernard's intellectual power is airily imaginative, which, while drawing an artificial dreamland, is but an unsubstantial simulacrum that cannot replace the earthy connectivity one can feel in her primal sensations.

Woolf's is most self-critical when she frankly points out that writing as an activity also paradoxically makes the writer more aware of herself. In order to observe things, invent plot, and provide a meaning, the writer will have to differentiate herself from the world she feels being part of, and her consciousness will transcend as a subject opposite to the world. She will also need an audience that listens to her and to gain attention means to gratify one's ego. In one of the revealing moments, Bernard comments on how writing will snap him back to identity:

> Yet behold, it returns. One cannot extinguish that persistent smell. It steals in through some crack in the structure—one's identity. I am not part of the street—no, I observe the street. One splits off, therefore. For instance, up that back street a girl stands waiting; for whom? A romantic story. …That is, I am a natural coiner of words, a blower of bubbles through one thing and another. And, striking off these observations spontaneously, I elaborate myself; differentiate myself and, listening to the voice that says as I stroll past, "Look! Take note of that!" I conceive myself called upon to provide, some winter's night, a meaning for all my observations. (82-3)

In one sentence, "I am not part of the street—no, I observe the street," Woolf lays bare the paradox between her desire to immerse herself in universal sensations, and her vocation as a writer to draw up such a dreamland—made only with words. Toward the end of the novel, when Bernard is already a dying man, he spells out the most difficult question for an artist, whose aesthetic ideal is to forsake the individual selfhood and to join the universal sensation, and who wonders constantly how to truly achieve this with his means of writing: "How describe the world seen without a self?" (204). Bernard seems to understand too well at this point that his individual consciousness will always be sharply demarcated simultaneously with his act of writing, and thus he vows to give up words: "There are no words…One breathes in and out with substantial breath" (*ibid*). The term "substantial breath," one that rhymes with Woolf's oceanic feelings and reminds us our basic connection with the universal motion, contrasts sharply to Bernard's writerly, imaginative, "unsubstantial territory" that is confined in an individual mind. Toward the end of the novel, Woolf seems to be mocking very bitterly at her own career as a writer:

> How much better is silence; the coffee-cup, the table. How much better to sit by myself like the solitary sea-bird that opens its wings on the stake. Let me sit here forever *with bare things*. (210, emphasis mine)

Bernard now only sits with bare things,[99] and is no longer obliged to provide things with human meaning, which, in the idealist tradition, will inevitably appropriate the thing seen and sublimate it into the unsubstantial territory of human consciousness. Such is Woolf's bitter self-mockery.

Woolf's auto-philosophical fiction sets her ideal of oceanic oneness in the context of her writerly vocation. But then she discovers that the major means through which she mends the disrupted order, that of writing, paradoxically prevents her from immersing herself in universal sensation. Auto-philosophical fiction serves to expose the backstage story of any philosophical ideal, while its positive purpose is to point out possible arenas of transformation. Proust's *Recherche*, which one might read as an allegory of idealist appropriation, brings to the foreground the issue of *the artist's receptive capacity*, as we see Marcel, in his anxieties to possess completely the object of love, ceases to receive the sensuous plenitude at the present moment, and can only later recuperate it in the edifice of his memory. Woolf's *The Waves* on the other hand accentuates the issue of *the practice of writing*, which is essentially dissociated from her cultivation of self, of relaxing her consciousness so as to immerse in universal

---

[99] As Bill Brown discusses, Woolf in her short story "Solid Objects" seeks to draw our attention to "bare things" extracted from the network of human usage and meanings. Bill Brown, "The Secret Life of Things (Virginia Woolf)," in *Other Things*, 1 edition (Chicago: University of Chicago Press, 2016), 49–78. Virginia Woolf, "Solid Objects," in *A Haunted House and Other Short Stories* (The Hogarth Press, 1944), 69–75.

sensation. The concluding question I will engage with in the final pages of the book is, then: How might we reconceptualize our practice of writing in a way that it would be related to our cultivation of the self? This is a question that can be best answered by the genre of auto-philosophical fiction, and in fact by one of Pater's imaginary portraits.

VI. Remembrance of the House

In his short imaginary portrait "The Child in the House,"[100] Pater articulates an ethic of remembrance, which might be read as a miniature of the consummate quest that Marcel in *Recherche* but dimply anticipates, but eventually falls short of articulation. This little piece reconceptualizes remembrance as an act that traces the origin of our individuality back to our material habitation and habituation, and therefore extricates art from its idealist domain. Like his *Marius the Epicurean* and Proust's *Recherche*, Pater presents his ideas through an auto-philosophical essay, for the concrete persona is the most effective device that serves to tell us, not so much the truth value of a certain philosophy, but the impact of adopting a certain worldview on one's life. The central questions for the auto-philosophical fiction, one that does not state any idea as absolute truth, but rather *explores through them* with *a concrete person*, are: what is the mode of self-cultivation required for my aesthetic ideal, and here most importantly as we keep Woolf's conundrum in mind, can writing be part and parcel of my aesthetic ideal?

Pater's hero Florian was by chance reminded of the name of his childhood neighborhood, and he starts a journey of self-reflection in which he traces back "the threads of his complex spiritual habit" to his hometown. Florian finds his habitual sentiments and the way he looks at things to be given by the atmosphere of the house: "*Florian* found that he owed to the place many tones of sentiment afterwards customary with him, certain inward lights under which things most habitually presented themselves to him" (15). It turns out Florian's impressions about his childhood hometown can be translated into a preference of "a well-recognised imaginative mood," and this mood would be so ingrained in him that it actually becomes "a part of the texture of his mind" (16). Childhood impressions can be translated into more generalized predilections, for example, Florian connects his preference in "a kind of comeliness and dignity," with "the pale people of towns" which he was accustomed to see (16). Florian insists that the child's taste is shaped by

---

[100] Water Pater, *The Child in the House: An Imaginary Portrait* (Thomas B. Mosher, 1896). First Published in Macmillan's Magazine, Aug. 1878.

its early, familiar habituation, and his theory is indeed quite radical that our habitual perception can be correspondingly translated into the structure of our inner life:

> Our susceptibilities, the discovery of our powers, manifold experiences—our various experience of the coming and going of bodily pains, for instance—belong to this or the other well-remembered place in the material habitation—that little white room with the window across which the heavy blossoms could beat so peevishly in the wind, with just that particular catch or throb, such a sense of teasing in it, on gusty morning. (18)

What we admit into our experiences, how we understand our powers, how we respond to experiences as we define their psychical impacts, to sum up, our psychological structure—Florian argues—is in the first place shaped by our early sensuous acquisition. It endows Florian with his aesthetic taste and habitual mood, and even defines his structure of desire and interprets for him his pains and passions: "the angle at which the sun in the morning fell on the pillow—become parts of the great chain wherewith we are bound" (18).

What Florian proposes here amounts to a theory of subjectivity that rebels directly against Cartesian dualism and the Kantian subject-object divide. Our life is not defined as an isolated brain floating in a vat; there exists a *substratum* of life that is deeply embedded in the material world, translating perceptions into predilections, and interpreting for us all experience to come. Our body, which through time receives the indelible imprints of environmental forces, thus shapes in us a unique sensitivity. That is, our sensitivity is not as ideal as the Romantics assume; it is in the first place shaped by our habitual material environment. Once Florian as a child encounters a magnificent hawthorn tree in bloomsome and, "for the first time, he seemed to experience a passionateness in his relation to fair outward objects, an inexplicable excitement in their presence, which disturbed him, and from which he half longed to be free" (30). His love for the hawthorn tree also inspires in him a desire to see its various incarnations on this earth. Things of crimson red, such as the color used "in the works of old Venetian masters, or old Flemish tapestries," would evoke in him "the recollection of the flame in those perishing little petals" (29). And further, this experience with the hawthorn tree also initiates his longing for "beautiful physical things," which is "a kind of tyranny of the senses over him" (30). Finally, such an impressive love of the hawthorn tree also compels Florian to affirm for him the reality of the material world, for he defines his empiricism as "the necessity he was under of associating all thoughts to touch and sight, as a sympathetic link between himself and actual, feeling, living objects; a protest in favour of real men and women against mere grey, unreal abstractions" (31).

Pater's theory that our sensibility is initiated by an intense instance of love also bears a conscious, although ambivalent, allusion to Plato's theory of love, as we see Pater evokes Plato's image of the swelling of the lover's soul when it is about to grow wings: "Was it some periodic moment in the expansion of soul within him, or mere trick of heat in the heavily-laden summer air?" ("Child" 29; cf. *Phaedrus* 251c). Pater keeps a distance from Plato here because Pater wishes to argue that the archetype of beauty resides not in the heavens, but belongs to our early habitation on this earth. Pater however borrows Plato's notion that our love toward one beautiful thing will *initiate* our sensibility and that we will expand our love to all things beautiful (*Symposium* 211c, Pater himself translates this passage in *Plato and Platonism*[101] p. 80). Borrowing from Plato's theory of love, what Florian articulates here is the presence of an inexplicable yearning whenever we are in the presence of beautiful things, for the structure of our sensibility is, in the first place, destined in the event of our original love.

In his famous "Conclusion" to *The Renaissance,* Pater urges us to unfetter ourselves from stereotypical habits so that we can always keep our eyes afresh to capture new, exquisite sensation in a world of flux:

> How shall we pass mostly swiftly from point to point, and be present always at the focus where the greatest number of vital forces unite in their purest energy?
>
> To burn always with this hard, gemlike flame, to maintain this ecstasy, is success in life. In a sense it might even be said that our failure is to form habits: for, after all, habit is relative to a stereotyped world, and meantime it is only the roughness of the eye that makes any two persons, things, situations, seem alike.[102]

Pater's position here in "Conclusion" is squarely oppositional with what he proposes in the imaginary portrait of Florian. But the power of the genre "imaginary portrait" is precisely to experiment with a certain idea in one's life, without ascribing to the idea the status of the only possible truth. By comparing the two propositions here, we see two conceptions about our

---

[101] Walter Pater, *Plato and Platonism: A Series of Lectures* (Adelaide: Cambridge Scholar Press, 2002).
[102] Pater, *The Renaissance: Studies in Art and Poetry*, 250.

individual sensibility, and two relationships between humans and the earth. One amidst the vortex of fleeting sensation and must sacrifice the structure of his habitual perception in order to welcome the unknown, while the other affirms one's unique sensibility as shaped by the earth. The two propositions lead to two completely different aesthetics, and Pater does not attempt to judge which one is right. Rather, reading through his oeuvre, we see his intellectual breadth, his capacity "to be for ever curiously testing new opinions and courting new impressions, never acquiescing in a facile orthodoxy of Comte, or of Hegel, or of our own."[103]

Building upon his theory of subjectivity, Florian connects his philosophical proposal to a writer's *ethical practice*, that of *remembrance*: to observe carefully the character of one's sensitivity and to attribute it to one's material formation.

> And it happened that this accident of his dream was just the thing needed for the beginning of a certain design he then had in view, the noting, namely, of some things in the story of his spirit—in that process of brain-building by which we are, each one of us, what we are. (10).

Only through the astute act of remembrance can we understand that our sensitivity, however unique and however it functions to shape our experience, is in the first place not ideal, but ecological. Writing for Pater is this remembrance of what we owe to the earth, and the act of writing itself should prompt the hero to turn this insight into aesthetic sentiments, experiences, and practices. This technique of self-writing, to borrow a notion from Foucault, has "an *ethopoietic* function,"—"it is an agent of the transformation of truth into *ēthos*."[104] Florian's remembrance through self-writing, then, is not merely a posthuman theory that posits our embodied subjectivity as a universal yet distant truth, it rather instills in the hero an abiding sense of gratitude, belonging, and longing for the earth. Florian would then give himself to the effects of beautiful things, and note carefully how these beautiful things might evoke in him an unutterable yearning, which is a sign that his sensitivity was first initiated in the event of his original love.

---

[103] Pater, *The Renaissance*, 250.
[104] Michel Foucault, *Ethics: Subjectivity and Truth*, ed. Paul Rabinow, trans. Robert Hurley, The Essential Works of Michel Foucault, 1954-1984 1 (New York: The New Press, 1997), 209.

> So he yielded himself to these things, to be played upon by them like a musical instrument, and began to note with deepening watchfulness, but always with some puzzled, unutterable longing in his enjoyment, the phases of the seasons and of the growing or waning day, down even to the shadowy changes wrought on bare wall or ceiling (33).

The exercise of our individual sensibility, the practice of watchful self-writing, is therefore not an act of idealist appropriation: it is rather a remembrance of our original love toward the earth.

In what way, then, is Pater's remembrance different from what we see in Proust's *Recherche*, or from Woolf's ecstatic memory of the waves flapping? The difference lies in *our structures of love, the ways we relate ourselves to things*. If, as Pater suggests, our structure of love is shaped by our earliest relations with our object of love, then we can read Marcel's desire for his mother's fleeting bedtime kisses, Woolf's oceanic oneness, and Florian's sensuous habituation as *metaphors* of how *each writer relates to the external world*. For one example, we may compare how Marcel's response to a beautiful hawthorn tree is so different from that of Florian. As a child, Marcel already feels compelled to enlist his memory to retain his sensuous pleasure even when, most tellingly, his object of love is a tree firmly rooted in earth, and never threatens to leave.

> Mais j'avais beau rester devant les aubépines à respirer, à porter devant ma pensée qui ne savait ce qu'elle devait en faire, à perdre, à retrouver leur invisible et fixe odeur, à m'unir au rythme qui jetait leurs fleurs, ici et là, avec une allégresse juvénile et à des intervalles inattendus comme certains intervalles musicaux, elles m'offraient indéfiniment le même charme avec une profusion inépuisable, mais sans me laisser approfondir davantage, comme ces mélodies qu'on rejoue cent fois de suite sans descendre plus avant dans leur secret. (V1, p. 188)

Marcel's relation to the hawthorn tree is a reproduction of his relation to his mother's unsatisfying bedtime kisses. Just as Marcel would be mentally prepared to receive his mother's bedtime kisses and then to retain their impressions every night, just as he already learned that his mental effort is the only means available to compensate for the fleeting pleasure, here he performs exactly the same ritual to the hawthorn tree. Marcel also feels he can never penetrate the mystery of the sensuous pleasure even as he is there to feel it, in the same way he can never understand the independence of his graceful mother, that she does not seem to be empathetic to his needs. For Marcel then, remembrance is the only available means to retain the images of things in one's mind so as to completely possess it, for his intuition is that only such mental retention can strip the material thing off its mystery, and that only this comprehension entails a real enjoyment of the thing. As an adult, Marcel finds that he can relish the sensuous plenitude only in the form of involuntary memory, assuredly contents of his mind. But Florian understands the grounding and initiative effect of the hawthorn tree, for the tree, like his childhood house, provides him shelter, security, and not without a sense of wonder. This sense of security allows Florian to regard his object of love with gratitude and respect.

In one of his letters, Pater comments that "Child in the House: voilà, the germinating, original, source, specimen, of all my *imaginative* work."[105] And if we read the theory Pater proposes in this piece as a premise to all of his imaginative works, including his impressionist criticism and his imaginary portraits, we come to realize that his subjectivism is not idealistic. For Pater, the most important virtue of the art critic is "the power of being deeply moved by the presence of beautiful objects."[106] The beautiful objects—including "all works of art, and the fairer forms of nature and human life"—all of these are "powers or forces [capable of] producing pleasurable sensations," in the same way we experience the powers of "an herb, a wine, a gem."[107] That is, Pater defines art as objects that produce strong or refined sensuous powers, rather than as representation or expression. As an art critic, the question that Pater asks in appreciation of a work of art is: "How is my nature modified by its presence, and under its influence?".[108]

Individuality is an important quality of being an art critic for Pater, but for him individuality is not purely idealistic. Pater famously asserts that art criticism is the mirror of the critic that reveals his sensibility: "The question he asks is always: in whom did the stir, the genius, the sentiment of the period find itself? Who was the receptacle of its refinement, its elevation, its taste?"[109] In "The Child in the House," however, as Pater argues that our subjective impression reveals rather our material formation, we might rethink his theory of artistic appreciation—not as an idealist appropriation—but as a rich interplay between an embodied sensitivity and sensuous powers produced by works of art. Just as Florian remembers his sensitivity is shaped by his material environment, Pater's idiosyncratic appreciation of artwork only

---

[105] Walter Pater, *Letters of Walter Pater*, ed. Lawrence Evans (Oxford: Clarendon Press, 1970), xxix, emphasis original.
[106] Pater, *The Renaissance*, xii.
[107] Pater, *The Renaissance*, xi.
[108] Pater, *The Renaissance*, x.
[109] Pater, *The Renaissance*, xii.

affirms his sensuous bond to the corporeal world. The "goodly crimson" in Flemish tapestries will remind Florian of the red hawthorn flowers that he as a child collected and perish in an old cabinet (29), but however idiosyncratic Florian's perception of the tapestries is, it serves to remind him his early aesthetic education by the earth, rather than, as is the case for Marcel, that the involuntary memory functions to appropriate things into the domain of one's imagination, disembodied.

Writing itself for Pater is this delineation of individuality, but this individuality always dimly suggests one's ecological history and material formation. This practice of remembrance that brings to mind the forgotten connection between individuality and material formation can evolve into a theory of art. The house that Florian lived in as a child, as it presents to him his predilections and explains his longings, "gradually becomes a sort of material shrine or sanctuary of sentiment; a system of visible symbolism interweaves itself through all our thoughts and passions" (18). Here the house is transformed into an object of art as it not only registers and shapes the hero's thoughts and passions; it moreover gives perceptible and palpable forms to our immaterial inner life. It is a concrete metaphor that makes external, explains and guarantees our connection to the material world. *What literature gives, then, is itself a metaphor of our material habituation.* In his essay, "Style," Pater differentiates between willful "mind," which is "his unreasoned and really uncharacteristic caprices, involuntary or affected," and what he calls "the soul," as an ineffable substratum underlying the true aesthetic expression, which only vaguely suggests itself.[110] For Pater, literature "does but suggest what can never be uttered, not as being different from, or more obscure than, what actually gets said, but as containing that plenary substance of which there is only one phase or facet in what is there expressed."[111] Our body is this "plenary substance," unique as each of it is shaped by a unique home, indelibly real as it has been shaped by manifold environmental forces, preceding our consciousness and reveals only a fraction of itself in literary expression. Literature, then, functions rather like the house that Florian lived in as a child, which gives perceptible form, and only vaguely intimates, a facet of our profound temperament and ecological history. Proposing that our memory is not immaterial, our individuality is not ideal, Pater finally allows remembrance to be the artistic practice that registers our connection with the material world: it is an endeavor that

---

[110] Walter Pater, *Appreciations: With an Essay on Style* (Landon: Macmillan, 1895), 34.
[111] Pater, *Appreciations*, 24.

remembers, with an ethical piety, that our individual expression really originates from our material constitution.

VII. Summary of Part Two

In Part Two, I explore the genre of auto-philosophical fiction through a discussion of Pater's imaginary portrait, which sets philosophy in life and serves as the most powerful measure to test how an idea feels, as well as what it reveals and compels. Pater's *Marius the Epicurean* is the purest auto-philosophical fiction in the formal sense that the hero does not affiliate oneself with any philosophical stance, but offers his life to a perpetual quest: the regime of Marius's aesthetic education consists of an expansion of his powers of reception in order to constantly court new ideas, new impressions. Then I have discussed how each writer, through their own auto-philosophical fiction, seeks to reveal the tensions between idea and life, which in turn discloses desirable arenas of self-cultivation.

With recourse to involuntary memory, Marcel answers the empiricist conundrum that our intellect has very limited access to our sensuous memory. Since the mechanism of involuntary memory is that it utilizes a present sensation to summon the edifice of his sensuous memory, it transports the real to the ideal, which Deleuze refers to as "the apprenticeship to art."[112] Yet, a thoughtful critic cannot read involuntary memory merely as a philosophical solution to the empiricist conundrum. Marcel's philosophical solution is set in the context of his amorous fiasco, and thus reveals what he sacrifices for the idealist transportation—sensuous pleasure and emotional intimacy of the present. Despite of Marcel's attempts to convince himself of the certainty that things exist only in the ideal realm of his memory, Marcel does not know how to change the condition of his life, as Pater would by expanding one's powers of reception. This distinction between mental conviction and self-cultivation is important, and my purpose is to show that only through a true transformation of the self might the artist escape one's original condition and create new subject-object relation, and that auto-philosophical fiction is a measure to test whether the idea leads to the transformation of the self.

In contrast to Marcel's futile mental conviction, for the rest of Part Two I have outlined Woolf's and Pater's methods of self-cultivation. Facing the same

---

[112] Gilles Deleuze, *Proust and Signs* (New York: G. Braziller, 1972), 65.

empiricist predicament that our individual consciousness is highly selective and registers only a fracture of fleeting sensations, Woolf's dreams of being part of the world—and her method is to relax her individual consciousness and to immerse herself in universal sensation. But in her auto-philosophical fiction, *The Waves*, Woolf tests her idea in the laboratory of life, and lays bare the conflicts between ideal and practice: her ideal of being one with the universal sensations is incompatible with her practice of writing, which sets her consciousness against the objects being described. That is, Woolf's auto-philosophical fiction reveals that she cannot incorporate writing as a regime of her aesthetic cultivation.

Finally, Pater reconciles this conflict between cultivation of the self and the practice of writing in one of his imaginary portraits, "The Child in the House." In the piece, Pater reconceptualizes writing not as an act of idealist transportation or representation, but as an ethic of remembering and revealing one's material formation. Only as Pater demonstrates that our individuality is in the first place embodied, can our unique and original expression affirm our connection with the material world.

Conclusion: Three Requisites to De-anthropocentrism

My book project answers to the topical debates on de-anthropocentrism, or how we might escape the Kantian ego and perceive the world in different ways. My answer is that we cannot seek to sketch a universal method through which we are guaranteed to earn the holy grail and see the thing-in-itself, as such universality would necessarily presume a human standard. I thus argue that de-anthropocentrism should be formulated as that each of us should seek our own individual approach to step out of the human center, to expand beyond the given perception, by recreating the self. The method of de-anthropocentrism cannot be metaphysical, universal, and a given; it, as a matter of concern, must always be ethical, individual, and dictate a program of re-creating the self.

This aesthetics of the self, such as that the artist works on one's structure of desires and seek to expand one's powers of reception, might be called art. The thesis of the book is such that art embodies this methodological paradigm of de-anthropocentrism, and that each work of art presents a new way of how a subject can relate to an object. De-anthropocentrism is achieved when the artist creates a new relationship with the world through transformation of the self.

Part One of the book, "Artificiality," therefore discusses how the Decadent artists seek to subvert the idealist pride by reinterpreting the idealist tenet that *art is superior to nature*, and in their reinterpretations we find them inventing ingenious ways of relating to materiality through recreations of the self: by loving the stone, by subjugating one's emotions and expressions under an impassive material surface, by suffering unknown sensations till the derangement of one's senses. Part Two, "Auto-Philosophical Fiction," discusses the works of Walter Pater, Marcel Proust, and Virginia Woolf against the intellectual milieu of empirical psychology, where the writers seek to expand beyond the Kantian ego and to experience the primal sensations of the phenomenal world. The genre of auto-philosophical fiction demonstrates that art differs from philosophy as self-cultivation differs from universal, theoretical truth. An auto-philosophical fiction tests philosophical ideas in the laboratory of life, and shows how each writer chooses an idea based on their temperament and experience, as well as how each idea yields a worldview as well as a regime of aesthetic education. Together, I study motifs of modernism—such as artificiality and sensuous memory—as arenas where the artists strive to subvert the idealist legacy, often through radical recreation and cultivation of the self.

Within the historical anchor of literary modernism, we have explored a new mode of thinking to approach the problem of Kantian finitude. I wish now to distill what we have gained in a definite form, and to put them into three requisites as the laws to achieve de-anthropocentrism. The three requisites are used to evaluate whether any philosophical or aesthetic thought actually answers to the call to de-anthropocentrism.

Requisite one: remove the illusion of knowledge, and stay where Kant acknowledges that we have no access to the thing-in-itself. We have seen that Kantian philosophy can be called anthropocentric only when he backpaddles from his insight on the perceptual finitude, and again elevates human reason as the measure of knowledge. Thus, if we want to defy anthropocentrism, the first step would be — not to break through the perceptual finitude and cut the correlation — but to remove the human measure of knowledge. This is not any kind of subjectivism or relativism, but to acknowledge that objects are much richer than what they present to human perception. With Baudelaire's metaphor of the stony sphinx, in which he defines the perpetual quest to the thing as the beautiful, we see that only as we recognize that the stone is incomprehensible and inaccessible, only as we relinquish the false claim to knowledge, can we, paradoxically, escape the Kantian *a priori* reason that confines us to the human ken.

Requisite two: know that our relationship with the world is not a given as Kant dictates it, but an ethical and aesthetic choice upon ourselves. After acknowledging that metaphysical truth is ultimately unattainable, we are left with an *ethical* question — how then do we posit our relationship with an object? This question is *ethical* in nature because after we remove the illusion of absolute knowledge, how we relate to the thing is *a choice entirely upon ourselves*. And by the term *ethics*, I mean that our relationship with the world cannot be defined by an absolute truth that we have discovered, which might even conveniently suggest to us a pre-defined moral system, but that *we have to create a relationship with the world*. This understanding of ethics, just as the absolute is removed, is akin to the spirit of aesthetics, as Nietzsche puts it,

> For between two absolutely different spheres, such as subject and object are, there is no causality, no correctness, no expression, but at most an *aesthetic* way of relating, by which I mean an allusive transference, a stammering translation into a quite different language.

> For which purpose a middle sphere and mediating force is certainly required which can freely invent and freely create poetry.[1]

Between subjects and objects, human reason is only one of the possible ways, the given way, of perceiving the world. But we are always creating other interfaces of perceiving the world, as our language, capitalist culture, and consumerist media do. The artists are the ones who consciously compose and invent the intermediate sphere between the subject and the object. This created relation between the subject and the object may be called aesthetics, while the value that we implement in the realm of the subject-object relation, such as whether imagination or materiality is ontologically more essential, concerns ethics. Our relationship with the object is fundamentally a created relation, and an ethical choice.

Nietzsche for himself chooses the ethics of nihilism as his relation to the world,[2] which is a determination to reject the possibility of any absolute truth. Levinas, for another example, chooses to be in a perpetual quest toward knowledge, even if we never attain it. In a way similar to Baudelaire's unrequited love for the stone, Levinas proposes a "metaphysical desire" that is strongest when the object of quest is an ultimate Other, forever beyond our possession: for it is precisely this separation from the Object that provokes our desire for it.

> Desire is absolute if the desiring being is mortal and the Desired invisible. Invisibility does not denote an absence of relation; it implies relations with what is not given, of which there is no idea.[3]

Throughout the course of the book, I have discussed concrete programs of how each artist creates one's own way to relate to the material world: Huysmans confuses the categories between concepts and unknown sensations, Woolf to immerse herself in the universal commotion, Proust to quest for the lost sensuous memory, and Pater to delineate how the sensuous earth shapes one's sensitivity. The paths to de-anthropocentrism are indeed diverse, but what matters is that each of these embodies the artist's aesthetic

---

[1] Friedrich Nietzsche, "On Truth and Lying in a Non-Moral Sense," in *The Birth of Tragedy and Other Writings* (Cambridge: Cambridge University Press, 1999), 148.
[2] Nietzsche, *The Will to* Power, p. 9, aphorisms 2 and 3.
[3] Emmanuel Levinas, *Totality and Infinity: An Essay on Exteriority*, trans. Alphonso Lingis (The Hague: Martinus Nijhoff Publishers, 1979), 34.

ideal and shape their self accordingly. De-anthropocentrism can be achieved only as theories are put into creative practices.

Requisite three: we might escape human finitude if only we affirm the possibility and the responsibility of subjective transformation. This is an often misunderstood, but in fact the most important element of de-anthropocentrism: *to step out of the human center and to be other than ourselves!* The book thus discusses ample examples of how the artist may consciously create one's desire (to love the inaccessible stone) or to cultivate one's powers of reception (to stay with the phenomenal impressions before they enter the Kantian reason). To subscribe ourselves to the demand of de-anthropocentrism means to recognize that our life should be consciously and creatively lived as a work of art, the author of this work must be ourselves, and the path must be of our own choice. The gist of the book is such that no philosopher can successfully find the way to escape the Kantian reason if he or she proceeds with the method of re-interpretating the given human perception. Instead, a transformation of the self—to depart from the human standard when we go on to this lonely and perilous path—is required to achieve de-anthropocentrism. The book proposes a new methodology for the question of subject-object relation, one that I call aesthetics—that the way each of us relates to the world is not a matter of universal truism, but rather of individual creation and of transformative encounters.[4]

---

[4] A version on the three requisites to de-anthropocentrism has been published on Wu, "A Dream of a Stone," 419–21, which I then have revised according to the needs of the book argument.

Bibliography

Abramson, Anna Jones. "Beyond Modernist Shock: Virginia Woolf's Absorbing Atmosphere." *Journal of Modern Literature* 38, no. 4 (2015): 39–56.

Auerbach, Erich. *Mimesis: The Representation of Reality in Western Literature*. Princeton University Press, 2003.

Aurevilly, Jules Barbey d'. *Du dandysme et de Georges Brummell*. Lemerre, 1879.

Banville, Théodore de. *Les Cariatides*. Paris: Pilout, 1842.

Baudelaire, Charles. *Les Fleurs Du Mal*. 2nd ed. Paris: Poulet-Malassis et de Broise, 1861.

———. "Notes Nouvelles Sur Edgar Poe." In *Nouvelles Histoires Extraordinaires*. A. Quantin, 1884.

———. *Œuvres Complètes de Charles Baudelaire*. Vol. I–VII. Michel Lévy frères, 1868.

———. *Selected Writings on Art and Literature*. Translated by P.E. Charvet. Penguin Books, 2006.

Benjamin, Walter. "On Some Motifs in Baudelaire." In *Illuminations: Essays and Reflections*, edited by Hannah Arendt, translated by Harry Zohn. New York: Schocken Books, 1985.

———. "The Image of Proust." In *Illuminations: Essays and Reflections*, edited by Hannah Arendt, translated by Harry Zohn. New York: Schocken Books, 1985.

———. *The Writer of Modern Life: Essays on Charles Baudelaire*. Translated by Howard Eiland, Edmund Jephcott, Rodney Livingstone, and Harry Zohn. Cambridge, Massachusetts: Harvard University Press, 2016.

Bennett, Jane. *Vibrant Matter: A Political Ecology of Things*. Duke University Press, 2009.

Bizzotto, Eliza. "The Imaginary Portrait: Pater's Contribution to a Literary Genre." In *Walter Pater: Transparencies of Desires*, edited by Laurel Brake, Lesley Higgins, and Carolyn Williams, 213–23. ELT Press, 2002.

Bogost, Ian. *Alien Phenomenology, or What It's Like to Be a Thing*. University of Minnesota Press, 2012.

Braidotti, Rosi. "Preface: The Posthuman as Exuberant Excess." In *Philosophical Posthumanism*, xi–xvi. London: Bloomsbury Academic, 2019.

Brown, Bill. *Other Things*. Chicago: The University of Chicago Press, 2015.

Brown, Stephen Gilbert. *The Gardens of Desire: Marcel Proust and the Fugitive Sublime*. SUNY Press, 2012.

Buckler, William E. *Walter Pater: The Critic as Artist of Ideas*. New York: New York University Press, 1987.

Buck-Morss, Susan. "Aesthetics and Anaesthetics: Walter Benjamin's Artwork Essay Reconsidered." *October* 62 (1992): 3–41.

Byrne, Romana. "Sadistic Aestheticism: Walter Pater and Octave Mirbeau." *Criticism* 57, no. 3 (2015): 403–29.

Carrier, David. "Walter Pater's 'Winckelmann.'" *Journal of Aesthetic Education* 35, no. 1 (2001): 99–109.

Carter, A. E. *The Idea of Decadence in French Literature, 1830-1900*. University of Toronto Press, 1958.

Code, Lorraine. *Epistemic Responsibility*. Hanover, N.H: Published for Brown University Press by University Press of New England, 1987.

Deleuze, Gilles. *Proust and Signs*. New York: G. Braziller, 1972.

Descartes, René. *Meditations on First Philosophy: With Selections from the Objections and Replies*. Edited by John Cottingham. Cambridge: Cambridge University Press, 1996.

Dolphijn, Rick, and Iris van der Tuin, eds. *New Materialism: Interviews and Cartographies*. Ann Arbor: Open Humanities Press, 2012.

Dorra, Henri. *Symbolist Art Theories: A Critical Anthology*. University of California Press, 1994.

Fairweather, Abrol, and Linda Trinkaus Zagzebski, eds. *Virtue Epistemology: Essays on Epistemic Virtue and Responsibility*. Electronic resource. Oxford: Oxford University Press, 2001.

Ferrando, Frabcesca. *Philosophical Posthumanism*, n.d.

Foucault, Michel. *Ethics: Subjectivity and Truth*. Edited by Paul Rabinow. Translated by Robert Hurley. The Essential Works of Michel Foucault, 1954-1984 1. New York: The New Press, 1997.

———. *Politics, Philosophy, Culture: Interviews and Other Writings of Michel Foucult*. Edited by Lawrence D. Kritzman. Paperback. New York: Routledge, 1990.

———. *The Hermeneutics of the Subject: Lectures at the Collège de France, 1981-82*. Edited by Frédéric Gros. Translated by Graham Burchell. 1st ed. New York: Palgrave Macmillan, 2005.

———. "What Is Enlightenment?" In *The Foucault Reader*, 32–50. New York: Pantheon Books, 1984.

Freud, Sigmund. *Civilization and Its Discontents*. Translated by Joan Riviere. London: Hogarth Press, 1930.

Fry, Roger. *A Roger Fry Reader*. University of Chicago Press, 1996.

García, Cristina Delgado. "Decentring Discourse, Self-Centred Politics: Radicalism and the Self in Virginia Woolf's 'Mrs Dalloway.'" *Atlantis* 32, no. 1 (2010): 15–28.

Gautier, Théophile. *Émaux et Camées*. Œuvres de Théophile Gautier. Lemerre, 1890.

———. *Mademoiselle de Maupin*. Paris: G. Charpentier, 1880.

Hagen, Benjamin D. "Feeling Shadows: Virginia Woolf's Sensuous Pedagogy." *PMLA* 132, no. 2 (March 1, 2017): 266–80.

Harman, Graham. *Object-Oriented Ontology: A New Theory of Everything*. Landon: Penguin Random House, 2017.

———. *Tool-Being: Heidegger and the Metaphysics of Objects*. 1st ed. Chicago: Open Court, 2002.

Hegel, G.W.F. *Hegel's Aesthetics: Lectures on Fine Art.* Translated by T. M. Knox. Vol. I. Oxford: Oxford University Press, 1975.

———. *Hegel's Phenomenology of Spirit.* Translated by A.V. Miller. Oxford: Oxford University Press, 1977.

Heidegger, Martin. *Being and Time: A Translation of Sein Und Zeit.* Translated by Joan Stambaugh. State University of New York Press, 1996.

———. "The Origin of the Work of Art." In *Poetry, Language, Thought,* translated by Albert Hofstadter, Perennial Classics., 15–86. HarperCollins, 2001.

———. *The Question Concerning the Thing: On Kant's Doctrine of the Transcendental Principles.* Translated by James D. Reid and Benjamin D. Crowe. London: Rowman & Littlefield International, 2018.

———. "The Thing." In *Poetry, Language, Thought,* translated by Albert Hofstadter, Perennial Classics. New York: HarperCollins, 2001.

Hext, Kate. *Walter Pater: Individualism and Aesthetic Philosophy.* Edinburgh, UK: Edinburgh University Press, 2013.

Hume, David. *A Treatise of Human Nature.* Edited by Norton David Fate and Norton Mary J. The Clarendon Edition. Vol. 1. Oxford: Oxford University Press, 2007.

Huysmans, Joris-Karl. *À Rebours.* Georges Crès, 1922.

Jaffe, Aaron. "Introduction: Who's Afraid of the Inhuman Woolf?" *Modernism/Modernity* 23, no. 3 (2016): 491–513.

James, William. *Essays In Radical Empiricism.* Longmans, 1912.

———. *Psychology: The Briefer Course.* Dover Publications, 2001.

Johnson, Barbara. "Poetry and Its Double: Two Invitations Au Voyage." In *The Critical Difference: Essays in the Contemporary Rhetoric of Reading.* Johns Hopkins University Press, 1985.

Kaiser, Matthew. "Marius at Oxford: Paterian Pedagogy and the Ethics of Seduction." In *Walter Pater: Transparencies of Desire,* edited by Laurel Brake, Lesley Higgins, and Carolyn Williams, 189–201. ELT Press, 2002.

Kant, Immanuel. *Critique of the Power of the Judgement.* Translated by Paul Guyer. Cambridge: Cambridge University Press, 2000.

———. *Kant's Prolegomena to Any Future Metaphysics.* Edited by Paul Carus. Chicago: The Open Court Publishing Company, 1912.

Lacan, Jacques. *The Ethics of Psychoanalysis, 1959-1960.* Translated by Dennis Porter. Norton Paperback. The Seminar of Jacques Lacan, Book VII. New York: W. W. Norton & Company, 1997.

———. "The Mirror Stage as Formative of the I Function as Revealed in Psychoanalytic Experience." In *Écrits: The First Complete Edition in English,* translated by Bruce Fink, 75–81. New York: W. W. Norton & Company, 2005.

Landa, Manuel de. "The Geology of Morals - A Neomaterialist Interpretation." Future Non Stop: A Living Archive for Digital Culture in Theory and Practice, 1996.

Lévinas, Emmanuel. "The Other in Proust." In *The Levinas Reader,* edited by Seán Hand, 160–65. New York, NY: B. Blackwell, 1989.

Lisle, Leconte de. "Vénus de Milo." In *Poèmes Antiques*, 134–36. Alphonse Lemerre, 1886.

Mach, Ernst. "The Analysis of the Sensations. Antimetaphysical." *The Monist* 1, no. 1 (1890): 48–68.

Mallarmé, Stéphane. *Poésies*. 8th ed. Paris: Nouvelle Revue française, 1914.

Man, Paul de. *Allegories of Reading: Figural Language in Rousseau, Nietzsche, Rilke, and Proust*. New Heaven: Yale University Press, 1979.

———. *The Rhetoric of Romanticism*. Columbia University Press, 2000.

Mathieu, Pierre-Louis. *Gustave Moreau:The Assembler of Dreams, 1826-1898*. Translated by Charles Penwarden. Courbevoie: Poche Couler, 2010.

Meillassoux, Quentin. *After Finitude: An Essay on the Necessity of Contingency*. Translated by Ray Brassier. London: Continuum, 2010.

Naremore, James. *The World without a Self: Virginia Woolf and the Novel*. New Heaven: Yale University Press, 1973.

Nietzsche, Friedrich. "On Truth and Lying in a Non-Moral Sense." In *The Birth of Tragedy and Other Writings*. Cambridge: Cambridge University Press, 1999.

———. "Truth and Falsity in an Extra-Moral Sense." *ETC: A Review of General Semantics* 49, no. 1 (1992): 58–72.

Ovid. *Metamorphoses*. Translated by A. D. Melville. Oxford: Oxford University Press, 2008.

Paladilhe, Jean, and José Pierre. *Gustave Moreau*. New York: Praeger Publisher, 1972.

Pater, Walter. *A Child in the House: An Imaginary Portrait*. Oxford: H. Daniel at his Private Press, 1894.

———. *Appreciations: With an Essay on Style*. Landon: Macmillan, 1895.

———. *Letters of Walter Pater*. Edited by Lawrence Evans. Oxford: Clarendon Press, 1970.

———. *Marius the Epicurean: His Sensations and Ideas*. 2 vols. Macmillan, 1913.

———. *Plato and Platonism: A Series of Lectures*. Adelaide: Cambridge Scholar Press, 2002.

Plato, and Benjamin Jowett. *The Dialogues of Plato*. New York: Random House, 1937.

Pridmore-Brown, Michele. "1939-40: Of Virginia Woolf, Gramophones, and Fascism." *PMLA* 113, no. 3 (1998): 408–21.

Proust, Marcel. *À La Recherche Du Temps Perdu*. 15 vols. Gallimard, 1946.

Regnard, M. "Sleep and Somnambulism. II." *Science* 2, no. 50 (1881): 270–74.

Regnard, M., and Clara Lanza. "Sleep and Somnambulism. I." *Science* 2, no. 49 (1881): 258–62.

Renan, Ary. *Gustave Moreau: 1826-1898*. Paris: Gazette des Beaux-Arts, 1900.

Rimbaud, Arthur. *Rimbaud: Complete Works, Selected Letters*. Edited by Seth Whidden. Chicago: The University of Chicago Press, 2005.

Russell, Bertrand. "The Ultimate Constituents of Matter." *The Monist* 25, no. 3 (1915): 399–417.

Ryan, Judith. "More Seductive Than Phryne: Baudelaire, Gérôme, Rilke, and the Problem of Autonomous Art." *PMLA* 108, no. 5 (1993): 1128–41.

———. *The Vanishing Subject: Early Psychology and Literary Modernism.* Chicago: University of Chicago Press, 1991.

Schopenhauer, Arthur. "Appendix: Critique of the Kantian Philosophy." In *The World as Will and Representation,* Vol. I:441–565. Cambridge: Cambridge University Press, 2010.

———. *The World as Will and Representation, Vol. I.* Translated by Judith Norman, Alistair Welchman, and Christopher Janaway. Cambridge: Cambridge University Press, 2010.

Surprenant, Céline. "Freud and Psychoanalysis." In *Marcel Proust in Context,* 107–14. Cambridge: Cambridge University Press, 2013.

Villiers de L'Isle-Adam, Auguste. *L'Ève Future.* Paris: Bibliothèque-Charpentier; Eugène Fasquelle, 1909.

Wagner, Richard. "The Art-Work of the Future." In *Richard Wagner's Prose Works,* Vol. 1. London: Kegan Paul, 1892.

Watson, Burton, trans. "Free and Easy Wandering." In *The Complete Works of Zhuangzi,* 1–6. New York: Columbia University Press, 2013.

Woolf, Virginia. *A Room of One's Own,* 1935.

———. "A Sketch of the Past." In *Moments of Being: A Collection of Autobiographical Writing,* edited by Jeanne Schulkind, 2nd ed. San Diego: Harcourt, 1985.

———. *A Writer's Diary.* Edited by Woolf Leonard. San Diego: Harcourt, 1981.

———. *Mrs. Dalloway.* London: The Hogarth Press, 1947.

———. "Solid Objects." In *A Haunted House and Other Short Stories,* 69–75. The Hogarth Press, 1944.

———. *The Waves.* London: The Hogarth Press, 1931.

———. *To the Lighthouse.* London: Hogarth Press, 1927.

Wordsworth, William. *The Complete Poetical Works of William Wordsworth.* Troutman & Hayes, 1854.

Wu, Tsaiyi. "A Dream of a Stone: The Ethics of De-Anthropocentrism." *Open Philosophy,* no. 3 (2020): 413–28.

Yeats, William Butler. *Poems.* London: T. Fisher, 1899.

Index

A

aesthetics of the self, xxv, xxix-xxxi, 27, 129
   aesthetic education, 78-80, 81-83
   ethical significance, xxxi-xxxii
   See also Foucault; receptivity; spirituality; transformation of the self; quest; *under* artificiality (dandyism); *under* memory (Pater)
art, the function of:
   create subject-object relationship, xxx, xxxii, 4-5, 19, 33, 49, 60, 62, 130-131. *See also* artificiality; auto-philosophical fiction
   Harman: experience the other, xxii-xxiii
   Heidegger: reveal the being of the thing, xx
art, superior to nature, 4, 5, 13, 32, 38, 41, 49
   See also artificiality
artificiality, 4
   android, 13-17
   appearance without inwardness, 13, 48-49
   cosmetics, 32-33
   dandyism, 28-31, 33
   ideal of inorganic materiality, 41-42
   ideal of sterile and eternal star, 36
   impassivity, 21, 29, 34-35, 37-38, 46-47

jewelry:
   as metaphor of art, 10, 45
   on Salome's garment, 44
   as sphinx's eyes, 35
   See also Baudelaire; Huysmans; marble statue; Moreau
d'Aurevilly, Jules Barney: on dandyism, 30-31
auto-philosophical fiction:
   the genre, 61-63
   Pater's imaginary portrait, 73-83
   Pater's remembrance, 119-126
   Proust's irony of absent Other, 83-85, 89, 92, 93-94
   Woolf's irony of writing, 116-119

B

Baudelaire:
   "L'Amour du mensonge," 48-49
   "Avec ses vêtements ondoyants et nacrés," 34-36
   "La Beauté," 17-24
   the flâneur, 52
   "Les Foules," 52
   "L'Homme et la mer," xi-xiii,
   "L'Invitation au voyage" (verse and prose poems), 50-52
   "Le peintre de la vie Moderne," 28-30, 69-70
   "Pourquoi la sculpture est ennuyeuse," 5-7
   "Rêve parisien," 41-42
   Romanticism, 1-2
   "Le Voyage," 82
   See also artificiality; decadence
Benjamin:
   the arcade, 53

on capitalist production, 107
the flâneur, 53-54, 114
phantasmagoria, 55, 114
on Proust, 94-95, 96
See also the crowd;
phantasmagoria; *under shock*
Bennett, Jane: *Vibrant Matter*, 48
Bogost, Ian: alien
phenomenology: xxii
Brown, Bill: Thing Theory, xx-xxi
Brummell, George. *See* d'Aurevilly,
Jules Barney.

C

the crowd:
Baudelaire on, 52
Benjamin on, 107-108, 109, 114
Guys's painting, 69
Woolf on, 107, 108-109, 115

D

de-anthropocentrism, xxiv-xxv,
xxx, xxxii-xxxiv, 63, 129-132
Harman on, xxi-xxii
See also aesthetics of the self
Decadence, 2-3
Delacroix, Eugène, 2, 30, 32-33
Deleuze, Gilles
vitalism, 48
on Proust, 84, 87-88, 93

E

empiricist crisis, 68, 78, 89
See also sensation, fleeting
empiricist psychology, 64-67

F

Foucault, Michel,

aesthetics of existence, xxxii,
122
on Baudelaire, xxxiii
ethopoietic self-writing, 122
The Hermeneutics of the Subject,
xxxi
Spirituality, xxxi-xxxiii
Freud, Sigmund, 112-113
Fry, Roger: impressionism, 71-72

G

Gautier, Theophile:
"L'Art," 9-10, 18
Preface to *Les Fleurs du mal*
(1868), 3, 10
"Symphonie en blanc majeur,"
10
See also under sphinx, marble
statue
Guys, Constantine, 29, 54, 69-70

H

Harman, Graham:
theatrical metaphor, xxii-xxiii
Object-Oriented Ontology, xxi-
xxiii
Hegel:
Buldung, 81
Idealism, xii, 28
Romantic art, xii, 4, 6, 16, 18, 20,
30
See also under marble statue
Heidegger:
Being and Time, xix
defamiliarization, xix-xx
"The Origin of the Work of Art,"
xx, 26
phenomenology, xix
too-analysis, xix
Huysmans, Joris-Karl: *À Rebours*

aesthetics, 58-59
artificial paradise, 53-54
artificial flowers (horticulture), 55
disorientation, 56-57
gilded tortoise, 45
sea voyage, 57
sensory correspondence, 57-58
See also under quest (of novel sensations); Salome; sensation

I

Idealism. *See under* Hegel; Proust (memory appropriated to the brain)
rethinking: see under autophilosophical fiction (Proust's irony of absent Other); Baudelaire ("L'Homme et la mer"); Mallarmé (L'Azur); Yeats, impressionism, 71-72
de l'Isle-Adam, Villiers: *L'Eve future*, 13-17

J

James, William, 64-66, 91

K

Kant, Immanuel:
 Prolegomena, xxviii, xxxi
 symbolical anthropomorphism, xxviii
 sublime, 56
 universal reason, xxxi-xxxii

L

Lacan, Jacques: *The Ethics of Psychoanalysis*, xxi
Levinas, Emmanuel, 83, 131

M

Mallarmé, Stéphane
 "L'Azur," 92
 "Hérodiade," 46-47
de Man, Paul, 19, 59, 83, 88
marble statue:
 Baudelaire on, 5-6
 Gautier on, 9
 Hegel on, 8
 Huysmans on, 7
 Parnassianism, 8
 the Pygmalion myth, 9, 11
 See also sphinx; Venus de Milo
Meillassoux, Quentin: xxviii-xxx, 50
 correlationism, xxix
 hyper-Chaos, xxix, 50
memory:
 Guys: of fleeting sensations, 54, 69-70
 Pater:
  Platonic initiation, 120-121
  remembrance as an ethical practice, 122
 Proust:
  appropriated to the brain, 86
  compensation for fleeting pleasure, 95-96
  involuntary memory, 86-87, 94
  metaphysical redemption, 69
  stored in the object, 85
 Woolf: oceanic rhythm, 99
 See also under Proust
modernism, xxvii
modernity
 à la mode (beauty of its time), 1
 See also Baudelaire; Benjamin; the crowd; Decadence; quest;

shock; *under* receptivity (of the unknown); sensation (fleeting)
The Monist (journal), 66
monument, 22
Moreau, Gustave, 36-45
 archetypical figures, 38
 "la belle Inertie et la Richesse necessaire," 37-41
 somnambulism, 39-40
 See also under Salome

N

New Materialism, xxiii-xxiv
Nietzsche:
 anthropomorphism, 55-56
 "a mobile army of metaphors," 58-59
 aesthetic creation of subject-object relations, 130-131

O

Object-Oriented Ontology. *See* Harman, Graham

P

Parnassianism, 7-13
Pater, Walter
 "The Child in the House," 119-126
 ethopoietic writing, 122, 125
 imaginary portrait, 73-83
 individuality, 124-125
 Marius the Epicurean, 74-83
 material habituation, 119-126
 See also under memory; Plato
phantasmagoria, 53, 55, 70, 114-115
Posthumanism, xxiv

Proust, Marcel: *À la recherche du temps perdu*, 83-97
 Benjamin on, 96
 compulsive possession, 84, 89
 Deleuze on, 84, 87, 93
 de Man on, 88
 metaphor, as the law of literature, 87-88
 See also under auto-philosophical fiction; receptivity
Plato:
 Pater on, 121
 Phaedrus, xxxi, 27
 Republic, xxxi
 Symposium, 27

Q

quest:
 of the absolute Other, 131
  See also under Baudelaire ("La Beauté")
 of the new, 82
 of novel sensations, 52, 55-57
 unrequited love, 20, 27
 See also flâneurs; Huysmans; *under* receptivity (of the unknown)

R

receptivity:
 Baudelaire on, 69-70
 Pater on, 68, 70-71
 Proust's deficiency of, 84, 90, 93-94
 See also under Woolf (stream of thought)
Renan, Ary: on Gustave Moreau, 37-45
Rimbaud, Arthur, 50

Index 143

Romanticism. *See under*
  Baudelaire; Hegel
Russell, Bertrand, 67
Ryan, Judith, 23, 64

S

Salome:
  Mallarmé: "Hérodiade," 46-47
  Moreau, 42-45
  Huysmans, 45
Schopenhauer:
  on absolute matter, 25-26
  on somnambulism, 39
sensations:
  fleeting, 52, 68-69, 84
  artificial manipulation of, 55, 56-59
  universal:
    Pater on, 97-99
    Woolf on, 99-100
  See also impressionism; receptivity; *under* quest; Woolf (stream of thought)
self-alienation: 4-5, 23
  love the android, 15-17
  See also under Baudelaire ("La Beauté")
shock:
  Benjamin, 96, 107-109
  Woolf, 109-115
somnambulism: 15, 39-40, 44
Speculative Realism, xxix
  See also Bogost, Harman
sphinx:
  Baudelaire, 17-24
  Gautier, 11, 21, 24
Spirituality:
  Foucault, xxxiii
  of dandyism, 30
  See also aesthetics of the self

T

The Thing:
  inaccessible, xxi, 20
  inexhaustible, xix
  mysterious charm, 22
  otherness, xvi, 16, 89
Thing Theory, xx-xxi
transformation of the self: xxii, 21, 27
  See also aesthetics of the self

V

Venus de Milo, 10-13
  as an android, 13-14

W

Woolf, Virginia
  the everyday, 109-111
  Mrs. Dalloway, 73, 102-104, 105-106, 109-110, 113-114
  To the Lighthouse, 104-105, 111, 113
  A Room of One's Own, 101, 106
  self-dissolution, 101-102, 104-106
  self as a social construct, 102-103
  "A Sketch of the Past," 99-100
  stream of thought, 72-73
  rhythmic order, 106
  The Waves, 116-119
  writing:
    the mission of, 111-112
    irony of, 112-119
  See also under crowd; sensation

Y

Yeats, William Butler:

"The Sad Shepherd," xvii-xviii
"The Song of the Happy Shepherd," xiv-xvi;
spurious correspondence, xvi

www.ingramcontent.com/pod-product-compliance
Lightning Source LLC
Chambersburg PA
CBHW070918180426
43192CB00038B/1746